THE TRANSFORMATIVE IMAGINATION

At the beginning of the twenty-first century there is an increasing tendency towards retrenchment within the Christian churches and among other world religions. Religious fundamentalisms are on the increase. In Europe, at least, there is an accelerated decline in church membership. In theology there is a corresponding move away from addressing basic theological issues in the contemporary world, towards increasingly technical interpretation of historical tradition. This book draws on the strengths in classical liberal traditions in theology, augmented by other perspectives, to present a creative proposal for the future of theology and society.

George Newlands explores the nature, scope and limits of an intercultural Christian theology, setting out a working model for a new open theology which relates theology and culture. Contributing to the cumulative effort to re-imagine faith in the contemporary world, a focus on the Christian understanding of God lies at the heart of this book. Exploring the interface between theology and particular cultural activities, *The Transformative Imagination* engages with politics, literature, philosophy and other humanities, and the natural sciences. The relationship between theology and the social and geographical sub-cultures which characterize human life is explored through diverse examples which make connections and initiate dialogue. Connecting Christian theology and human rights, religion is seen to link constructively with some of the most intractable problems in contemporary global conflicts of interest. Theology is re-situated as a team player, a catalyst to facilitate dialogue in contrast to triumphalist theologies of the past.

The Transformative Imagination

Rethinking Intercultural Theology

GEORGE NEWLANDS
University of Glasgow, UK

ASHGATE

Published by
Ashgate Publishing Limited
Gower House
Croft Road
Aldershot
Hampshire GU11 3HR
England

Ashgate Publishing Company
Suite 420
101 Cherry Street
Burlington, VT 05401-4405
USA

Ashgate website: http://www.ashgate.com

British Library Cataloguing in Publication Data
Newlands, George M., 1941–
The transformative imagination : rethinking intercultural theology
1. Theology, doctrinal 2. Religion and culture 3. Hospitality – Religious aspects – Christianity
I. Title
230'.01

Library of Congress Cataloging-in-Publication Data
Newlands, G.M., 1941–
The transformative imagination: rethinking intercultures theory /George Newlands.
p. cm.
ISBN 0-7546-3827-8 (alk. paper)
1. Theology, Doctrinal. 2. Christianity and culture. 3. Religious pluralism. I. Title

BT78.N45 2003
261—dc21

2003052246

ISBN 0 7546 3827 8

Typeset in England by Author & Publisher Services, Calne, Wiltshire
Printed in England by MPG Books Ltd, Bodmin, Cornwall

Contents

Preface

This study explores the nature, scope and limits of an intercultural Christian systematic theology, especially within modern Western society. Such a theology respects particular commitments within the religions and facilitates dialogue between communities of belief and other dimensions of culture in society.

One way of focusing the quest for an intercultural theology is to understand it as a version – not the only version – of a theology of hospitality. This represents a development of the concept of a theology of generosity. Generosity in a Christian context involves a commitment to giving, unconditionally and with an emphasis on those who are most in need. It also means an intellectual generosity, a willingness to look for the best interpretations of strange cultures and beliefs and to be open to learning from them. Hospitality embraces all that can be said of generosity, and underlines the need for concrete interaction. Hospitality involves the risk of inviting others into our own environment, and being prepared for reciprocal hospitality. It is a particularly suitable metaphor for Christian theology, which has a dual focus on word and sacrament, on concept and embodiment. Like generosity, hospitality is not confined to one aspect of life. It does not only happen with material commitments, but also carries an intellectual commitment, a commitment to a meeting of minds. It is this intellectual dimension of hospitality which will be the main subject of the following chapters.

At the beginning of the twenty-first century there is an increasing tendency to conservation and retrenchment within the Christian churches and among other world religions. Religious fundamentalisms are on the increase, and these may sometimes, though by no means always, lead on to terrorism. This state of affairs is accompanied, in Europe at least, by an accelerated decline in Church membership. In academic systematic theology there is a corresponding move away from addressing basic theological issues in the modern world, towards increasingly technical interpretation of historical tradition. Rather against this trend, this book is understood as continuing in the path of liberal orthodoxy, in the tradition of Schleiermacher in Germany, the Baillies in Scotland, Geoffrey Lampe and Keith Ward in England, David Tracy and Brian Gerrish in the United States.

Recent theology has been dominated by perspectives loosely defined as neo-orthodoxy and radical orthodoxy. There has been much exciting theological exploration under these banners, and they continue to contribute constructive avenues for theology. Both movements have had something of the colourful and exotic flavour of the tropical greenhouse. They have produced vivid and striking fruit to brighten up a dull world. But they have had some of the disadvantages of the hothouse plant, and are not easily cultivated outside a carefully controlled environment. We can never jump into the same river twice. But I believe that there are strengths in classical liberal traditions in theology which can be explored, suitably augmented by other perspectives, in a creative research tradition for the future of theology and society. This book is an attempt to set down a marker in such a tradition, a progressive orthodoxy.

We have to recognize the fact that theology faces real difficulties in the modern world. None of the recent schools of thought has resolved these problems, but most have contributed new insights to the nature of the task, which it would be unwise to ignore. As we shall see, not every sort of liberalism has been fruitful in theology. Minimalist systematizations of belief do not produce good theology and are often simply tedious. Neo-liberal economic systems are often questioned by Christian faith, and radical individualism can be immensely selfish. On the other hand, liberal evangelical and liberal catholic theologies share a common tone of openness, including openness to traditions from which they differ, and an awareness of their own provisionality, together with a firmly Christological focus, which has yielded and may yet yield a rich harvest for Christian theology. Both the evangelical and the catholic dimensions add a vital spiritual depth to the liberal frame. Such a liberal theology may also be understood as a progressive theology, though with a more sober view of progress than that concept has sometimes suggested.

Hospitality is a concept and a reality vital to the flourishing of a humane society. It denotes a wide dimension of trust and of openness. But it is not without limits. It indicates a texture of compassion and care which is not compatible with many aspects of human living – in violence, coercion and manipulation, in the systematic neglect of the marginalized, in triumphalist ideologies of every sort. With advocates of such values there will be dialogue but not agreement. In this sense hospitality is a challenge as much as a willingness to embrace. Hospitality may be strengthened by long tradition, but it is also a strategy which has inherent within it the constant possibility of surprise and of new beginning. Outcomes cannot always be predicted. A theology of hospitality is inevitably a theology of risk and a theology at risk. That is also of the essence of the Christian gospel.

The relation between theology and culture will always exhibit a dialectical tension. Theology seeks to be self-critical, and not to confuse its critical engagement with culture with a triumphalist perspective which is often itself no more than the reflection of a particular cultural reading of Christian faith. It reflects on the scope and limitations of the language and imagery of its tradition. It seeks to criticize culture in society which is inherently coercive, contrary to the central elements of the gospel, and which has sometimes been echoed and reinforced by theology itself. There is no escape from absorption in a particular culture for human language and human activity. The task is to try to remain as self-aware and as critically constructive as possible. This is most likely to happen through conversation and dialogue.

This tradition cannot be faithful to its own best insights without radical renewal which involves critique of past tradition, openness to quite different and often conflicting traditions, and input from fresh sources. I find in the various emancipatory theologies such a stimulus to new dimensions of the Christian vision, also in inter-faith, comparative theology and in political theology. I am grateful to the University of Glasgow for study leave, and to the Claremont School of Theology for its generous hospitality. No books are written without the support of friends and the list can never be exhaustive. My thanks especially this time to David Jasper and the Centre for Literature, Theology and the Arts in Glasgow, to Alan Brown, Paul Middleton and David Smith, to Alex Wright, Ian Markham, Martyn Percy and John Hick, to Jack Fitzmier and James and Jane Barr in Claremont, to our son Craig in Los Angeles, and to the Ashgate team.

George Newlands, Glasgow

I
THINKING INTERCULTURAL THEOLOGY

CHAPTER 1

The Quest for Intercultural Theology

Faith, Culture and Civil Society

This study explores the nature, scope and limits of an intercultural Christian theology, especially within contemporary Western society, which both respects particular commitments and facilitates dialogue between communities of belief and other dimensions of culture in society. The primary focus of the Christian understanding of God remains at the heart of the project. It is understood as part of a cumulative effort by many scholars to re-imagine faith in the modern world.

The word 'intercultural' is the most useful term to describe the dialogue which I want to examine. Intercultural and cross-cultural theology is most often used to describe dialogue between different religions. I shall concentrate here on the Christian religion. 'Multicultural' often emphasizes the heterogeneity of different ethnic groups in society. I am concerned to look for continuities while respecting the discontinuities. There is a need to go beyond fragments towards a genuinely integrative theology, while avoiding the colonization of other disciplines which has been an unfortunate characteristic of much traditional theology. 'Intercultural' emphasizes a relationality beyond relativism, while refusing the standardization inherent, for example, in much transnational corporate enterprise. The intercultural is closely related to interdisciplinarity, which can be pursued through many disciplines other than theology. Christian theology, through its claim to be relevant to all human well-being, has particular reason to pursue an intercultural approach.

Intercultural theology has tended in the past to concentrate much on inter-faith issues and on non-Western cultures. Christian systematic theology is increasingly focused on particular Church community and confessional loyalties. The aim here is to develop *a programmatic approach to theology in dialogue*. There are two distinct but connected issues to be faced here. One is the interface between specific theological frameworks and particular cultural activities. An example might be the relationship between theology and English literature. Here it is naturally important to look at both sides of the dialogue. How has literature in its diverse modes understood the religious and theological imagery with which it has often worked? Only a listening theology is likely to be able to achieve a constructive engagement.

A second major issue is the relationship between *theology and the social and geographical sub-cultures* which characterize human life. What characteristics might a theology which arises from a community of Hispanic women in Latin America contribute to the understanding of God in other cultures, or indeed to a more cosmopolitan perspective, or are their reflections only intelligible within a local group? These questions are not of course exclusive. We live in increasingly overlapping and cosmopolitan sub-cultures, in which some Hispanic women also have qualifications in English literature.

In the face of such almost infinite possibility for diversity it might be thought best for Christian theology to stick firmly to an agreed classical pattern of expression, which may be appropriated everywhere in the same way. It is increasingly clear that such a strategy is only effective in very limited circumstances, and is, or may be perceived to be, coercive in ways which are contrary to the nature of faith itself. Christian theology is by definition concerned for the relation of faith to the whole created order. It is equally clear that not every strategy for relating faith to culture will do.

Overview

Intrinsic to the approach is the aim both to respect cultural particularity and to facilitate dialogue between diverse cultural groups. This entails a repositioning of theology's traditional self-understanding, to become a catalyst or facilitator in a constantly developing conversation with a wide range of disciplines.

Part I, 'Thinking Intercultural Theology', considers the role of theology in the postmodern era. This introductory chapter examines the need for an intercultural theology today as a collaborative effort, not least in the light of the continuing challenge of secularization. There is analysis of types of correlation between theology and culture. Chapter 2 examines the legacy of liberal theology, and evaluates the success of the recently revived perspectives of Barth and Tillich in relation to culture while avoiding the pitfalls of *Kulturprotestantismus*. Chapter 3 opens up the intercultural project further, in interaction with philosophical proposals from Bernstein and Berlin, and considers the ambiguities of culture, religion and talk of God.

Chapter 4 considers the collapse and retrieval of the classical hermeneutical tradition, following the explosion of emancipatory theologies and their accompanying new awareness of cultural diversity. This leads to Chapter 5, focusing more sharply on the specification for an intercultural theology. The profound, though fluctuating, impact of the secular, together with social fragmentation and the need for political engagement, renders traditional theological triumphalism obsolete. There need be no contradiction between effective *political* action and theological engagement with the cultural and the aesthetic

Part II, 'Focusing Intercultural Theology', focuses upon the specific topics of human rights and Christology. It develops the structure of a theology which draws integral connections between political engagement and transcendental affirmation. Chapter 6 is devoted to a critical study of the relationship between theology and human rights. This reflects a distinctively but not exclusively Christian approach to God and the world. It points to a God who is not the dominating subject of triumphalist theology, yet remains the creative source and goal of human life. Unapologetic stress on the humane and on human rights is the hallmark of a theology which is neither tribal nor supracultural but intercultural.

Chapter 7 focuses on the distinctively Christian contribution to the understanding of the human through Christology, and the relation of a postmodern theology to morality.

Part III, 'Integrating Intercultural Theology', is devoted to the tensions between traditions and interruptions, transculture and sub-culture. Interdisciplinary dialogues are examined in Chapter 8, on cases in theology and literature, philosophy and intellectual history in the humanities, and Chapter 9, on theology and science, underscores the differing impacts of the pure sciences and technology on the theology/culture interface. Chapter 10 draws together the findings of the section in the application of *postfoundational* theory to the intercultural, to suggest a theological perspective which is *metamodern* but not anti-modern.

Chapter 11 sums up the project, reflecting on the mystery of God in a critical culture, as a credible way of speaking about divine action and about God.

Facilitation and Resistance

Discussion of theology, culture and society often lacks specificity and criteria. It has to take account both of cultural pluralism and of relations between the aesthetic and the practical. Theology and culture are not separate worlds: there has always been mutual interaction and critique. There is no simple key to this issue, with which theology continues to struggle – in a classical tradition from Aquinas and Augustine to Schleiermacher and Troeltsch. What may critical theology contribute (a) to the understanding of God in a pluralistic culture, and (b) to the resolution of conflict in specific social and political issues, involving human rights and values? Can theology help us distinguish in practice between legitimate and illegitimate strategies for change and development in cultural and social structures? How is the dimension of religion and transcendence to be appropriated in a constructive way in the modern world?

As well as listening, Christian theology has an obligation to make a distinctive contribution of its own in dialogue with culture.[1] What exactly does it have to offer? The widespread turn in Christian theology from religion to Christology as the central Christian theological motif in the twentieth century suggests the possibility of a fresh critical hermeneutical exploration of the symbols of the Christian tradition. The results of this exploration may then be correlated to an analysis of human values within conflicting cultural frameworks. Concepts of facilitation and resistance may be explored as potential paradigms for a transformative theology. There is an increasingly wide gulf to be bridged between many of the professional concerns of the guild of systematic theologians and the major issues, ethical and political, which often polarize society.[2]

What is offered here is not an overarching postfoundational theory of the relation of theology to culture, but a series of suggestions which may facilitate the practice of an intercultural theology, and provide pointers in the direction of a deeper interaction. Our concern is not just with the inculturation of traditional theologies in different cultures, but with a critical interaction between tradition and culture. Not every contextual theology is an adequate theology. Our concern will not be for the local but for the best perspective. Theology needs to benefit, always, from the whole Christian tradition, from conservative and liberal elements, but in a self-critical framework.

Culture and Society

Theology, as traditionally conceived, is a function of the Church. Faith as the Christian faith is the logic of redemption, the self-accountability of Christian community. But redemption is intimately connected with creation. Faith is given, in Christian understanding, not as therapy for the individual or even the elect group, but for *the service of all humanity*. Grace is given to be given away, and God is love, characterized by generosity and hospitality. Grace should be central to intercultural theology.

Theology reflects on God as creator and reconciler. In the sphere of humanity, *creation involves culture*. It encompasses the communal habits, quest for meaning and behaviour of people in groups. What is culture? There have been numerous definitions, all of them themselves embedded in particular cultural contexts, and themselves limited and somewhat arbitrary. In his famous definition of 1871, E.B.Tylor held that 'Culture or civilisation, taken in its wide ethnographic sense, is that complex whole which includes knowledge, belief, art, morals,law, custom, and any other capabilities and habits acquired by man as a member of society'(*Primitive Culture*, I,1).

Geertz (1973,5) put it like this:

> Believing, like Max Weber, that man is an animal suspended in webs of significance he himself has spun, I take culture to be those webs, and the analysis of it to be therefore not an experimental science in search of law but an interpretive one in search of meaning.'

Culture is about webs of meaning. Geertz explores the task of 'thick description', of setting down the meanings which particular social actions have for those who perform them, and then asking what these meanings tell us about the societies in which they are found, and about social life as such.

Among the hundreds of studies of the nature of culture among cultural anthropologists and others, definitions have been the subject of fierce controversies, not least those around Marxist theories of culture. Surber (1998) provides a useful overview of critical discourses on culture. He distinguishes the critical discourse of liberal humanism, the tradition of hermeneutics, the materialist critique, based on Marx, the psychoanalytic critique, the critical theory of the Frankfurt school, formalist and structuralist analyses, postmodern discourses and present-day cultural studies. Schafer (1998) characterizes culture as embracing holism, context, value, identity, conflict, criticism, vision, creativity and power. An intercultural theology will be open to learning from each of these critiques, without necessarily being committed exclusively to any of them, in the world of late modernity.

The study of culture should enable us to understand the world in which we live a little more clearly. It should also help us to see ourselves in better perspective:

> To see ourselves as others see us can be eye-opening. To see others as sharing a nature with ourselves is the merest decency. But it is from the far more difficult achievement of seeing ourselves among others, as a local example of the form human lives have taken locally: a case among cases, a world among worlds, that the largeness of mind, without which objectivity is self-congratulation and tolerance a sham, comes. (Geertz, 1983, 16)

The importance of trying to see ourselves in perspective, however difficult this may be, is obvious in view of theology's traditional tendency to triumphalism:

> The objection to anti-relativism is not that it rejects an it's-all-how-you look-at-it approach to knowledge or a when-in-Rome approach to morality, but that it imagines they can only be defeated by placing morality beyond culture and knowledge beyond both. This, speaking of things which must needs be so, is no longer possible. If we wanted home truths, we should have stayed at home. (Geertz, 2000, 65)

There is a continuing dialogue between theology and culture. It takes different forms, is explicit or implicit, and depends on a continually changing perception of both theology and culture. Talk of God and experience of divine presence is articulated within particular cultures in different ways. There is always a new quest for a better understanding of God in each generation and in each cultural group. However, the search for appropriate relationships between theology and culture has never been easy. There have been patterns of correlation and patterns of conflict. There is need for connections between theologies and cultures. There is need, too, for awareness of disjunction and difference.

In the search for understanding of the theology/culture dimension there has been much unclarity, and with this an understandable tendency to scepticism, and to *abandonment of the issue* in favour of more obviously profitable projects. But the relationships between theology and culture remain unavoidable for any theology which aims to relate faith to the world outside the church in which the great mass of humanity lives.

Theology is also related to *society*. Society and culture overlap. In society we are dealing with the institutions, the commercial, political, economic, legal and geographical institutions by which life and work are determined, from leisure industries to town planning. Each of these institutions has its own cultures and sub-cultures, considered in microcosm and macrocosm. Within societies there are debates about social and moral values, about the nature of human goods and human dignity. The relationship between church and society has always been an evolving one. The last century has seen continuing debate about these issues, for example from the critical realism of Reinhold Niebuhr to the emancipatory theologies and the debates about civil society and the public square in North America. Conflict over religion and family values has led to 'culture wars' in which the ethical content of Christian faith is hotly disputed. The conflict over specific social and political issues – capitalism, family values, racial discrimination – has usually been more focused than the most intangible and amorphous reflection on 'culture'. But the cultural divides set the tone which affects the specific social and political agendas. A theology which understands God as creator as well as reconciler has to pay serious attention to the different levels and textures of human relationship, at cultural and social, communal and individual levels. Not least, it has to reappraise its understanding of God as the source of faithful engagement in the world.

As human activity using human language theology can never be acultural. Christian theology understands revelation, knowledge of God which can come only from God, as part of its basis. Revelation comes in, with and under human reflection and activity, and is integral to the dynamic process of critical engagement with culture. A dialectical understanding of the relationship between the human and the divine is central to the long-standing discussion of the connections between theology, religion and religious studies.

I have reflected elsewhere on a culture of generosity. Generosity implies justice and fairness, and going beyond what is required in giving. It implies hospitality, spontaneity, grace. It needs to have its own content; it has to have something worthwhile to give. Christian faith contributes the gospel of God in Jesus Christ. But if it is to be saved from elitism, generosity also requires mutuality and reciprocity. Generosity is paradigmatically open to listen, to learn, to share mutual hospitality. That is not always easy. Faith seeks to move forward by reflecting imaginatively on all the paradigms of the past, in their continuities and disjunctions.

Theologians sometimes need to reappraise their roles in relation to culture and society. They may have to learn to play more convincingly and effectively as contributors to a team, while at the same time making a decisive and distinctive contribution. Theology may not often be done by a group, as in the natural sciences, but it should not be done in isolation. We must be willing to learn from society and culture as well as contribute to it. We may have to acknowledge that our internal tradition has sometimes got things wrong, and has been rescued despite itself from outside. Critics often point to what they see as the appalling record of Christendom, and they note that the Church has often changed its mind on theological and social issues only in the face of overwhelming rejection of its tradition from society beyond the religious community.

It is possible to see this dialectic as the providential divine correction of theology from the created order. To use one popular set of metaphors, here the values of the Church are corrected by *the values of the kingdom.*[3] Sometimes it has mainly been through the action of humanist or non-Christian agencies, sometimes through Christian action outside and in opposition to official Church policies, that theology and Church has changed its mind. Obvious examples are slavery, capital punishment, racial discrimination and family planning. It is through such dialectical interaction that a generous faith is deepened, and a new understanding of God and humanity is reached.

What does the understanding of humanity have to do with the understanding of God? Classical theology has always understood that there are deep interconnections. The understanding of humanity may help us to correct and enlarge our limited understandings of the mystery and the disclosure of God. The understanding of God may help us to keep ourselves human, and preserve us from dangerous divine pretensions.

Types of Correlation

How are the interactions between theology, culture and society best to be explained and understood? Here there are a myriad possible questions, of which we can hope to tackle only a few, although we must try to expose the basic ones. Anthropology, sociology and cognate disciplines encompass huge domains of research, and generate endless debate and disagreement at every level among themselves. It is not for theology to sit in judgment on these discussions. Theology may listen, learn and perhaps on occasion contribute. But it cannot usefully *take over* the content or the direction of these other disciplines.

What have been the most common approaches to the relationship of theology and culture?

Correlation

The relation of theology to culture has sometimes been addressed by a theology of correlation, famously by Paul Tillich, but also by Paul Knitter and others. From the side of culture, this has had the advantage of producing a useful general framework, a small-scale map. But it has left the particularity of local cultures, of the small-scale communities, unclear. For these are not fractal patterns in which the small scale mirrors the large scale; the local cultures have widely divergent characteristics and overlaps. From the side of theology, it has often seemed that theology has become too much the servant of culture, too enmeshed in the cultural grid to be able to offer an autonomous critic of culture. The standard horrid example is *Kulturprotestantismus*, leading up to the *Gleichschaltung* with Nazi ideology in the 1930s – though it should be noted that Tillich himself had a very different attitude to Nazi ideology, attacking fiercely the theology of Emmanuel Hirsch in the 1930s, and brilliantly correlating theology with authentic German humane culture against Nazi ideology in his wartime broadcasts.[4] Alternative stances to Tillich's model were succinctly set out in Hans Frei's typology of theology.

Inculturation

A further popular model has been the idea of inculturation. This has been much used in African theology in the twentieth century, for example by Aylward Shorter. The scope and limits of inculturation, and the criteria for decision, remain hard to specify.

Liberation Theology

Liberation or emancipatory theology employs a variant, where the cultural correlation is not with an indigenous cultural model but with political and economic programmes. Here the problems are those flagged up by Berlin in his discussion of negative and positive liberty. It is important not to impose upon people what others perceive that they would want if only they knew better, thus limiting individual freedom from coercion.

Multicultural Theology

Here the diversity of cultures and the rights of particularity are respected, in ways which may not appear in general theologies of correlation. There is a danger of a kind of tribalism, and an inflexibility which inhibits natural change in cultures. There may be an indifference which enables different cultures to exist side by side, never engaging with and perhaps neglecting the needs of one another. An example might be the relationship of black and white congregations in the United States.

Cross-cultural and Intercultural Theology

Theology in this mode has usually been concerned with inter-faith dialogue, between different religions, often on different continents. It is important to evolve strategies for dialogue in situations where there may be strong disagreement and a disinclination for dialogue. Conflict has to be managed and turned to constructive purpose. The aim here will not be so much final agreement as the development of mutual respect and, it is hoped, reciprocity in action towards the achievement of maximum human dignity.

Intercultural Theology

I want to use this term to suggest dialogue between the diverse segments of overlapping and diverse cultures. Here, different religions and ethnic groups may or may not be involved. More immediately significant may be conflicts of interest between different Christian groups, as in denominational differences through the ages, differences on race and gender issues, differences connected with economic status and social class. As we become more aware of cultural diversity the need for effective intercultural theology becomes more acute. This may be, not a single theological programme, but a cluster or constellation of lines of theological research which have common emphases while respecting the diversity of cultures. It is with the notion of intercultural theology that this study will be especially concerned. It will be concerned to explore the frontiers between the late modern and the postmodern in the changing relationships between theology, culture and society.

Pluralism and the Intercultural

Theology and culture: here is a proverbial minefield of ambiguity and generalization. Also problematic is the recent emphasis on the pluralism of culture within all of our societies. We can no longer think of intercultural study as involving primarily different ethnic and religious groups on different continents, or even of ethnic multiculturalism in our cities. Within apparently monochrome cultures there are often very different sub-cultures, overlapping in various ways. Even within a typical Western country or city, we can no longer think of the interaction between a monochrome theology and a monochrome culture.

How is theology to respond? We may think that the attempt to relate multifaceted theologies to multifaceted culture is doomed to endless ambiguity and lack of precision. Better, perhaps, to accept that each sub-culture will quite legitimately appropriate a theology in its own chosen way, and offer a distinctive theology to be retrieved in different ways. An example might be the way in which the very particular and largely self-contained theology of Karl Barth has been retrieved in particular theological traditions. Here is one way to retain specificity and focus. The universal always arises out of the particular. Theology makes its own substantive and intrinsic contribution.

Yet the need for a theology of correlation between the gospel and culture remains, not necessarily as an exclusive alternative but as another essential characteristic of a modern theology of engagement. *The theology of the exclusive designer label is not enough.* It belongs to a theology of grace that it is always oriented towards the other. It is not self-absorbed but other-related. It derives its existence not solely from an ancient tradition of being or from a modern tradition of universal rational principles, but also from a postmodern tradition of being in interactive relationship. Theology makes its contribution not simply in application to a context but in interaction. Such a theology of engagement we find, for example, in the writings of Eduard Schillebeeckx (Schillebeeckx, 1987).

Theology has a core and a unity, but that is an eschatological unity. Here God's presence to faith is through fragments, parables and icons of faith. There is ample recognition of this eschatological completeness together with residual mystery in all the classical theologians.

From the side of culture, too, there is a reluctance, especially in Europe, to be controlled by what is perceived to be a *hegemonic* network of religious doctrine. What is welcome is participation, reciprocity and dialogue in which the course of the journey to be undertaken remains open. The other side of this is a willingness to bring to the dialogue a distinctive contribution. In an authoritarian framework such an emphasis would be and is implicitly threatening, an attempt to pre-empt and control the direction of dialogue. In a partnership of genuine equality, each of the members has a duty to contribute as much of an original and particular input as possible.

Notes

1 It is basic to an intercultural progressive theology that it focuses on the huge positive contribution that Christian faith may make to human well-being. John Cobb (2002) and David Griffin (2000) have noted perceptively the often negative effect of some traditional liberal theology, which has masked the positive contribution which it seeks to make.

2 Case studies reinforce the argument here, including examples of interaction between theology and culture from the work of the Centre for Theology, Literature and the Arts in Glasgow, between theology and society from a Masters course in Emancipatory Theology, and from current debate on religion and human rights.

3 The notion of the kingdom may itself require rethinking, suggesting expectations of being ruled, which may not appropriately reflect relationships with God.

4 At stake was the question of divine particular action in history and the notion of Kairos, where Tillich felt that his views were misrepresented by Hirsch.

CHAPTER 2

Discernment: Beyond Liberal and Confessional Theologies

The Drive for Critical Theology

Theology in the modern era has attempted to be *critical theology*. Of course theology in the ancient world also sought to be critical, in that the foundations were clearly developed and premises built in a scholarly manner on these foundations. The modern period was characterized by the development of methods of historical understanding, which have driven the quest for a new scientific and, as far as possible, objective basis for knowledge. In turn the critical theologies inspired by the modern have been attacked for being anything but critical. On the contrary, the liberal theologies of the nineteenth century were steeped in cultural assumptions which tended to make God simply a mirror of their social manners. In the anti-moderns, in the work of Barth and von Balthasar, and in the post-moderns and post-liberals like Lindbeck, Frei and Hauerwas, there was a fierce reaction against the pretensions of Enlightenment. Among the postmoderns there has been a recognition that all human thought is immersed in culture. The work of Barth and von Balthasar, for all its denunciation of accommodation to culture, is itself deeply rooted in particular cultural assumptions, and employs language with very specific cultural roots.

Sometimes there has been a retreat from engagement with the universal to focus on the particular. The Christian Church sometimes has to concentrate on its own inner self-understanding, and its worship, in order to renew its energy, in order to serve in the world more effectively. This turn inwards has also had its negative side, appealing to a tribal mentality which creates a coercive form of inner community which excludes divergence of opinion and cuts itself off from society, becoming sectarian. The universal dynamic of the Church has brought the opposite problem of a dilution of the gospel within society, so that it ceases to have a distinctive contribution to make. The problem recurs in every age of how to combine faithfulness to the gospel with openness to serve in the whole created order

There has never been a simple route from accidental truths of history to eternal truths of reason, but my contention is that there are important aspects of truth which emerge from the engagement, intellectual and social, of individuals in the series of overlapping communities in which they live, with the major social and intellectual issues of their time. The issues vary from one profession to another: history, politics, physics. In this case the issues are in essence theological, concerned with the contribution of Christian faith to Church and society.

How is theology to engage most effectively with culture in the future? It is clear that different approaches have their own advantages and disadvantages, and there are no infallible ways. For theology, the problems of a disengaged, purely academic liberalism on the one hand, detached from the life and worship of the community, are clear. A monolithic, organic appeal to a touchstone of revealed authority is even more problematic. There is no single middle way, more *a variety of possibilities* between these opposites, and there are things to be learned from the extremes. There are also more continuities between contrasting theological styles in a particular period than is often imagined. Theology needs its prophetic, protesting figures like Kierkegaard and Barth. It also needs people like the Baillie brothers in Scotland, to discern connections, to build bridges between different styles of theology, between theology and society, to underline the continuity between creation and reconciliation. Part of the value of the postmodern is to stress the web of connection between the basic pillars of different programmes.

There are many ways to build bridges, depending on the conditions. The values of tolerance, universal human rights, openness and liberal democracy have been lasting benefits of the Enlightenment. When they have been denied, the results have been catastrophic. Postmodern thought has brought us new perspectives: the importance of recognizing and respecting otherness, minority communities, distinctive cultural identity, the self as embodied in particular social relationships. We may learn not to seek artificial harmonies but to live in constructive tension. In the perspective which this study explores and affirms, these are not opposed but reciprocal values. The postmodern is valuable as an extension and development of the modern, not a denial. A liberal evangelical theology may develop into a critical liberal theology which is also a liberal catholic theology. But this will be a catholicity which respects subsidiarity, which avoids the kind of organic holism which is coercive. Such a theology will be committed to engage with multicultural community, both within and beyond Christianity and the world religions. It will be concerned with human rights in an intercultural hermeneutic of engagement. For Christians this will be understood as a central strand of the nature of discipleship.

'Liberal' means different things in different cultural contexts, though there will be 'family resemblances'. It can mean attitudes or it can mean specific programmes. In the United States debates about liberalism have often taken colourings which are less familiar in Europe. Paradoxically, liberal has there been a term of abuse used by the political right in relation to the left, and by the left in relation to the right. These colourings have been echoed, with variations, in theological debate. There can be 'thick' or 'thin' construals of liberal values, narrower or broader, exclusive or inclusive perspectives. These debates have often centred on notions of justice and human rights, to which thousands of volumes have been devoted. Theology is not best qualified to do the work of philosophers or political scientists for them, but it can introduce the distinctive perspectives of the gospel to these debates, and seek to make innovative contributions to their resolution. In many contemporary contexts, faith may often be best articulated in relation to justice. I am concerned here to engage with this field, and to construe further the central impact of the gospel in terms of generosity.

There are considerable similarities between theological exploration of the distinctiveness and uniqueness of the Christian message and discussion in political theory about the limits of liberalism: how far there are core liberal values and to what extent relativism can be taken to embrace respect for uncongenial positions. There may be attitudes which can be tolerated but which cannot be respected. There are actions which so curtail the freedom of others – violence and oppression – that the freedom to perform them has to be denied. To use Berlin's language, we must have the negative freedom to be free from oppression. We may wish to advocate positive freedoms which we see as social goods – full employment, comprehensive health care – but we have to take care that these do not in turn become coercive.

Such a programme should in principle be helpful to any Christian community. But it ought to be encouraging in particular to the 'mainline' churches, which have suffered great numerical decline in the twentieth century. Of course they too may learn from the dynamism of some of the newer denominations. But they should not undervalue the excellence of their achievements over a very long time scale. That would not be faithful to their own witness. What has been said in America by Charles Bayer (1996) and by Weeks, Coalter and Mulder (Weeks, 1996) is worth emphasizing. There will have to be continuing radical change, not least in the ossified structures of Church organization. But the mainline Church should not put short-term gain before long-term constancy.

Bayer noted that the mainline churches are been squeezed by secularism on the one hand and religious fundamentalism on the other. Both should be resisted. Theology has become too divorced from the life of the Church. Anti-intellectualism in the Church is a consequent danger. We should be alive to the historic dangers of the connection between very conservative theology and very conservative politics. We should continue to engage with social theology and human rights, while not neglecting a dynamic attention to worship and to ecumenical effort. We should remain constant and consistent.

There is an excellent construction of an agenda for the Church in the future in Robert J. Schreiter's *The New Catholicity* (Schreiter, 1997). Schreiter examines concepts of culture and theology on a global and on a local scale, and reflects on the possibility of a critical liberation theology 'between resistance and reconstruction'. What would an intercultural hermeneutics look like? It would facilitate effective communication, negotiating issues of truth and meaning within a recognition of relative incommensurability. A new catholicity will recognize the asymmetries of power, through solidarity with the poor and the oppressed, with minority cultures which experience risk and contingency. It will involve, as it has always involved, retelling the Christian story through a variety of new codes and signifiers, and showing how the story is not only recited but lived. The intercultural will privilege conversation as a basic strategy for research.

Beyond the Frontiers of Liberal Theology: The Era of the Christian Realists

When we extrapolate from the particular to the universal, in so far as there are anything like universals any more, we have to underline the imaginative and selective elements in our argument. I have tried to examine the theological and cultural roots of one version of a liberal theology in *John and Donald Baillie – Transatlantic Theology* (Newlands, 2002). The Baillies in their early writing concentrated on the relation of a particular Scottish philosophical and literary education to theology, and later on wider ecumenical and social themes. With a different educational background and working in a different context, both the substance and the methods of inculturation would have varied. The suggestion here is that this particular example has features which may help us in the task of relating theology to Church and society in the present.

The specific proposals and methodological moves made by the Baillies cannot usefully be repeated in a quite different context decades later. Is it then possible to distil an essence of their work, from whose elements new theological programmes can somehow be cloned, as in the dinosaurs in Jurassic Park? Clearly not. Dinosaurs will only flourish in an appropriately contemporary environment, as will theologians.

In the hands of the Baillies the evangelical liberal approach to theology sought to combine critical openness to modern scholarship at all levels with commitment to Christian faith. John Baillie often said that the basic problem with liberal theology was its illusion of finality. This was true, and a new critical liberal theology would have continued to learn from its critics, including Marxist, liberation, neo-orthodox and post-liberal theology. But the illusion of finality is scarcely exclusive to liberal thought. The management of radical change is a continuing challenge to all human activity. An evangelical liberal theology would also have to learn from the catholic dimensions of Christianity, especially in the area of worship and liturgy, in which its contribution has often been rather shallow and unimaginative, transforming the mystery of God into a bland concert performance.

Above all, a new critical liberal theology has to be confident in developing its own response to the divine transcendence. To be essentially reactive is often to be dull. A theology of transformative Christian practice will shed new light on the mystery of faith, changing the contours of the landscape to produce surprise and devotion. It will not simply add critical footnotes to unsatisfactory texts. I have tried to contribute to this in *Generosity and the Christian Future* (Newlands, 1997). I hope to have succeeded in suggesting that such an enterprise is part of a well established tradition whose credentials are at least as solid as any other candidates in the theological tradition, and whose potential for deployment in a theology of the future is still immense.

There were severe problems with liberalism as a theology by the end of the 1920s, and these were exacerbated by the fundamentalism/modernism debate. The Christian realism of Niebuhr and his friends addressed these problems, as the Barthian movement was to do in Europe. Realism was essentially a development and corrective of liberal theology and not a reversal. Realism in turn was to run into huge problems when its brand of political pragmatism met opposition from more radical and idealist groups. In the liberation theologies we may perhaps see again the appeal to the Kingdom and to the character of Christ which characterized the liberal theology of the early part of the twentieth century.

It is often said that the liberation theologies were distinctive in emphasizing the relation of theology to praxis, but Baillie and his friends were equally concerned about these connections. They were aware of the dangers of modern forms of high scholasticism, of the sort sometimes espoused later in the century by the followers of Barth, and by elegant studies in Patristics and in Biblical Studies with no real contemporary impact. It is of course possible for theology with a high theoretical content to have important practical consequences, as with the potential impact of Duns Scotus on the entire medieval pentiential system. But it is not clear that the liberal tradition was any less profound than the anti-modern theology which was to come increasingly into fashion.

Theology has to be able to criticize current social trends. The gospel is often a word of judgment on the collective immorality of society. But theology must also be able to offer a contribution to social dialogue where that is required. In a pluralist framework where the way forward may be through the recognition of incommensurable goods, attention to an ever-changing context is of the essence.

We may need a *theology without frontiers*. For faith, everything in the created order is to be transformed, and brought into God's future for creation. Of course, all our theology is part of a human religious construct, and religion reminds us of the need for dialogue with other religions than our own. Religion indicates the limits of theology. But, at the same time, theologians reflect that religion involves a response to transcendence, for Christian faith to the incarnate God of Jesus Christ. Theology points to the limits of religion. In seeking truth conditions and comparing religious phenomena with methods, norms and sources, it functions as a critique of religion, even though it cannot adopt a role outside a particular culture.

In this critical and dialectical mode, theology may engage in constructive dialogue towards the development of the human future with other disciplines in the human and natural sciences, with history, with law, with the arts, with the natural sciences and the life sciences. The notion of a critically realistic dialectical theology, to borrow a phrase from Bruce McCormack, may take many different forms in different circumstances. As soon as it assumes the illusion of finality, whether in liberal, neo-orthodox, postmodern or any other mode, it ceases to be either critical or realistic or dialectical.

What happened to the liberal critical theology of the Christian realists? This is a complex issue involving many cultural changes. There were some basic factors. In America it was significantly affected by the Vietnam war and its aftermath. The realism of the Niebuhr generation could justify a war in which there were no absolutes, but only the lesser evil. Limited force might be applied to achieve limited objectives. The realization that it had been a major political error to enter the war in the first place put a question mark against the wisdom of the wise men who had been able to justify it. The more liberal wings of the churches began to develop liberation theologies, with a new sensitivity to what was happening in the so-called 'Third World'. The theology of the white Anglo-American consensus could seem both dated and arrogant. As more radical theologies developed there was a loss of confidence in the mainline liberal theology, a willingness to practise self-criticism which could be overdone and have a paralysing effect.

On the more evangelical wing of the Church, a new social ethics began to emerge, not least in connection with opposition to nuclear weapons. New Catholic–Protestant alliances were to be forged, which changed the agenda and the culture of debate. Disillusion with too close an alliance between Church and society led to the development of post-liberal theologies and more tightly focused understandings of the Church as community. Conservative scholars sometimes saw the opportunity to take over from the liberal establishment and advance the eternal, unchanging truths of the gospel as they saw them. Taking over the Southern Baptists in 1975, they have continued to make steady progress.

If Americans had any doubts about the obsolescence of liberal theology, they need only look to Europe, where secularization was much more advanced. This is the effect of Troeltschian synthesis between gospel and culture – disappearance of the gospel. In Britain the radicalization of the Student Christian Movement (SCM) in the 1960s, long a source of candidates for theology and ministry, was perhaps a sign of what could become experimentation to destruction within the mainline synthesis. Linguistic philosophy often appeared to have destroyed the basis of the liberal appeal to faith and experience. History raised increasingly difficult issues. There was a perceived need, too, for more serious engagement with Catholic and Orthodox thought.

The decline of the SCM meant a loss of a major traditional source of more liberal Christians into ministry and priesthood and academic theology. The new intake came increasingly from more conservative cultures. At the end of the twentieth century the theology of Karl Barth took on a new attractiveness, as a bulwark against secularism. In France, Germany and Italy, church attendance dropped sharply.

There was a further significant factor. Throughout Europe, there was an increasing awareness of the problematic nature of 'Christendom', with its hegemonic attempt to colonize culture in the name of a self-assured Christianity. Christendom and the imperial legacy were seen to be uncomfortably close to one another. The appeal to 'Christendom' was in some respects similar to the Christian Coalition of later American religion, and in some respects paradoxically close to the anti-Christendom isolationism of some postmodern conservative Christianity. It ran the risk of hubris, triumphalism and institutional violence. If there was to be continuing dialogue between theology and culture, more self-critical models were to be required.

The centre of Christianity is shifting rapidly, to Africa, Asia and Latin America. This change is reflected in all the world-wide ecumenical bodies, and in all the denominations. The major presence of Orthodox and Catholic members in ecumenical forums, often representing traditional and conservative theological positions, makes new alliances with conservative Protestantism possible. Understandably, those who have felt subordinated in the past are enjoying the sense that it is their turn now. It may in time be possible to interact with similar traditional perspectives in Islam and other world religions. All of these factors suggest that, at least in the medium term, there may be little scope for a new critical liberal understanding of theology and Church of the kind that would take up the legacy of John and Donald Baillie. At the same time, the limitations may be thought precisely to suggest the urgent need for such a theology, not least as a bridge towards those who will not go down the traditional paths.

Perhaps more constructively, it is in the engaged dialogue between different perspectives that human understanding of God, and of Christian discipleship in the modern world, is most likely to be enlarged. A truly critical theology will always be a dialectical theology, not fixed on one track solutions, but ready to listen and to learn new truths from unexpected directions.

Three Ways of Dialogue: Schleiermacher, Barth, Tracy

There are many different ways of entering into dialogue between theology and culture. Characteristic of the nineteenth century, of the modern age in theology, not least in the work of its founding father, F.D.E. Schleiermacher, was interdisciplinary study of theology and the humanities. The great theologians of the twentieth century were usually resolutely anti-modern, and their legacy in various editions of neo-orthodoxy has been an isolation of theology within its own bounds, accompanied by a marginalization of the study of theology and the arts. The greatest of the anti-moderns, Barth and von Balthasar, were not unmindful of the humanities: Barth and Mozart, von Balthasar and aesthetics. Yet the trend has been to isolationism, or at best to an ideological makeover of the realm of culture, as for example in some of the writings of Leslie Newbigin. On the credit side, there have been some modern systematic theologians who have not followed this trend – I think of David Tracy. But on the whole, the field has been relegated to marginality. This has had profound consequences, for the important task of dialogue between the disciplines, but also for the understanding of the nature of theological inquiry itself. Beyond this, it is highly instructive to reflect on the kinds of theological and ecclesiastical perspective which have influenced the works of poets and playwrights, musicians, lawyers and scientists. Eliot and Auden, Mozart, Blackstone and Einstein – all were much affected by particular religious doctrines, and not always, we may think, for the better. This book seeks to create at least some pointers towards bridging the gap once more.

It is of course true that theology has assimilated with culture in ways which have been profoundly contrary to the Christian gospel and damaging to humanity. But if theology is not to be a private language for a privileged tribe, there have to be bridges and there must be dialogue with all human culture. The Christian faith itself contains guiding pointers to such dialogue, not inaccurately summarized in I Corinthians 13. Love, patience, longsuffering and kindness, these are of the essence. Where assimilation involves opposite values to these, such as violence and coercion, the dialogue will involve critical questioning and protest. Attempts at communication will still be required.

Karl Barth represents an immensely useful critical question against any easy accommodation of theology to culture. His work is therefore of great importance for the development of a new critical theology of culture. At the same time, Barth's work is itself, like all theology, heavily inculturated, sometimes consciously but very often unconsciously. It is therefore in no sense *the* criterion for the shape of dialogue, which must come out of its own dynamics (to paraphrase Barth's own understanding of *Sachlichkeit*). To use Barth again contra Barth, the gospel means not humanity for God but God for humanity. That in turn raises sharp questions about Barth's own interpretation of this profound statement.

A different, but in my view at least equally important, perspective on theology and culture is to be found in the work of David Tracy. Owing much to Schleiermacher as well as to the catholic tradition, Tracy explores the development of the classic as a paradigm of theology. This tradition has a kind of double vision, standing firmly within a particular tradition but being sensitive and open to other traditions. It is this kind of bridge (or perhaps more appropriately active interaction) between theology and culture, based on the understanding that theology has a distinctive contribution to make, but has also a genuine expectation to learn, that we are trying to explore.

Dialogical Theology and the Intercultural Challenge

Karl Barth, Intercultural Theologian?

Let us return to the yield for intercultural theology of these different approaches to dialogue. It would be a serious omission to analyse resources for a new critical theology without some reference to the work of perhaps the dialectical and also most influential of modern theologians, Karl Barth. If we bear in mind Berlin's reflection that truth is usually to be found in the tensions between the positive and negative effects of great philosophical ideas, then we see this paradox classically displayed in Barth, who has been the inspiration of an often highly intolerant scholastic orthodoxy, and at the same time a consistent, and indeed insistent, advocate of the perfect freedom of the grace of God in Jesus Christ, always surprising and unexpected. How did Barth stand in respect of diversity and creativity? *To what extent* could we even describe him as a liberation or even an intercultural theologian? How did he relate, subjectively and objectively, to the culture within which he wrote and lived?

There would clearly be arguments in favour of Barth as a supporter of cultural diversity and of freedom. He came from a country with a long tradition of independence, espoused liberal politics and wrote a commentary on Romans which was centred on the free and sovereign grace of God. The Reformed tradition had a long history of opposing authoritarian regimes – typical were the Huguenots. He was the chief author of the Barmen Declaration, which stressed the authority of Jesus Christ, against all fascism. In his *Church Dogmatics* he opposed the death penalty, and considered such issues as war and peace from the standpoint of grace. Later writers on liberation, like Moltmann and Cone, were dependent on his work.

On the other hand, Barth could become for some Protestants what Aquinas became for Catholics, providing the certainty and the answers which we all long for. He gave Christians self-confidence, as Reagan and Thatcher provided political self-confidence. Swiss culture at the end of the nineteenth century, like ours, was partly generous and outgoing, partly introspective and isolationist, partly reflected political self-interest.

When he spoke of freedom, was this to be for Christians alone? What of Moslems, Jews and humanists? There was no word about the persecution of Jews in the Barmen Declaration. Later in the *Church Dogmatics* there was very little on the Holocaust.

The emancipation of women came very late in the Swiss cantons. Barth has been much criticized for supporting in theory and in practice the patriarchal picture of woman which came down to him from the biblical narratives. Woman is there as a helper for man, who remains the central figure. He has also been criticized for homophobia in the *Church Dogmatics*. Here the image of God is immutably male and female.[1] Did Barth represent a viable approach to the relationships of theology and culture? There would not appear to be much account taken of cultural diversity in the magisterial narratives of the *Church Dogmatics*. Like all of us, he came from a particular background and wrote within its limitations. He often emphasized, rightly, that all theological statements are eschatologically open, and not the final truth. As with all theology, the advantages and disadvantages of his proposals emerged with the passage of time.

Barth stressed the freedom of the divine Word. Indeed this must be a warning against bewitchment by neo-orthodox or liberal theologians alike. There will always be a need for further struggle to understand the concrete implications of love, peace and justice in particular situations. He was a European, with European strengths and limitations. It would seem clear that an intercultural theology has to come from a concrete situation and address that situation, but it should avoid automatically prescribing the approaches appropriate to one culture to others. *Grace is central*, and suggests a dialectical relationship to nature. Human rights are understood by Christians to be centred in Jesus Christ. But grace suggests also a dialectical relation to scriptures. The incarnation of the grace of God was not in a text but in the person of Jesus Christ. Grace is larger than our culturally limited ideas, and also our culturally limited theological and Christological concepts.

There is, too, a positive as well as a negative ambivalence in Barth. He did see the Jews as a people to be respected in their particularity, and not to be dismissed in an Enlightenment assimilation. He was prepared late in life to comment in his letters that the Pharisaism of those who insulted homosexuals was much worse than the sin of which they complained. He did try within the limits of his biblical images to emphasize men's responsibility to be just to women.

To illustrate something of the problem, let us try to throw a different imaginative light on the contextuality issue here. We might imagine that Switzerland is a small Caribbean island. Barth is born here, and has early contact with European missionaries from Goettingen. They constantly accuse his father of worshipping his ancestors, namely the old Reformed theologians and exegetes. Barth is at first tempted by these impressive people. Later he himself returns to ancestor worship and defends his father's position. Contrary to the negative stance of the Europeans, he wants to defend the Reformed faith. He wants, in politics, recognition and equality for his community and culture. He wants to speak of the uniqueness of his theological method and his Christological concepts. *Extra ecclesiolam nulla salus*. He wants to commend the biblical interpretation which finds resonance in his community. He wants to raise the God of his fathers against the relativizing of the present. In this he was quite right.

What remains problematic is the fact that he now wanted to impose his own culture upon the rest of the world, whether in Norway or New Zealand. But the 'island' of Switzerland is not New Zealand. Therein lie the necessary tensions in our human society, between more universal and more local relationships. Both are important. The task is to utilize effectively the constructive tension between the two.

The above example is of course a considerable exaggeration. But there are problems in Barth's approach to these issues. It would be unwise to conclude, however, that nothing more can be learned from this tradition for an intercultural theology. To choose a mainstream example, Paul Lehmann's *The Decalogue and a Human Future* (Lehmann, 1995), is a sensitively developed theological ethics based on a neo-orthodox perspective, and is particularly relevant to some of the human rights issues which we are considering in this book. He stresses the importance of seeing the law within the framework of the gospel rather than the gospel within the framework of law. The gospel is a force beyond hierarchy and beyond equality, leading us towards reciprocal responsibility. Responsibility is related to power. Properly understood, 'Power is the gift of the possibility, energy and ability to respond to and take responsibility for the freedom to be human in the world' (77). The true apperception of the human denotes 'a sign of the transfiguration of the mystery of experience in the experience of mystery' (95).

Responsibility to God joins God and humanity and nature in 'a humanizing concern of authority and gratitude and trusteeship' (148). Within this responsibility the nature of the family and civil society can be rethought. The imago Dei as male and female can be seen, not as a limiting image, but as a foundational image (174), underlining the values of otherness in differentiation and commitment, reciprocity and fidelity, privileging no particular sexual orientation. As far as economic issues and property values are concerned, what matters is that ownership rests ultimately in God, 'who bestows the goods and determines their fruitfulness' (192). Beyond property rights there is the absolute need for justice rather than judicial manipulation of the courts, and for the human rights of marginalized people such as asylum seekers (205). Luther understood the decalogue as an apperceptive description of what the gospel affirms about life in this world and about what a realistic assessment of life in this world involves. 'The gospels are apperceptive affirmations' (225). There is, then, a reciprocal responsibility between rights and responsibilities:

> When rights take priority over responsibilities, politicization takes priority over humanisation in and of the common life. For rights tend to focus upon limits as hindrances to be removed. When responsibilities take priority over rights, humanisation takes priority over politicisation in and of the common life. For responsibilities presuppose limits as the boundaries within which the freedom to be human in the world is experienced as a foretaste of fulfilment. (227)

In essence Lehmann's thesis is that the decalogue is not a catalogue of proscriptive law but a picture of how the world in its unfallen state would operate, indicating the shape of God's purpose. In the world as it is, the gospel provides a framework of grace and forgiveness within which life may be lived in *freedom* within the limits of the possible.

Tillich: Counter-cultural Theology?

There are alternative approaches. We have stressed that it is very difficult to address culture in general. For culture is always divided into many areas of sub-culture. It is always possible, however, to address a particular issue which has a deep impact on a culture. A striking example of this approach in the same period, from a theological perspective, may be seen in Paul Tillich's wartime radio broadcasts into Nazi Germany, *Against the Third Reich* (Tillich, 1998). Tillich has often been associated in popular theology with assimilation of theology and culture, and contrasted with the robust *contra mundum* approach of Barth, not least in relation to the Nazis. Here, however, we see a concentrated but carefully differentiated attack on a culture, which is careful to distinguish between good and bad elements and to combine judgment with hope. A powerful address on 31 March 1942 dealt with the question of the Jewish people:

> The depth of the Jewish question is that the Jews are the people of history, the people of the prophetic, future-judging spirit. This means that we ourselves sin against the meaning of our own history if we bear guilt against the Jewish people … What is important is that the eyes of the German people should be opened, that the German people should realize this: the Jewish question is the question of our own existence or nonexistence as Christians and human beings. It is the question of our redemption or our judgement. (13f)

Tillich probes the depths of cultural presumptions. In a sermon on Internal and External Freedom of 20 April 1942 he notes, 'In classical German poetry, no word has a stronger ring to it than the word freedom.' But he goes on to assert that 'German philosophers fell back on internal freedom without making serious efforts towards external freedom. Freedom in spirit, bondage in life: this contradiction rests as a curse over German history … Protestantism has not been able to defeat this curse' (21). Here is a source of fear and of hope. 'Allow the Protestant protest to become strong among you, as it did among your fathers in their time. Internal and external freedom have proven to be one. The struggle for both is what your time requires of you' (24).

He writes on the ninth anniversary of the German book burning, on 18 May 1942: 'Book burnings are as old as books … But again and again the books are victorious. The thoughts that have become embodied in them rise up out of the ashes, more powerful than before' (33). He speaks of the German tragedy: 'The difficulty and the double tragedy for Germany is that it has surrendered itself to it [National Socialism] – half-willingly, half unwillingly – and became its instrument and as a result, was itself the instrument of a destroying and self-destroying destiny' (50). At Christmas

1942 he writes, 'Whoever follows National Socialism must persecute the child in the manger. Whoever obeys the Fuehrer who has become a Fuehrer unto death must turn aside from the star that points to Bethlehem' (98).

For 'A German Good Friday' (1944) he can say, 'Millions of people have been nailed to the cross of the most profound suffering and the most agonizing death by the henchmen of National Socialism. And the German people stood by and looked on, just as in the old pictures of the crucifixion.' But things are changing. 'If, at the beginning of this war, the German people were now almost exclusively among those who crucified, they are now, with every day, themselves moving closer to the cross.' It is possible that light may come from this darkness. This cross must be borne without bitterness. 'And if you are reconciled to your fate, which is guilty and innocent at the same time, then you can reconcile that fate to yourselves' (240).

This is a profoundly challenging reflection, in the form of sermons, on the relation of faith to culture. It is relatively easy for us now to identify with Tillich and with the justice of his critique. It remains of course always a much greater challenge to identify the injustices in our own cultures, not least when they are widely popular and supported by the powers that be, when to challenge them is to invite at best disdain and at worst destruction.

The relationship between internal and external changes within cultures has important consequences. In a theological context, for example, the understanding of revelation may be internalized or externalized, When revelation is thought to be publicly available, as in doctrines of the external clarity of scripture, people who choose to ignore publicly available truth can be held publicly accountable. When revelation is internalized, a matter of inner light, public accountability becomes less clear. There may be occasions, as in the later Auden's plea for individual space, when it is appropriate to pay attention to the internal. But in situations like those examined by Barth and Tillich, at least for Christian theology, the internal and the external become one.

Rudolf Bultmann

In this context it is instructive to recall another, perhaps the most neglected, of yesterday's theologians, Rudolf Bultmann. The world of Rudolf Bultmann has almost completely vanished from the pop charts of modern theology. In the brave new world of radical orthodoxy and the second coming of Karl Barth, it is hard to think of Bultmann without instant recollection of his faults which, it seems, are legion. Protestant fideism, Cartesian and Kantian dualism, Augustinian individualism, Eurocentric Enlightenment foundationalism, expressivist experientialism and numerous other dragons of modern giant killing can be slain in recalling Bultmann. Yet it may be well worth looking at the debris of the bombardment to see what, if anything, remains of his achievement for the theological future.

Bultmann shared Barth's concern for a theology of the Word. But he was clear that modern people must be presented with the scandal of the gospel, and not simply a scandal of interpretation, because the gospel was obscured by the concepts of an ancient culture. Bultmann did not wish to jettison the ancient thought forms. It was necessary first to demythologize them, in order to understand the true message, then to remythologize, in order to bring the biblical passages to bear on present-day issues.

Bultmann was to be much criticized. He was denounced in some Church circles as a heretic and a Marcionite. His existential philosophy was attacked as inadequate. From other perspectives he was attacked as not going far enough. His approach was thought too Christological and too biblical. More recently, literary and sociological analysis has questioned most of Bultmann's specific conclusions and proposed new methods of research. But scholarship is always a continuing process, and theology is greatly indebted to Rudolf Bultmann for giving a huge stimulus to New Testament study.

Central to Bultmann's thought is the category of faith. He wrote the famous article '*pistis*' in Kittel's *Woerterbuch*. Faith is a constant theme, too, in the great commentary on the Fourth Gospel: cf. Bultmann on John 15, 1–10 (412). Faith is faith, without objective security. Though his famous insistence on the non-objectifiability of faith is traced by critics to Kant, and criticized as fideism, it is also firmly in the tradition of Luther and central to Christian theology. For a rounded picture of his contribution, the rather sceptical posture of some of his critical scholarship must be balanced by the deep piety of his sermons (translated as *This World and Beyond*), especially in the war period, for example for December 1939. Bultmann was a member of the Confessing Church circle in the Marburg area, which included Hans von Soden and other theologians.

In the last decades the prevailing trend has continued to move away from Bultmann's themes. But there have been attempts to reassess critically his legacy. In his *Christus praesens*, James Kay challenged Hans Frei's critique of Bultmann's work through a reading of a 'realistic narrative,' which is only loosely related to the historical context of the text. David Fergusson's judgment is instructive.

> If we fail to appreciate that Christian faith and intellectual criticism were for him harmonious pursuits we shall not understand his theology. If we cannot follow many of his conclusions, we can do no better than pursue his intention of faithfully representing the word given to the Church while simultaneously relating it to the questions and insights of the world around us. (Fergusson, 1992, 147)

Is there a case for seeing value today in Bultmann beyond the pulpit? Bultmann is often seen as the quintessential theologian of that 'modern' form of Protestantism which is decaying fast and which, within the cultural dialogue to which it aspires, has long been overtaken by postmodern concerns of a radically different nature from the old. I have much sympathy for Charles Taylor's view that the postmodern does not abolish the modern but is an extension of the modern. Postmodern developments that too quickly become palaeo-modern may easily lead us back to patterns of tribalistic and coercive religion. Nevertheless, any reassessment of Bultmann ought to face squarely the postmodern challenge in theology.

We may doubt whether Bultmann would have enjoyed a weekend break in the Aladdin Hotel in Las Vegas, the fantasy land where it is always twilight and always time for food and drink, impulse buying and impulse gaming. Even in Marburg he was an essentially socially and academically conservative scholar who found it hard in some ways to adjust to contemporary dislocations. In his diaries John Baillie recalled a visit to Marburg in 1946, where the great scholar explained wearily that students were simply not up to standard these days, and knowledge of New Testament Greek among the new cohort of students was quite lamentable. Clearly, grammar books were not read assiduously in the trenches.

There is, then, no instant reconstitution of Bultmann for the twenty-first century. Troeltsch, too, was a socially conservative figure in the German academic tradition, yet his work remains important for a radical reappraisal for the development of Christianity. What of Bultmann? I want to suggest that Bultmann remains important for the future of an intercultural theology for several reasons. First, the whole question of the relation between faith and history remains a continuing central issue of Christian theology and practice. It was inevitable that the debate should move on from the arguments of the 1960s to eschatology, to postmodern readings of the Bible, to postfoundational philosophy and emancipatory theology. Yet the relation of faith to history, however intractable, continues to be central to the issue of divine action, where there will remain elements of mystery but where attention always needs to be focused.

Faith is a central concept for Bultmann. It is possible to become obsessed with the doctrine of justification by faith. Yet the abuse does not take away the proper use, and this always remains a central strand of Christian theology, whether it is highlighted or neglected. Without faith all notions of transcendence become academic in the most esoteric sense. Faith can collapse into fideism. But it retains an element of paradox. It is always related to mystery. Bultmann was always unwilling to unpack the nature of the 'Christ event' which he understood to be opened to us in the act of proclamation and reception. This reticence may be seen to have a value in underlining the mystery at the heart of faith. The theology of the Word is of a word which involves both revelation and concealment. When we stress too much the revelation, we are always in danger of creating an ideology which turns out to be coercive.

Where can we look for a retrieval of fruitful elements of Bultmann's thought? We have mentioned Protestant theologians. But it is also within the Catholic tradition, very early in the study by G. Hasenhuttl and, more recently, in the writings of Schillebeeckx and David Tracy, that we find a remarkable development of the twin themes of faith and mystery which in a sense combine the Protestant and Catholic traditional ways. The revealed word is also the concealed word, the word of power in powerlessness, of the theology of the cross.

Power in powerlessness. Dialogue may lead in directions which would have surprised earlier generations. The emancipatory theologies of the millennium have brought sharply into focus the sexist, racist and other discriminatory attitudes which have made our theology parochial and tribalistic, not least in its universal aspirations. These were not pressing issues for Bultmann, though his strenuous opposition in the Marburg faculty to the Aryan laws of the 1930s showed how he felt about racism. If we are to be faithful to Bultmann's intention, the emancipatory dimension will become urgent. Bultmann might well have been inclined to characterize a theological programme such as that of James Cone as 'enthusiasm', yet faithfulness to a tradition of dialogue may be expected to change perceptions on both sides of the dialogue as it proceeds.

Bultmann's theology is a theology of redemption as much as of revelation. What are we redeemed from, and what are we redeemed to? Perceptions of sin are one of the areas in which we are seeing a major shift in Christian, and indeed in human, consciousness. For almost two millennia we have produced impeccable treatises on moral theology while exploitation in various guises continues unchecked. Bultmann's theology was for the individual rather than the corporate structure. Yet individual perception has been, and always will be, vital in changing corporate cultures.

Bultmann's intention of open dialogue remains a valuable reminder, yet his world was not the world of the millennium, and the world will change again and again. To maintain the momentum of dynamic Christian discernment, we must renew theologies with a critical edge, with the courage to retain what is non-negotiable and to recognize fresh insights into the truth of God, strategies almost unthinkable in the circle of the Alt-Marburger half a century ago. Faith is concerned with this world as God's world, in which there is God's presence in unconditional love despite the appearance of things. In his focus on Christian faith for this world as it is, Bultmann remains an advocate for faith without frontiers.

Graham Ward

Are these the only available approaches? Theology continues to produce new avenues, a continuing warning against complacency. Graham Ward's *Cities of God* is closely related to the 'Radical Orthodoxy' and suffers from many of the problems of radical orthodoxy. But it has the great merit of recognizing the profound changes which Western society, especially urban culture, has undergone in the last quarter of a century, and seeking for intelligent solutions to new situations.

Ward's programme is pursued with insight and energy. The introduction argues for a Christian theology of signification, connected with the cultural metaphors of social semiotics, in order to produce a new analogical world view. This is a lively but, in its own way, rather exclusive paradigm for the nature of knowledge. The postmodern perspective now established led to a sharp, provocative and timely analysis of the contemporary cityscape, under the heading of 'cultural atomism'. Beginning from a critique of the *Faith in the City* document of the 1980s, Ward seeks to show how the city has changed, and has become radically secular. 'This city has no need of God (or religion) for its values (aesthetic, moral and spiritual) lie all at hand' (42). Postmodern cities are 'cities of endless desire'. Las Vegas and Los Angeles are the modern heteropolis, Disneyland as reality. 'The culture of seduction, simulacra and death, which we see played out in the contemporary heteropolis, is both godless and fearful, self-possessed and self-destructive, embattled and belligerent' (68). The Christian response can be neither to accommodate with the world nor to renounce it, retreating into neo-tribalism. We need a new understanding of analogy, involving the divine participation in the particular and social, thus combating atomism.

How may we move from the corporeal to transcorporeality? The body, the mystical body and the sacramental body are all refigured by Christology. Broken, disabled, despised bodies are healed: 'Through the brokennness of the transcorporeal body God's grace operates through his creation' (96). Through resurrection and eucharist we may participate in the displaced body of Jesus Christ. A new construal of incarnation becomes possible (116). The Church as the body of Christ becomes a new community of desire. Desire, though it often takes on sexual connotations, is ultimately desire for God. In the Enlightenment this desire was often directed to the self and the awakening of self-consciousness, and thence to postmodern virtual communities. But it is possible to construe the Church as the authentic God-given erotic community (152). Participation follows fragmentation and creates community. The eucharistic presence is not so much real presence as true presence. It is part of the erotics of redemption. This leads to reflection on sacred sex, a theology of desire and a critique of Barth's theology of sexual difference: 'It is as if he returns to a natural theology his whole theological system is designed to refute' (197) – Irigaray's 'hom(m)osexuality', seen from the perspective of men. Love relates to otherness and difference, whether between different or same sex couples. The Church must sanctify, then, genuine sexual difference through its liturgies, whether that sexual difference is evident between two women, two men or a man and a woman (202).

Postmodern cities are described as cities of angels, but these are virtual angels in cyberspace, of a science fiction sort, and need to redeemed. This may happen in cities of the good, with the help of reflection on de Certeau's critique of the modern alienated city, and Augustine, for whom all earthly loves point to the eternal love of the Trinity. Liberal Christian pluralism has had its day, lost in cultural atomism. We must build new confessional Christian communities (258). The theologian does not have all the answers and cannot produce solutions: 'The theologian's task is to keep alive the vision of better things – of justice, salvation and the common good – and work to clarify the world-view conducive to the promotion of these things. (260).

This is a powerful and suggestive account of the position of the theologian in the postmodern world. Its insights into the ambiguities of the contemporary city are searching and illuminating. The stress on the love of the other as basic to a Christian understanding of reality provides a persisting focus. But the preferred solution, shaped around eucharistic communities as islands of refuge in the darkness, may not be sufficient. It is, in my view, important to any strategy for the Christian future that there should be worshipping communities centred on the love of God in Jesus Christ. But somehow these communities tend all too often to become introverted and to view the world beyond as basically a threat. This world is also God's world, and may be seem as an opportunity, with many shades and colours, not by any means all black. To value traditional Christian worship is not to disparage more humanistic understandings of worship and of a religious dimension in the service of humanity. The earthly city is indeed not the heavenly city, but by God's grace the city may come to move in the direction of the heavenly city to come, in the development of a few grains of mustard seed.

Note

1 Cf. *Church Dogmatics* III, 4, para. 54.1; III.1.p.166ff, and the discussion in Badham (1995, 35ff).

CHAPTER 3

The Intercultural Turn: Shaping the Envelope

After Pluralism and Relativism

Bernstein

In thinking about conceptual frameworks for doing theology which combine precision with flexibility I have been particularly encouraged by the work of two philosophers, Richard Bernstein and Sir Isaiah Berlin.

Richard Bernstein does not do the theologians' work for them, and dialogue would not be helped by responding in terms of a theological repetition of his own philosophical reflections. But he does have things to say about the nature of rational inquiry which are extremely helpful for the definition and particularization which has to define the effective engagement of theology with culture. Let me pick up just a few points.

In *The New Constellation*, Bernstein highlights the word 'constellation' to suggest a way of reflecting on the interactions between a loose but significant cluster of data. For me, that echoes my own approach to theology in partnership, and it chimes in with ideas which I have found profoundly helpful in David Tracy, notably in his talk of theology in fragments, and in Wentzel Van Huyssteen, in his work on postfoundational theology. Bernstein also talks about engaged fallibilistic pluralism. I have commented elsewhere on the appropriateness of this suggestion for a programmatic generosity in theological work at all levels. Engagement is not excluded by rationality, but promoted. *Fallibilism* is always appropriate in a theology which is by definition eschatologically open, which does not pretend to finality in its present apprehension but which does have specific commitments, positive and negative. These commitments include values which are non-negotiable, such as the privileging of love, justice and peace. However, the interpretation of these values is vulnerable, open to risk in reciprocity and further experience. Pluralism is a *sine qua non* for a dialogue of partners who are to be treated as equals. But, as Bernstein is careful to stress, there may be unhelpful pluralisms (he cites fragmenting, flabby, polemical and defensive pluralisms). This critique of certain sorts of pluralism and relativism is especially relevant to any intercultural project.

He is also concerned to stress that a postmodern commitment to fragments does not automatically exclude learning from modern and premodern paradigms, as though our most recent thoughts effectively disable the historical tradition of critique and reflection.

Berlin

Very similar suggestions are made in a number of works by Isaiah Berlin, through his notion of an 'agonistic liberalism', a liberalism which struggles with constructive tensions. Berlin characteristically sees truth as something to be arrived at through making a judgment based on the constructive tension between incommensurable values. It seems to me that the Christian icon of Christ on the cross is just such a commitment by God to holding in tension competing values and bringing an effective reconciliation out of suffering love. God's love in Jesus Christ is the same divine nature which is named in the major world religions, and which creates light in darkness in endless different ways. What we may also be reminded of from Berlin's philosophical reflections (Berlin was of Jewish family and not observant) is that to speak of God, of the love of God, of Jesus Christ, is not in itself to resolve these tensions. History shows that all human imagery is eminently capable of creating *destructive* as well as constructive tensions. It requires careful engagement, as much at a theoretical as at a practical level with the interfaces of theology and culture, to produce communicative action which leads towards rather than away from goodness and the enhancement of human dignity. It is partly in the reimagining of traditional paradigms, and partly in reassessing new situations which have arisen in today's world, that we are likely to find clues to the perennial questions of truth and value which shape civil society.

In his essay on *Two Concepts of Liberty* Berlin famously demonstrated that both 'positive' and negative' liberties had potential advantages and disadvantages. Negative liberty could become a self-absorbed search for individual freedom from constraints which could neglect social responsibilities and ignore the other. Positive freedom as emancipation to a particular desired state could become a tyranny in which individual choice could be threatened. Enlightenment rationalism can create freedom from irrational prejudice and a search for common human values. It can also lead to new technocratic oppression. Romanticism suggests mystery and openness, but can also lead to oppressive nationalism.

Faith as Contribution

Nothing is guaranteed. I try to speak as a Christian theologian, and I want to reflect on the content of an intercultural theology. Theologies of culture have often been constructed as theologies of correlation. These have been illuminating in the work, for example, of Paul Tillich and Paul Knitter. But they become harder to formulate as culture becomes ever more complex and diversified, as layers of global culture produced by mass media interact with fragmenting local cultures. With what aspects of culture are the correlations to be made, given that the theologies are themselves products of complex cultures? There are generic theologies which seek to build up dialogue with universal human values. The stress on what binds human beings together is important, yet it is the specificities in these human commitments which produce constructive engagement in dialogue, and to which theology has always to return. There are confessional and communitarian theologies which stress basic beliefs, but they must always guard against various sorts of tribalism and fideism.

Theologies of correlation between theology and other disciplines are likely to be more successful when they respect firmly the autonomy of their dialogue partners. Science, literature and medicine, for example, may engage in issues which dialogue with theology on occasion, but they are not theology. Interdisciplinarity is not a form of intellectual colonialism. Many disciplines are exercised by the dilemma of how to respect mystery and relativity, and at the same time to justify claims about universal human rights and/or values, which are a practical necessity for continuing human flourishing. There is unlikely to be a single means of resolving these issues. It may be more effective to look for a continuing conversation between different models, through which fragments of different paradigms may advance the discussion, not through any process of continuous tradition, but in a rather less predictable order. Theology which uses human language is always vulnerable to these problems and continuously in development.

Dialogue with culture must strike a balance, it would appear, between the tyranny of the universal and the tyranny of the particular. There may not be strict identity between the beliefs and practices of particular groups, but there may well be resemblances. It is in the exploration of identity, resemblance and difference that dialogue, communication and mutuality may develop. This is a process in which Christian faith and theology can play a role which is both collaborative and distinctive. It will deploy a theology which has core characteristics. But it is also *porous*, in being open to learning from other traditions and other identities. As such it is open to the future, aware that our awareness at the present moment is not God's last word on anything.

Faith as contribution, Christianity as team player: am I advocating a form of process theology, in which the power of God is at work throughout the created order, sharing in its outworking? I have much sympathy with such theologians as the late D.D. Williams, who was happy to use process concepts to illuminate theological issues.[1] This does not of course entail some kind of strict correspondence between divine action and human action. On the other hand, Christians will see all that takes place as within the economy of creation and reconciliation, and so as part of God's purpose for the cosmos.

Theology, culture and human rights – it might be thought that this is a particularly ephemeral and politically correct combination. I think, however, that the area of human rights, understood in the context of the crucified Jesus Christ, is an immensely powerful image grasping the significance of faith in modern society. It relates culture to politics in ways which stretch well beyond the barriers of cultural politics, and may be a focus for apprehending the significance of the God of kenotic love in a world which is as much secular as it is religious.

Paul Tillich in his *Theology of Culture* (Tillich 1959, 159f) wrote of the need for a conquest of intellectual provincialism, between Europe and America. Much of this is still relevant today, but there is a need for a much wider intercultural dialogue. The problem of theological provincialism is perhaps even greater.

Faith and Fallibility

An intercultural theology is part of a team effort. Mention has been made of tensions between Church and kingdom, between what theology may contribute directly and what it may learn by listening to the world. There may be issues in which theology is simply not suited, out of its own traditional resources, to see the best solutions most quickly. That is an admission which theologians are sometimes reluctant to make. Theology may learn to receive as well as to give.

There will be other areas in which theology has a leading role, notably in reflecting from its tradition of worship and service on the understanding of God. Again, there will have to be discernment between *legitimate and illegitimate imagery*. God in Christian faith is pure self-giving love, characterized in the person of Jesus Christ. Not every appeal to transcendence focuses on kenotic love. Visions of transcendence which reflect this core focus will tend to reflect the practice of vulnerable love in culture and society.

This core is non-negotiable, because it reflects the character of God in Christ. It is capable of further interpretation. But it is not infallible. It could in theory be falsified if faith turns out to be in the future or eschatologically mistaken. Faith is faith, not to be identified with irrefutable knowledge. It retains the character of 'nevertheless'. It is not based on compelling logic. But Christian faith is confident that this situation, while rationally conceivable, will never in fact arise. Faith trusts in the divine promise. How to articulate with maximum imaginative force faith's understanding of God remains a standing new challenge in every generation.

Intercultural God

God is God. God in Christian faith is traditionally understood as creator and sustainer of all that is. God, creator, sustainer and faith are all notions with a particular cultural background. But Christian faith has always maintained that human language about God reflected in part a response to God's prior approach and presence to humanity. Our language reflects in human expression awareness of that which transcends our expression. Transition from ancient and medieval concepts to modern and postmodern concepts of what there is has been reflected in the struggle to articulate this sense of the other who is beyond, within and before us. Ontologies and metaphysical frameworks have been tested to destruction, and often shown to be illuminating precisely in the ways in which they break down. Aesthetic choices have been attracted to wholeness and to brokenness, to symmetry and to randomness, to the mystical and to the prophetic. Philosophical and doctrinal commitments naturally shape these preferences. Much modern theology looks for *a way between* the paradigms of the late modern and the postmodern. It will be in this space that we shall look here also.

The reasons for such a choice may be summarized quite succinctly. Traditional ontologies retain considerable explanatory power as ways of imagining the concreteness of being and existence, but they will not work in the ways in which they were intended to, because their conceptual foundations have been shown, at least to many people's satisfaction, to be minimal. Postmodern negative dialectics usually suffer from being universalizing mirror images of the theories they are concerned to refute. They are equally hegemonic and are therefore equally unacceptable. The truth seems to lie between these poles. But this is far from illuminating in itself. What sort of betweenness, intersubjectivity, or whatever else it might be is envisaged?[2]

Engagement between theology and culture involves ambiguities. There is a natural reluctance on the part of Christian systematic theologians to become involved in such ambiguities. There is always the danger of a disastrous dilution of the central content of faith. However, these ambiguities, as we shall see, are not always on the side of theology. There are considerable ambiguities in the conception of culture. It will be a major contention of this study that exploring the interface between theology and culture can illuminate rather than dilute the profile of faith, and help us to understand better its distinctive contribution. Faith is concerned with *the mystery of the hidden/revealed God*. This is indicated but not defined by the various narratives which our changing and disparate cultures construct.

Locating the Ambiguities of Culture and Religion

Culture

Theology needs to engage with culture, but culture has been and is a much disputed notion. It would be unwise to ascribe finality to any of these interpretations. Theology needs to engage with different construals of culture in different ways. And culture is not everything. We have to be aware of the many ambiguities of culture.

Terry Eagleton's *The Idea of Culture* is one of the sharpest recent studies of this complex subject. It is important to hear voices such as Eagleton's, since they do not come from a theologian, and they are not designed to facilitate a comprehensive hermeneutical theory for the theologian. Eagleton begins by relating culture to nature:

> The idea of culture then, signifies a double refusal: of organic determinism on the one hand, and of autonomy of spirit on the other. It is a rebuff to both naturalism and idealism, insisting against the former that there is that within nature which exceeds and undoes it, and against idealism that even the most high-minded human agency has its humble roots in our biology and natural environment. (5).

It is not a substitute for politics: 'Nothing could be less politically innocent than a denigration of politics in the name of the human' (7).

Eagleton says of culture in crisis that, 'It is hard to resist the conclusion that the word "culture" is both too broad and too narrow to be greatly useful' (32). The closest he comes to a definition is that 'Culture can be loosely summarized as the complex of values, customs, beliefs and values which constitutes the way of life of a specific group' (34). Culture is often in fact a battleground of conflicting values: 'At its worst, the result is a kind of pluralized conformism, in which the single universe of Enlightenment, with its self-sameness and coercive logic, is challenged by a whole series of mini-worlds displaying in miniature the same features' (42).

Eagleton comments ironically: 'Whereas high culture is the ineffectual opposite of politics, culture as identity is the continuation of politics by other means. For Culture, culture is benightedly sectarian, whereas for culture Culture is fraudulently disinterested' (44).

Is everything, then, entirely relative without remainder? The issue is faced in a chapter on 'Culture and Nature'. Is the belief that everything is culturally relative itself relative to a cultural framework? 'It belongs to the peculiar kind of cultural animals we are to sit loose to our cultural determinants ... The "essential" self is not one beyond cultural shaping, but one which is shaped in a specific, self-reflexive way' (95). Humanity is poised between nature and culture, and neither culturalism nor naturalism is enough.

Can we or should we move towards a common culture? Eagleton contrasts T.S. Eliot's view of a common culture, which is Christian and elitist, with that of Raymond Williams, which is of radical socialist change: 'For Williams, then, what matters most is not cultural politics, but the politics of culture' (122). Noting that 'The primary problems which we confront in the new millennium – war, famine, poverty, disease, debt, drugs, environmental pollution, the displacement of people – are not especially "cultural" at all' (130), Eagleton concludes that culture is important but not the answer to every social and political issue – a conclusion with which the theologian, from her own standpoint, will readily agree.

Essays in theology and culture, as we shall see, have tended to concentrate on 'high culture', and have not always recognized the extent to which theology is itself embedded in specific cultures. There is probably no one appropriate paradigm for the interaction between theology and culture. On occasion theology, somewhat like law or medicine or other fields, may be more directly, sometimes more indirectly, engaged with particular cultural issues. Theology may be engaged with local, national or global cultures. It may be engaged with cultural issues external to itself, perhaps moulded by other professions, law or business, finance or economics, global media or the Internet. When questions of the nature and purpose of the created order arise, there will be interaction with the professional cultures of the natural sciences, of mathematical physics and of biology.

Religion

Culture is a multifaceted concept. This complexity applies equally to theology and religion. These terms are understood very differently. Sometimes theology has been understood almost as equivalent to religion. Theological studies have been understood as religious studies. But there have also been variations. In the nineteenth century much was made of the concept of *religion* as a means of both raising the subject to a 'scientific' level and of controlling, perhaps domesticating, theology within the humanities. In the twentieth century reaction set in. Barth stressed that theology and religion were not the same thing, elevating the unique status of Christian theology above 'the religions'. In mid-century there was talk of religionless Christianity, and of the secular meaning of the gospel. This was paralleled by the study of the phenomenology of religion in religious studies departments.

Theology may include such areas as the study of religions as phenomena of human society and of religious language, ecumenical or confessional theology as the exploration of affirmations of faith. There will be a reciprocity between the methods pursued and the understanding of God implied or suggested. Where God is understood as an external divine transcendent referent, theology will be shaped in one way. Where God is understood as a term for the human religious imagination without remainder, theology will be shaped in other ways.

Despite the postmodern insistence that 'there is nothing outside the text', it is clear that, for Derrida at least, 'text' may be wide enough to include reason, revelation and experience. Narratives alone, whether regarded as divinely inspired documents or as purely human documents or as some combination of both, can scarcely be the basis for a viable theology, since the range of available texts is enormous and the grounds for selecting one text rather than another are likely to involve appeal to factors outside the written text.

In the course of the development of theological and religious traditions, premodern, modern and postmodern, all kinds of *concepts basic to talk of God* have been developed and modified: talk of substance and accident, transcendence and immanence, presence, revelation, mystery. Though some of the concepts of classical theology may not be sufficient to provoke the kind of dialogue between theology and culture for which this book is arguing, they may be necessary. It is hard to recommend the vision of the compassionate, vulnerable figure of Jesus Christ for human flourishing if there are no grounds for connecting Jesus with a personal source and goal of the created order.

It may of course be that we can so modify our talk of God as to cut out notions of presence, transcendence and grace, and still speak of divine love. There are Buddhist religious notions of immanent compassion which might take us in this direction in developing dialogue, but without some notion of ultimate meaning and purpose in the created order it would appear difficult to deploy the central distinctive contributions of any of the major world religions.

In thinking of the justification of religious belief we cannot act as though the postmodern turn in philosophy had not occurred, any more than we can ignore the modern. That way leads nowhere. But we need not allow a particular area of a complex problem to set and shape the agenda for the whole. There are very different sorts of postmodernity, some more destructive and some more constructive, which can be deployed in different ways. Learning from the postmodern, for example in its critique of notions of transcendence, we may still learn from the premodern in addressing the challenges which face us today. This is part of the value of hermeneutics, *as a tradition of continuity and irruption*. Though the development of a full-scale postmodern doctrine of God inevitably lies outside the scope of this study, we note here the issue as a reminder that theology is as much an enterprise under constant dialectical reconstruction as culture. It is my view that in such reconstruction the more unspectacular reflections on theological method of such writers as H.R. Niebuhr, Basil Mitchell and David Tracy, reinterpreted and developed in a postmodern framework, are likely to stand the test of time better than some more drastic alternatives. My own preference will be for a construal of God which seeks to retain the classical framework, modified by continuous critical reflection. More will be said later about the value of both transcendence and human rights, about both divine presence and divine mystery, in discussion of the contributions to this area by Charles Taylor and David Tracy.

Truth and Culture

I have suggested that from a Christian theological perspective *there is an intrinsic connection between theology and culture*, since the gospel is for all humanity, and there is an intrinsic connection between reconciliation and creation. This connection has been expressed in different ways, which in turn raise new questions.

For Paul Tillich, 'Religion is the meaning-giving depth of culture: culture is the form of religion' (I am indebted here to a stimulating paper by David Klemm on 'The Problems and Prospects of a Theology of Culture'). This makes sense, if it is understood in an inclusive and not an exclusive way. Religion, we might want to add, is also politics. This can have positive and negative connotations. One might ask if Tillich's model of culture is a culture that floats above politics and economics, at a level of comfortable abstraction. Tillich would reply that the model is instantiated in concrete political situations: see his war sermons (Schleiermacher might make a similar reply).

Religion is also concerned with truth and values, which are not separable from but are distinguishable from culture. A religion may be culturally significant, perhaps as a form of social glue or as a vehicle for raising political awareness. But if it is not thought to be true, as far as it is possible to ascertain truth, then it will not have great impact.

We might then explore the triangle, religion, culture, truth, a little further. How could the relationship be developed? We might perhaps speculate that part of the *truth* of a religion is a function of its ability to connect with a particular culture or sub-culture. But some very oppressive cultures have been underwritten by religion. Is such a notion of truth ultimately vacuous? Most members of a given culture believe that truth is influenced by culture but not entirely determined by it. There are other criteria, of coherence and correspondence, which are not absolute but which remain important. The truth of what happens when a motor car hits a bridge at 120 mph may be perceived differently in different cultures, but there will be constant physical effects – deformation of the bodywork – regardless of the perception. The physics largely shapes the impact, including the cultural impact.

The same might be said of theology. It is often argued that theology has its own substantive content and method which it brings to culture. The primary business of theology is to bring its own expertise to bear upon diverse cultures and to shape them. Of course in the case of theology, more than in the case of physics, it will soon be noted that it is inseparable from its own internal cultural texture, based on selection of tradition and ecclesial ethos. The dialogue of theology with culture may be at least a little like the DNA model, with a double helix of one sort of traditional cultural amalgam interacting with another sort of traditional cultural amalgam, except that here there is no repeatability, as in different strings of DNA. Instead, there is rather a chaotic and haphazard (rather than random and therefore partly predictable) interchange. However, the chaos is modified by the recurrence of certain core characteristics of both the more narrowly theological cultures and the wider social cultures. The wider cultures reflect the basic needs of human organization for survival and development. The theological cultures reflect core religious phenomena, such as appeals to reason, revelation and experience in respect of spiritual dimensions of transcendence and/or immanence. A more open theology will understand its core affirmations as inclusive and provisional. A more conservative theology will understand its core affirmations as foundational and precisely authoritative.

Is theological truth appropriately conceived when categorized in terms of religion? We have already mentioned the danger of attenuating the claims of classical Christian faith through the use of the categories of religion. Faith is concerned with all human life and experience, not simply with religious experience, narrowly conceived. It is also concerned to relate its concepts of God to the whole created order, in order to avoid an anthropocentric narrowing. This is not to say that one set of descriptions is always preferable. But it is important to note historical trends and nuances. If 'theology' tends towards triumphalism, 'religion' tends towards diminution of the divine mystery. Both trends have positive and negative aspects.

Religious Truth?

Is culture best understood in terms of religion, as Tillich suggests? I would agree that all human life and activity is ultimately understood by Christian theology *coram Deo*, before God. But this may perhaps be seen best as an ultimate rather than a penultimate perspective, to use a distinction much employed by Bonhoeffer. It is not clear that the religious dimension is or should be the immediate context of all engagement with culture. Culture is related to all human experience, religious and non-religious, secular, economic, social and political. The religious dimension will be integral to such a vision, but not necessarily organically and holistically pervasive. There is something important in Barth's somewhat paradoxical assertion that in the name of God we are called to seek for *human* justice, peace and love, since only God can bring about God's justice in society. This is the constructive dimension of the secular meaning of the gospel.

It may then be asked whether the secular meaning of the gospel implies especially in a postmodern context, the abandonment of anything like the personal God of classical theism, the external divine referent who is ultimate being, substance and love. We may be driven to the *kenosis of kenosis* in some traditions of deconstruction, in which only a purely negative theology remains. Yet this may be too simple, a mirror image of a concept which was itself provisional and multifaceted. A more appropriate model for God is perhaps always likely to be a much more dialectical model, in which fragments of presence and absence in tension with one another are acknowledged in ways which open up, rather than close down, the mystery of God, and which continue to relate to the effectiveness of transcendent kenotic love. The notion of fragment also has its limitations: fragments need to be seen to be related if they are to have value. The appropriate role of religion in culture, including Christian religion, is *to contribute purposefully but not to dominate.*

To contribute: this brings us to the urgent need for an intelligent, interactive intercultural theology, which seeks to be self-critical, respects particularity and retains the objective of engaging in a mutually enriching dialogue with different cultures. The full realization of such a programme may always be beyond us. But the project should at least be able to take constructive steps in the right direction.

Notes

1 Williams' *The Spirit and Forms of Love* (1968) remains a classic exposition of the love of God. He uses process concepts without being limited to a process framework here, and in his posthumously published collected essays (Williams, 1985).

2 Concepts of 'the between' and of intersubjectivity have been explored extensively, for example, by Eric Voegelin and Michael Theunissen. Though they tend to lack precision, they are helpful in pointing to different degrees of connectedness.

CHAPTER 4

Reappraising Hermeneutics: Theology without Frontiers

The Collapse and Retrieval of the Hermeneutic Tradition

Undoing the Past

How are we to develop a legitimate intercultural theology, a theology which has a critical sense of its own use of language and imagery across cultural, historical and political divides? One of the most important tools for understanding theology has been hermeneutics, from Schleiermacher on. This tradition has been severely challenged in recent years by the emancipatory theologies, coming often from outside Europe. Where do we now stand with the hermeneutical project? In this section I want to look at the task of interpretation or hermeneutics today, in the light of the critical questions raised by emancipatory theology, notably black and feminist theology, towards traditional European traditions of philosophical and theological hermeneutics. I shall try to open up the issues as sharply and provocatively as possible.

The world in which we live is often complex, *puzzling*, ambiguous. There has always been a need for interpretation. From a modern perspective we are inclined to see *interpretation* up to the recent past as *monolithic*, corresponding to the authoritarian nature of most ancient societies – until the Enlightenment. Then there was liberty, equality, fraternity. We were free from the chains of dogma. We were able to develop a new hermeneutic, a new hermeneutic of critical rationality. From Richard Simon to Wilhelm Dilthey, we developed a new, highly sophisticated way of dealing with the texts in which our culture articulated itself in its most considered and precise ways. There were, it is true, other theories of understanding, for example in the natural sciences. Einstein and Dirac developed theories of the nature of the physical cosmos which appeared on occasion to challenge some of our hermeneutical axioms. But still, we could see that the philosophy of science was part of the same intellectual culture which had created an intelligible and moderately definitive map of the way things are, banishing superstition and ignorance. Ernst Troeltsch showed how to understand culture as a totality, from psychiatry to jurisprudence. We knew where we were.

Then came the fall: postmodernism. Every man did what seemed right in his own eyes. A kind of fog of epistemological winter descended over the civilized world. Lyotard taught us to rejoice in alterity: we should rejoice in the distinctiveness of our particular culture. Feminists told us that we were intellectually dead in a male chauvinist world. Black philosophers demonstrated our oppressive behaviour. Gay theorists showed that even our new talk of complementarity was radically abusive. Religious fundamentalists rejoiced to find that the ghetto mentality was suddenly radical chic. Platonism was dead. Communicative action was also dead.

What of the future? I want to go back for a moment beyond Plato, beyond the pre-Socratics to Homer. It is not without reason that the *Iliad* is regarded as one of the great classics of human literature. There may be no simple solutions. The outlook is bleak. The world is as the prophet's scroll, full of war and the sounds of war, as John Henry Newman said. Values are incommensurable. But there is a sense that there ought to be values somewhere, that it would be desirable to work towards some kind of reciprocity, that the irrationality of the gods is a kind of outrage against human flourishing. And so a kind of provisional way of coping with the irrational had to be attempted. God may appear to be absent. But for Aeschylus there is hope of an ultimate justice of Zeus, beyond the appearance of radical uncertainty.

The world of ancient Greece was very different from our own, and we have to take care not to minimize its strangeness. Yet we do not find its literature utterly unintelligible. We find resemblances between the values, dilemmas and questions which it raises and our own. Moving into Christian literature, we find that the surd element, the irrational negative which destroys relationship, is traced by Augustine to the Fall, and is overcome in the incarnate Word. In Anselm's famous line, *Nondum considerasti quanti ponderis sit peccatum*. For St Thomas the word is the source of being, of *analogia entis*. For Luther the word brings life out of death, *Deus vivifacit occidendo*. For Schleiermacher, the word must be understood both in its grammatical and its psychological meaning. But it is a text, too, which points to a human being as the incarnate word. Christ brings us into his own sense of the divine presence, and through this presence creates community. *Christus praesens* as word event is at the heart of the gospel for Barth and Bultmann.

Yet this word is a word articulated in the reality of historical events as much as in literary texts. It is for Troeltsch a word in history, for Rahner a sacramental word, for Ebeling a wordless word event. Wittgenstein reminds us that we cannot take the high way to understanding, for we are not God.

Emancipatory Theology and Cultural Diversity

Communication through Cultures

How can we begin to make sense of communication, how can we engage in *actual communication*, in a fragmented world? If we listen to Isaiah Berlin, once we have abandoned the illusion of totality and finality we can develop a technique of agonistic liberalism, in which the constructive tensions between incommensurables may lead us to a dialogue which preserves human freedom. This will be a venture with risk. It will not be us and them but us and us. No party to the hermeneutical engagement is privileged over against the other. In some respects at least, there are no professionals. All are amateurs, all are learners. But some cultural traditions may be more fruitful than others, for historical reasons, at times more by luck than by judgment.

Through the eyes of the modern we can see the limitations of classical paradigms of thought. Through the postmodern we can see the limitations of the modern. Through the varieties of the postmodern we can also see the limitations of the postmodern. Intercultural dialogue develops respect for both minority cultures and majority cultures. It creates a future in which present structures are unfrozen and not refrozen, in which change and variation become the energy of growth to greater maturity. Monochrome cultures tend to stagnate. Cultures are enriched by comparison and contrast. But too rapid change produces new dangers of distortion and destructive conflict. Hermeneutics involves the understanding and the management of constructive change.

One of the disadvantages of postmodernism has been the impression it has sometimes created that there is no possibility of shared values, and of notions of a common good. But on the other hand it has alerted people to the importance of the recognition of *the other* in society, to the dangers of dominance by a monochrome majority culture. This awareness has encouraged the development of liberation or emancipatory theologies, for example Black, Hispanic and feminist theologies. At the same time, there has been a perceived danger of stereotyping the other, so that all Black or feminist theologies are judged by one model, thus defeating the object of a true multicultural enterprise. It is often the case that the otherness of the other will express itself differently in different circumstances, creating room for argument and debate.

It seems to me that classical theology still has much to learn from other cultural perspectives, not least in the present, where 'liberation theology' is often seen as a phase which has passed and can be safely disregarded. We may illustrate the importance of an intercultural approach with reference to the relevance of some aspects of Black theology in Britain today. Readers familiar with the American development of Black theology, with its transition from a civil rights-based call for integration to a militant assertion of Black power, may be somewhat surprised by the prevailing patterns of Black theology in Britain. Black Christians in Britain were for a long time practically invisible, and in many areas remain so because they are very few in number, for example in Scotland. But from the 1950s there was a significant influx of Black Christians into Britain from the West Indies, especially Jamaica. Their development has been well documented in Roswith Gerloff's two-volume *A Plea for British Black Theologies* (1992). The development of this community was shaped by the experience of exclusion from existing local churches, and by the need to affirm continuity with their heritage in the Caribbean. White Western theology has contributed significantly to the involuntary invisibility of Black people, to Black oblivion. In sum, 'white theology is an entrapment which leaves the Black Christian without hope, without recourse and without identity, and leaves White Christians with unrealistic views about themselves' (ibid., I, 45).

The problem is not persecution but neglect. Gerloff quotes some fairly well known lines read at an Apostolic Church service in Watford, England (ibid., I, 75).

> When Jesus came to Watford/They simply passed him by
> They never hurt a hair on him/They simply let him die
> For men had grown more tender/and would not cause him pain
> They simply shut the door on him/And left him in the rain.

Despite the long tradition from Augustine to Gadamer, there remains no communication. This sense of alienation led to the development of independent churches in the charismatic/apostolic tradition, with a great emphasis on holiness and personal piety, notably the Pentecostal Oneness Church, representing Apostolic Pentecostalism. A strong sense of community was reaffirmed in the sphere of charismatic worship. More recently there has been a greater awareness of the social and political dimensions of the gospel, coupled with a radical stress on issues of justice and poverty (Patel, 1990). Paul Grant has said this of traditional Christology:

> What is the point of a personal relationship with someone who apparently does not want to understand how and why you live as you do? It is pointless to be freed form 'sin', only to be enslaved by a Saviour who does not want to live in the backstreets, does not know what it feels like not to have enough cash or can only condemn or patronize those who defend themselves against the incursions of the police and racist attacks. Give me Someone I can trust.

It might be thought that in this respect the British churches are far behind their American counterparts, in which pietistic community was transformed into Black Power in the 1970s, yet that would be an inappropriate stereotyping. The reaffirmation of traditional Caribbean worship may itself be an effective means of coping with marginalization, while the 'Black Power' approach to justice issues has not always led to progress, and may often have to be supplemented by more assimilative approaches in order to achieve long-term goals. A simple division into 'Black' and 'White' theology may well suppress the variety and argument which is intrinsic to a process of engagement with the task of searching for common human goals.

In a new preface to his *Black Theology and Black Power* James Cone noted too a curious omission. There was no mention of the widespread oppression of women in Black churches. 'Amnesia is an enemy of justice. We must never forget what we once were lest we repeat our evil deeds in new forms. I do not want to forget that I was once silent about the oppression of women in the church and in society. Silence gives support to the powers that be' (xi).

Here is another example of the complexity of cultures, in which even apparently radical stances can mask structures of injustice. Eloquent testimony has since been given about the '*triple jeopardy' of women who are women, black and poor*, by Dolores Williams, Jacqueline Grant and others (Grant, 1989). We might also reflect further on the hermeneutics of the phrase 'amnesia is an enemy of justice'. Churches today are much concerned to present a caring, compassionate face to the world. It is important that there should not be a huge gap between public political correctness and private resentments, and that the lasting damage caused by the damning rhetoric of the recent past should be acknowledged.

The whole issue of the role and status of women in theological perspective is another striking case in which awareness of multicultural complexity is vital. Advocates for feminist and womanist thought have opened up whole areas in which traditional theology has been silent, usually oppressively so. Alison Webster (1995) in her study *Found Wanting* has highlighted the ambiguities of notions of the complementarity of men and women, especially in the case of lesbian Christian women for whom the other is also in a sense the same. She argues that 'the logic of imposed complementarity is imposed heterosexuality', and this applies particularly to common exegesis of the imago Dei in terms of the complementarity between man and woman. She quotes from an interviewee, 'Jackie': 'Women in general are seen as dangerous temptresses, with single women being the greater danger since there is no man to control them' (65).

In the lives of Webster's subjects a traditional theological understanding of the role of women will not do: ' With one and the same breath the church invites me – and all others – to journey in discipleship with all its risks and uncertainties – and then warns me that in no way can it partner me on that journey except in safe and restricted terms' (134). It will not do either to class male and female same-sex relations together: 'Lesbians have historically been deprived of a political existence through inclusion as female versions of male homosexuality' (150). She concludes that 'Mainstream Christianity is in danger of making an idol of heterosexuality' and has excluded many people's experiences, particularly that of women. We need a new sexual ethics which is astute about power and committed to provisionality (195).

The Hermeneutics of Generosity

These examples raise sharply the whole issue of hermeneutics in a future society, and, for my subject, hermeneutics in the churches. An effective modern theology must bring together the emancipatory authority of Jesus as the Christ with the shape of the concept of a God for whom to be is truly to be self-giving. and in doing so give fresh meaning to the understanding of life in the spirit. None of this is new to the tradition of the gospel. But it does need to be spelled out in language to fire the imagination in each new generation. Bernstein's 'engaged fallibilistic pluralism' and Berlin's 'agonistic liberalism' seem to me to offer philosophical categories helpful for the expression of such openness. I suggest that human rights and Christology may be mutually illuminating concerns.

Generosity needs to focus on specific application if it is be effective. It is possible to focus on rights and still lack sensitivity and critical self-awareness. 'If I have faith to move mountains, and have not love …'

Diversity and Uniqueness

Reflection on hermeneutics brings us back constantly to the continuing relation between the gospel and culture. I find helpful much of what Kathryn Tanner (1997) says in her *Theories of Culture*. In this study Tanner explores the development of notions of culture in the modern world. Culture was often seen in the past as 'high culture', the development of an educated sensibility, or as a description of the character of a society as a whole, in which there was considerable identifiable uniformity. Beyond this description there are postmodern views of culture, in which different segments of society are seen as discrete units, insulated from one another. Tanner prefers a view of society which takes note of the differences and conflicts *within particular cultures*, which among other things breaks up their insularity and makes engagement between different cultures possible and desirable in a search for common human values and practices.

Tanner relates the cultural quest to the quest for an appropriate understanding of the role of theology in society. Neither classical modern nor postmodern or postliberal views of Christian community as comparatively homogeneous entities will do: 'Theological judgement has to be exercised in order to give meaning and structure to the cultural materials that figure in Christian social practice: those materials are vague and circulate in many versions, with many different potential or actualized associations with other cultural materials and with particular patterns of social action' (160). She concludes that 'Diversity is a salutary reminder that Christians cannot control the movements of the God they hope to serve. It helps them remain open to the Word by keeping them from taking their own point of view for granted. … The recognition of God's free and uncontrollable Word, which respect for Christian diversity spreads, desocialises Christians, so to speak; it breaks the habit of the normal, and thereby frees them for renewed attention to the Word' (175).

I return to the tension between the one and the many, the universal and the particular. It might be thought that, in arguing for an agonistic liberalism on the one hand, with a constructive tension and conflict between sometimes incompatible positions, and at the same time privileging a version of a kenotic Christology of generosity, I am simply recommending a contradiction. My response to such a position would be that I see the Christ symbol, reflecting the reality of God, as intrinsically relational, hospitable and generous. I find recent support for this perspective in Paul Knitter's *Jesus and Other Names* (1996). Jesus is appropriately understood as universal, decisive and indispensable, rather than full, definitive and unsurpassable. Such a perspective is of course invaluable in opening up dialogue with the major world religions, and in defusing the sense of disloyalty which has often inhibited Christians from being fully open to dialogue. In a correlational Christology, Jesus has a relational uniqueness, though these relationships will not always be easy. An intercultural theology seeks conversation with rather than domination or exploitation of alternative perspectives.

In all such dialogue the future is likely to be longer and more significant than the past, though the past will of course contribute to the shaping of the future. The presence of God before, in and after time is a signal of an openness which is always an openness of generosity, not a licence for exploitation. It may be expected to produce surprise, to encourage imagination, to encourage a *theology without frontiers*. In his book, *Jesus and the Reign of God*, C.S. Song has some striking things to say about God which intensify the imagery of a theology without frontiers:

> There is, in the last analysis, one question that is essential to religion, and one only: does it or does it not show to the world and to the people the true face of the God who forgives, comforts and makes alive, the face of the God who is love, justice and freedom? (35)

> God is non-God insofar as there are outcasts. God is non-God as long as outsiders remain outsiders … And as long as certain men, women and children are treated as outcasts and outsiders, God chooses to be the God of outcasts and outsiders. (38)

> God is like a great painter who deeply appreciates each and every color and who approaches each and every shade of a color with deep reverence. … God has to be, then, fully and completely technicolored. (51)

Empowerment, self-giving and generosity: are these not also incommensurable? They are. Yet in the perspective of crucifixion–resurrection they may support a theology without frontiers in which fear and oppression are reduced, in which dialogue and recognition are achieved, in which love and justice are served.

Cultural Complexity and Paradigm Shift

Tanner emphasizes that, on a postmodern understanding, 'the distinctiveness of cultural identity is therefore not a product of isolation. Cultural identity becomes, instead, a *hybrid*, relational affair' (Tanner, 1997, 57). Christian identity is itself essentially relational: 'Christian identity hinges on being open to direction from the free grace of God in Christ' (ibid., 150). Diversity is bound up with creativity.

Tanner offers an immensely stimulating and challenging analysis. We may want remind ourselves, however, of a long tradition of fear of diversity, an understandable and sometimes justified fear. Human life has from the beginning involved enormous dimensions of uncertainty. From the struggles of early hominids to the carnage of twentieth-century wars there has been doubt about survival, about values, about meaning. To this uncertainty religion has traditionally brought consolation. It has provided hope, and it has often provided answers. Religion has provided certainties, and these have inspired and given courage and resilience to continue. Religion has contributed to the skills required for humanity to make astonishing progress in self-development.

The core beliefs of religion, like other core beliefs concerning basic human issues, tend to become fixed and often inflexible. Human beings need to have *core values*, however formally or informally expressed. Without some confidence in sufficient reason and the ability to get things done through empirical deduction from experience, humanity would not have developed in the way it did. Nature and nurture, culture and genetics have brought us to our present human state.

Up to the early modern period, perhaps the seventeenth century in European culture, there was a general belief in a fixed structure of the nature of things in the cosmos, all under the ordinance of a supreme being, God. The Enlightenment was to some extent at least an attempt to assert human independence and the role of reason against the role of divine revelation as the arbiter of faith and morals, channelled through the churches. But still there was the expectation that there was a single system of truth and value, already partially exposed. This framework of reality would eventually be uncovered by the power of reason.

Postmodernism changed all this picture. Now there was celebration of diversity and plurality. There could be no single legitimate world view. There are numerous disparate forms of life within different communities, each with its own perspective. All is relative. Yet the new scheme of things could also bear considerable similarity to the old. Even this kind of negative dialectic could develop a holism of its own, in which all is fragmentary in the same way, a kind of fractal landscape. In the thoroughness of its protest it could become a systematic mirror image of the old totalities. Secondly, postmodern hermeneutics could be employed to conceal a residual hidden agenda of core beliefs which remained somehow inviolate amidst all the relativities.

It seems to me crucial to any attempt to construct a new paradigm of intercultural theology should be firmly grounded in the reality of the interaction between different sub-cultures. It is always easier to prescribe than to listen, yet prescription without at least an attempt, however inadequate on the theologian's part, to listen to this engagement is not likely to be effective.

Intercultural Poetics

It is not the purpose of this chapter to review the vast ranges of current discussion of hermeneutics. My main point has been to underline how voices from the margin are often neglected, not consciously but simply because of the nature of the process, in much classical discussion of hermeneutics. One writer who provides a useful pointer towards overcoming some of the problems is Paul Ricoeur whose work has been discussed by theologians and appropriated in many directions, not all of which would be consonant with the present programme of intercultural theology. But his writings may help us to develop a hermeneutics of dialogue and reciprocity in a number of ways.

Theological readers will be familiar with Ricoeur's basic themes. He is always sharply aware of the dialectical nature of reading and understanding. On the one hand, we are always in danger of reading our own prejudices and assumptions into texts, and hearing from them only what we want to hear. We need to develop a hermeneutic of suspicion, in order to be more self-critical in our approach, to be more objective. On the other hand, we need to be open, to be able to listen to discover what new things the text may be able to tell us. We need to move, as it were, from suspicion to suspicion of suspicion, so that we do not shut ourselves off from discovery through our own critical self-understanding. We need critical openness, suspicion and yet also hope.

Learning about suspicion from Marx, Freud and Nietzsche, Ricoeur envisages a move from an initial critical process to a 'second naïveté', through the power of metaphor, which moves from the literal to an openness to the unfamiliar, given to us in biblical texts (Ricoeur, 1979). We listen, but at the same time we remain in an open process. This is faith – faith without compulsions of any sort. Such an open theology, which unmasks ideologies and remains open to change, has proved attractive to emancipatory theologians as well as to more traditional theologians, the one stressing the openness, the other stressing the call to listen to the specificities of the text. This constructive tension is reflected in much of Ricoeur's other work, in which, for example, he can criticize Gadamer's stress on tradition in the name of suspicion and the need for a political consciousness, while affirming the need to be aware of the heritage of the past (Ricoeur, 1981, 63ff).

For Ricoeur the notion of a symbol is an important hermeneutical device. The symbol is a gift given together with others in community. Through symbol the human being can be pointed from her actual condition to her essential condition, bringing together suspicion and hope in a form of poetics. Poetics enables appropriation of biblical symbolism, but this remains as a suggestion, a possibility open to faith and to continuing philosophical struggle. Ricoeur may not provide us with a conclusive rational template for intercultural theology (indeed such a universal concept would itself be problematic) but he may encourage us to think that an open-ended, interdisciplinary conversation does in fact produce insights which are new discoveries, valuable to all parties in the conversation.

Paradigm Shift without End?

Myth and metaphor, symbol and poetics – these may seem like an invitation to abandon traditional theology, steeped in its ontological and analogical strategies, and to begin all over again. There is a sense in which such a clearing operation, a hermeneutic of suspicion, continues to be necessary and there is still much to be learned from deconstruction in its various forms. I believe that this process still has some way to go, not least in a time of widespread theological retrenchment and resurgent fundamentalism.

There is also then the task of reconstruction, not in the original frameworks, but with the benefit of both the traditions and their interruptions. This re-imaging process has huge implications for intercultural theology. Neither a fixation on classical language usage, steeped in its own cultural particularity nor a mirror image opposite will achieve the task of intercultural communication. The appropriate method will involve the development and modification of both traditional and novel imagery and conceptuality. It will involve new selections of data and new priorities in response to changing political and cultural perceptions. But the new rhetoric will seek also to be faithful to the subject matter of the substance of the faith – that is part of the continuing paradox and challenge of intercultural Christian theology.[1]

Hermeneutics constantly renews itself, but in intercultural perspective renewal goes beyond the linguistic and the philological to wrestle with overtly cultural and political developments in which our language is embedded and in which our communication has power, and involves negotiation between the more powerful and the less powerful in society. Here we must consider, however inadequately, religion within the matrix of that 'thick culture' within which at least in part we live and move and have our being, and which is the subject of the huge enterprise of the social sciences.

Note

1 There are excellent descriptions of the work of Ricoeur, Habermas and liberation hermeneutics in Anthony Thiselton's *New Horizons in Hermeneutics*, (1992). Any theology which takes up emancipatory models must face up to Thiselton's critique of 'the self-contradictory nature of socio-pragmatic liberation "theology" in which the oppressed take up the tools of the oppressors'. Genuine liberation 'de-centres both the individual and corporate self' (ibid., 450). For Thiselton, the cross relativizes all self-interests (617). (This must be true, for Christian faith. But of course the cross has itself been subject to all sorts of subversion in Christian tradition, so that its meaning has to be constantly re-imagined.)

CHAPTER 5

The Secular and the Religious: Culture and Politics

Faith and Culture in a Secular Society

I have suggested that mutual appreciation and constructive interaction between theology and culture may be facilitated by reflection on the notion of generosity. There is a sense in which, for Christian faith, *generosity is an eschatological concept*. Only God is truly generous. Our generosity has always an element of the incomplete, the self-interested, the coercive. This study is concerned with interactions of faith and culture in a number of specific instances. It deals in fragments. At the same time, it is designed to be an integrative theology in which the clusters of fragments are seen to have an ultimate coherence.

The delicate task of dialogue is full of potential hazards. For example, when we look at the relation between Christianity and literature, we see an interesting ambiguity in the role of such central images as incarnation, for example in inspiring great poetry and at the same time perhaps in reinforcing authoritarianism in the work of Eliot. Questions of ethics and of truth in corporate and individual life are constantly thrown up by these interdisciplinary explorations, and they require answers. In addition, there are endless different sorts of connections between Christianity, theology and the humanities. Poets and novelists may often be influenced by religious practice and by doctrine, without ever reading formal theology. There are some who did read theology and were consciously influenced by it – Eliot, again, by Niebuhr and Barth, Auden by Niebuhr and Kierkegaard. Beyond this, the whole discussion is deeply influenced, at least in Europe, by the increasing effect of secularization.

The Secular

We must note that very different sorts of interactions occur in different cultures. Though 'intercultural theology' very often suggests to us interreligious comparisons across the major world religions and in different continents, there are, as we have noted, also numerous overlapping sub-cultures in European and American societies, and in predominantly Christian contexts. And there is continuous change. It is often said rightly that the Bible has an enormous influence on literature and the humanities. It may be, however, that this influence will be nothing like as great in the next century as it was in the past. It is true that the 'secular Christianity' which many expected to appear in the 1960s did not happen, and the last decades of the twentieth century brought a renewed interest in religion and spirituality in many parts of the world. Yet, in Europe at least, church attendance continues to plummet. This distancing from the churches is bound to have an effect on the role of the Bible in society. The novels of the 1980s and 1990s in Europe and even in the United States rarely make Christian or biblical themes central.

The influence of theology in Europe and America has diminished over the last decades. Theology has in general turned to various forms of orthodoxy. This could be construed in different ways, from a necessary return to the essentials to almost a kind of commodification, which has filled the internal needs of the churches. One result has been a tendency to an ever-greater chasm between the guild of the theologians and the world which billions observe and assess through the mass media.

In the United States there is an understandable concern not to go down the same secularizing route as Europe. How far this will succeed is not clear. It seems likely that postmodern fragmentation will preserve different patterns of observance, more and less secular, among different groups. In the remaining two-thirds of the world there may be increasing polarization between secular and religious world views. There is scope everywhere for tension and conflict, constructive or destructive.

In considering the problems of theological engagement with contemporary society we should not hesitate to avail ourselves of the insights of the sociology of religion. In his work on secularization the British sociologist Steve Bruce (1996) documented in a striking manner the decline of religion in the modern world. He noted everywhere the erosion of the supernatural. In Britain in 1900, 22 per cent belonged to Protestant denominations; in 1990, the figure was 7 per cent. Belief in God is increasingly diffuse. There is fragmentation and eclipse of community. Stress on rationality appears to leave less space for God. Modernization generates secularization except where religion finds or retains work to do other than relating individuals to the supernatural. Religious adherence remained strong mainly as an expression of protest, as a rejection of alien values and domination, and of cultural and social integrity. Churches decline into sects and cults. *Liberals decline.*

Religion finds social roles only in cultural defence and cultural transition. Examples are seen in the ethnic church – Poland, and in 'the threatened elect' – Afrikaaners and Ulster Protestants. Religion survives in cultural transition, migration and social change, but disappears in the third generation. Only where people still possess a traditional religious world view are they likely to respond to social dislocation by seeking and being attracted to religious remedies.

America is only an apparent exception. Religion here provides a way of maintaining American values with ethnic distinctiveness. But there are now changes in US religion. We are seeing the secularization of the mainstream:

loss of specific content and distinctiveness. There is a kind of secularization of conservative Protestantism in the culture of some fundamentalist groups. The New Christian Right presents itself as a discriminated-against minority. Ethnicity is very important. The 'New Religions' of the 1970s represent only very small numbers. The individual is sovereign. Religion will now be mainly a matter of pick and mix.

Even if only a fraction of this challenge is true, it represents a serious challenge to theology. Large swathes of modern society are not particularly religious, and people do not spend their lives locked in Kierkegaardian angst, looking for religious illumination. A theology and a Church which is content to remain self-contained and self-reflexive is unlikely to avoid further marginalization.

The Global, the Particular and the Secular

We may reflect that Bruce's argument represents only one side of a complex picture. Even where it is not today as powerful as it was, religion is part of a complex and fragmented culture. It may be much more than this, a human response to a divine initiative. It is affected by the impact of contemporary cultural trends, at this time *globalization* on the one hand and *fragmentation* on the other. The development of modern mass media assists globalization. 'Cultural studies' in many university courses has in recent years involved the analysis of 'popular' culture, sometimes in conscious contrast to the 'elite' culture of the European academic tradition. Religion has its place in this revolution, alternately pursued and marginalized by television, and now by the Internet. There is not, and perhaps never has been, a single stream of universal culture even in Europe.

I shall concentrate almost exclusively on Christianity. Christianity has had much influence on human civilization, and Christians have been involved in numerous professions. Theologians have a distinctive relationship between personal belief and professional output. In the world of literature, and in the visual arts, there has often been a direct reflection of faith in relation to art. In the ancient world there were direct correlations between religion and such areas as law, medicine, science and politics. In some instances these direct relationships remain. The law of marriage in Britain is still much influenced by theological considerations. Discussion of medical ethics often includes a religious input. Politics is affected by Christian traditions, with good and bad effects.

But often, at least in the modern world, the relation between religion and culture, between theology and professional life, is much more indirect. Though lawyers, historians, bankers, civil servants and medical professionals often have religious views, it is not usually thought appropriate for these views to impinge directly on professional work. Religion remains as an implicit framework for their understanding of life, their private views of integrity and their personal and family relationships.

They may use their professional skills to assist in humanitarian work which for them has a religious underpinning. The result is that religion is on the one hand much less manifestly operative as a factor in modern cultures than, say, in the ancient world. But it may still have an effect much greater than external evidence would lead us to suppose. The impact of religion is less likely to come from direct engagement with theology – how many non-theologians regularly read theology today? – than from the impact of Christian worship, and from the continuing effect of a long tradition of Christian values shaping many societies. Even in countries where church attendance is very low, as in Denmark, there would appear to be a deep *continuing respect* for Christian values in society. In speaking, then, of the correlation of religion and culture, we are considering a dialogue which takes place on innumerable levels of different intensity and visibility in different cultures.

We have stressed the need for theology and the churches to build effective bridges to other dimensions of culture, against the anti-modern trends of much current theology and practice. But of course not everything that is, is good. For Christians there can be a bridge only to link up with the basic human values at the centre of the gospel: love, peace, justice, forgiveness and reconciliation. Coercion, oppression, racial discrimination and the like are always wrong. As is often noted, churches which have practised apartheid have been perfect examples of the involvement of Christianity with evil. But the abuse does not take away the proper use.

Is this in the end just one more form of cultural imperialism, advocating an acculturated modern liberal faith based on the Western secular values of one highly particular culture? We need not undervalue the positive role of Christianity in fostering important aspects of liberal democracy, humanistic culture and cosmopolitan values. Indeed the tradition of Christian humanism has been hugely beneficial to humanity. But we shall always have to bear in mind that our contribution to dialogue will depend not on our self-perception but on how we are perceived by others.

Church attendance, at least in Europe, is in sharp and apparently irreversible decline. There will always be the need for Christian communities to gather around centres of worship, but it may be that in the future at least some of these communities may see themselves, not as self-sufficient sources of salvation for those who come in, but as resources to contribute, in a paradigm of humility and mutuality, to a continuing human task of constructing values and constructing wider societies. Here the aim would not be to dominate or to shape society in the manner employed by traditional Christendom, but to offer fragments of vital resource: to act as *catalysts*, as the salt of the earth. Within such a framework the interaction of religion and culture, both at the margins and at the centres of cultures, becomes highly significant. It is impossible to bring support to the margins without adequate support from the centres.

For Christian theology to take this step towards reciprocity, and to abandon its traditional claim to absolute priority in any joint exploration, requires considerable courage. It requires both generosity and an understanding of hospitality which is open not only to give graciously but also, and this is often much harder, to receive graciously. It seems to me that such a body as the Red Cross, which originally came into being largely under Christian influence, though it has now been paralleled by the Red Crescent, has been such a generous host to social and political life, exerting influence out of all proportion to its size. It is this transformative function, not necessarily turning everyone into traditional Christians, but offering a deeply Christian envelope for thought and praxis, which seems to me to be a vital role for Christian theology and community in the future. It also requires a measure of confidence that an intercultural theology is not simply an attenuated version of more confessional theologies, but is concerned equally to articulate the huge positive contribution of the Christian faith to the human future.

The Continuing Influence of Religion?

When we consider the influence of religion and Christianity in particular on culture and the arts we think of the influence of religion on science and medicine in the ancient world, of Christianity on painting and prose up to the early twentieth century. Yet it would be hard to think of a decisive influence of Christianity on the humanities after, say, 1950. By this time the lawyers, historians and the like are doing what the natural scientists did earlier – producing their research *without any reference to religion*, though they may have private religious beliefs.

Yet there is this paradox, that there is still a strong interest in religion in society, in large areas of the world. In North America churchgoing remains buoyant. Private religious feeling remains. Theologians still write theology, often engaging with culture. Where, then, is the cultural outlet for other Christians and people of religious conviction? Christian convictions about justice and compassion still influence the conduct of professional life in almost every area. Religion can still be a source of management of change in these areas, as either a conservative or a progressive force. Religion has both inhibited and supported the development of human rights. For example, many of those who work for Amnesty International are Christians. Religious people are often at the forefront of campaigns for social reform, in the name of justice and peace, even though the churches' past record on these issues is very ambiguous.

If religion is to be a force for good in society – and the major religions are all committed to such a vision – then it is important that not only theologians should be involved in trying to build bridges between religion and culture. What is needed is a reciprocity of dialogue and of effort to promote common human values.

There has been much concern in the liberation and emancipatory theologies for a close correlation of theology to *praxis*, in the name of love and justice. Yet it will be strange if there is no corresponding engagement from other disciplines, for example from the arts. This may take the form of postmodern pluriformity, such as feminist theology in dialogue with Women's studies and Black theology with Black studies. It has to be noted here that poetry and drama are themselves not as central to modern culture as they were in previous centuries. The impact of the mass media has created its own culture, and though this has not neglected traditional art forms, it has led to a kind of marginalization of them. Football, TV chat shows and soaps, pop music and even the national lottery arguably have a much greater role in the shaping of culture. It would be important in all areas of the humanities to provoke constructive engagement with theological themes on a much wider front, as Kierkegaard had an impact on Auden or Anglican incarnational theology had on Eliot. Charles Taylor, a philosopher, is a model example of dialogue with contemporary theology. Here is a task that has hardly begun.

Fragmentation, Theology and the Politics of Culture

Seeking to balance an audit on the relation of Christianity to culture at the end of the twentieth century, we may say that, in Europe at least, *the fairly homogenous pervasion of culture in Christendom is definitely over*.

That is by no means to say that the contribution of Christian faith is over. On the positive side of the account, the radical pluriformity of modern culture may provide new opportunities for imaginative initiatives at different levels in specific sectors of particular cultures. These fragments may involve concentrated areas of Christian transformative symbolism, as often envisaged in Christian evangelical postmodernism. But this is not the only possible alternative. They may also involve concrete and local instances of intercultural dialogue between faith and society of a more liberal sort. Such dialogue may involve the setting out of unapologetic Christian perspectives. To describe such engagement I am inclined to prefer the word 'liberality', to indicate a critical development beyond classical liberalism. Liberality involves generosity, unconditionally open to mutuality and reciprocity. To identify and pursue such avenues will involve both reference to areas of significant interaction in the present and comparison with modes of interaction in the past. In this way we may hope to arrive at guidelines for more effective intercultural dialogue between Christianity and society in the future. In seeking to examine response to the presence of God within the fragments of multicultural pluralism we shall be pursuing further the discipline of theological intercultural hermeneutics.

Dangerous Dialogue?

The ways in which Christian theology has interacted with different layers of culture and different disciplines are endless. Encounters which seem particularly fruitful to one Christian perspective will seem unfruitful to others. In this study I shall concentrate on areas which have appeared to me to be significant, and explain why this should be so. I shall then draw conclusions which I hope may be helpful in future dialogue between theology, faith and culture.

In this dialogue, as I see it, none of the partners has a privileged point of view. The theologian, the poet, the historian, the political scientist – all have contributions to make, and none has *the* master narrative which can encompass all else in an authoritative way. This is something which the theologians, at least, have been slow to learn. But the phenomenon also occurs in other forms of academic positivism, for example in the natural sciences.

We have noted that modern literature, and modern public life in general, rarely reflects a specific emphasis on Christian faith. But faith and theology continue to have an impact on public life. There is a continuing effect of the historical legacy of Christianity in many cultures, notably in Europe and America. There is a considerable silent influence of Christian belief on public and private life, an influence which certainly includes love, peace, justice and generosity. This may be hard to confirm, but it does have an impact on theoretical and practical action in the public square. Sometimes the most articulate expressions of traditional Christian faith are the least effective instruments of Christian action in society. We may compare the often anonymous attempts at reconciliation on a personal and social basis in Northern Ireland with the orthodox dogmatic rhetoric of a figure such as Ian Paisley. Striking the appropriate balance between faith and culture is rarely easy, but an effective interaction of faith and culture remains central to human flourishing.

The Public Sphere and the Recognition of Values

Different sorts of theologians, historians and others will inevitably reflect very different interactions between theology, faith and culture in their work. Theologians naturally tend to become increasingly absorbed in a purely theological framework of reference: this is evident, for example, in a reading of Wolfhart Pannenberg's impressive three-volume *Systematic Theology*. The social historian will naturally have a different field of interest from the ecclesiastical historian, or the historian who is seeking to reflect on issues of fundamental theology.

Theology, Culture and Values: Modern Britain

A major focal point of the study of theology and culture is the role of the Christian community in relation to social issues. In his excellent *Churches and Social Issues in Twentieth-Century Britain*, G.I.T. Machin gives a condensed and highly instructive perspective on the complexity of the interactions of theology, faith and culture in our time. He sets out from the church and social questions, 1900–1918. He considers that, in this period, part of the churches' continuing influence lay in their contributions, some highly conservative, some fairly liberal, to the current growth of social reform. Such bodies as temperance societies, a National Purity Crusade and a National Anti-Gambling League set the tone. The Nonconformist Lloyd George was able to pronounce that 'we are fighting Germany, Austria and Drink, and the greatest of these deadly foes is drink'. The Lambeth Conference of 1908 produced a fierce and detailed denunciation of artificial contraception. The First World War produced a National Mission of Repentance and Hope in the Church of England, and its reports, such as the fifth on Christianity and industrial problems, were much criticized.

Moving on selectively, 1945 brought the welfare state and increased ecumenical effort. The churches' efforts to limit divorce legislation continued. Artificial insemination by a donor was long combated. The churches strongly opposed the Wolfenden Report of 1957 which promoted greater sexual tolerance. A new source of temptation increased: television.

In the 1970s and 1980s church membership declined. Women's ordination began to make some progress. AIDS provided the more conservative with new arguments in favour of tradition. As divorce increased, the 'culture wars' on family values from the USA became echoed in Britain. The churches laid stress again on social justice, in opposition to the Thatcher administration. Machin ends at 1996. Attitudes in social ethics tended to harden at the end of the 1990s, notably at the Lambeth Conference in 1998.

We should remember too that social change in the West takes place against the background of a fast developing pop culture, accelerated by media expansion and technological development. We shall look at this phenomenon again in considering the impact of applied science in society. There is a good account of mass and popular culture, and of its critique in the Frankfurt school of criticism, in its notion of commodity fetishism, in Strinati (1995). Strinati discusses the theory of a breakdown in the distinction between culture and society, in which culture no longer mirrors society but is society, as the mass media constitute our sense of reality as virtual reality.

'Neither consumerism nor television form genuine sources of identity and belief, but since there are no dependable alternatives, popular culture and mass media come to serve as the only frames of reference available for the construction of collective and personal identities': Strinati suggests that the idea that the mass media take over 'reality' clearly exaggerates their importance (239). There is a discussion of the increasing role of virtual reality in Graham Ward's *Cities of God.*

The Political Imperative

How is faith to contribute intelligently to the issues which often have provoked the 'culture wars' that are an inevitable part of the process of human social development? How are the relationships between theology and culture to be related to the relationships between theology and *society*? Some comments by David Tracy appear to me to shed much light on the issue.

> Without *a critical social theory*, the link between the debates about rationality and the debates on modernity (and postmodernity) are difficult if not impossible to clarify. That methodological failure has important substantive consequences: first, the correlational category 'situation' (as with Tillich in the systematics or most of my own work) has the strength of allowing for good cultural analysis. Yet most 'situationalist' analysis is in danger of being trapped in purely 'culturalist' or even 'idealist' categories unless the correlational theologian can show the links between the cultural resources of our situation and the materialist (economic, social, political) conditions of our society. (Tracy, in Browning, 1992, 26)

Tracy goes on to stress the importance of both dialogue and solidarity in action (ibid., 41). It is important not to see culture as something which floats mysteriously above society, but rather as something constantly present within society. The question of a critical social theory leads me back to Charles Taylor.

In his well known essay on 'The Politics of Recognition' (Gutmann, 1994), Charles Taylor analysed the delicate balance between the importance of the Enlightenment concern for the search for universal human values on the one hand and the need for the recognition of the cultural values of particular, often minority, groups on the other. He underscored the suggestion that we are in any case very far from being able confidently to assert that we have the correct criteria for evaluating the claims of different cultural groups, though we must continue to do what we can, aware that this is a learning process. The subsequent debate, notably in the volume, *Multiculturalism*, edited by Amy Gutmann, stressed both the importance of the issues for debate on human values and the need for constant critical reflection on the ways in which judgments are made.

When we then remind ourselves of the other twentieth-century voices which we have heard – Bernstein, Berlin and Taylor – we may appreciate that there is much to be learned from critical study of multiculturalism. As human beings we must continue to search for common human values. But we become aware that we are very far from identifying perfect criteria, and we require a considerable degree of humility. As theologians we must seek to understand further God's desire for the salvation and reconciliation of the whole created order, and the role of Christian community in this wider purpose. For the sake of the Christian gospel we shall want to look at the scope of intercultural rationality in articulating the meaning of the divine reconciliation present in the gospel. We shall seek to combine both recognition of cultural particularity and limitation with awareness of the need for connection of these fragments in communicative action.

However inconvenient, the gospel is radically inclusive, reciprocal, encouraging of mutuality. Christians will continue to believe that God, the God of Jesus Christ, is and remains for ever the creator and redeemer of the cosmos. But that does not mean that his followers have any kind of divine right to control human affairs. They are called to serve, to contribute, to advise, to persuade, but not to rule. Church history past and present makes it clear that this is a pretension which the Church finds it immensely hard to lose, which it tends to mask in an ever more complex rhetoric of self-justification. Justification by faith alone is a concept which modern theology often finds obscure, but it does point to the self-sufficiency of God's grace for Christian life and thought.

Reference to justification by faith, however, itself points to an area in which theology must be ever vigilant. Justification was a focal point of the theology of Martin Luther, for whom Christian freedom was also a central issue. But concentration on the theological complex of justification in an ahistorical or pietistic context could and can act as a kind of immunization against the practical implications of justification in a wider society. It can also produce sterile repristinations of traditional confessional orthodoxies. Both strategies are a form of abdication of theological responsibility in the world before God. That is why concepts of *agonistic liberalism* and engaged fallibilistic pluralism, and the debates about multiculturalism and recognition of particularity, are so fruitful for precisely theological reflection.

It may be objected that recognition of ambiguity is not always helpful. Luther could stress *simul justus et peccator*, and still offer unambiguous condemnation of the Jews and the peasants in the name of God. Charles Taylor has noted importantly that talk of multiculturalism is not the end but the beginning of a conversation, which remains open and which recognizes the provisionality of our judgments, while continuing to defend and support central core human values. In the sphere of Christian community, communicative action between Church and the wider society, Church in the public square, will remain a pressing commitment.

The Politics of Culture

Charles Taylor provides an always illuminating paradigm for intercultural thinking. I want to look again more closely at his argument in *On The Politics of Recognition*: 'A number of strands in contemporary politics turn on the need, sometimes the demand, for recognition' (25). There are thought to be links between recognition and identity. Where past societies spoke of honour, today we speak of dignity. Since the Enlightenment we speak of individualized identity, and think of ourselves as beings with inner depths. We seek authenticity, being true to ourselves. But human life has a basically dialogical character. It is partly formed by the people we love. It 'is vulnerable to the recognition given or withheld by significant others' (36). There are two consequences in the public sphere. With the move from honour to dignity has come a politics of universalism, emphasizing the equal dignity of all citizens. There is also a politics of difference, inviting us to recognize 'the unique identity of this individual or group, their distinctiveness from everyone else. … The universal demand powers an acknowledgement of specificity' (39).

For the politics of equal dignity, all share a universal human potential. For the politics of difference, one should accord equal respect to all actually evolved cultures. The difference blind society can be highly discriminatory. Rousseau is important to discussion both of dignity and of recognition. Where there is stress on a very tight common purpose, 'the margin to recognize difference is very small'; there is a danger of too much homogenization. There is a tension between individual rights and common goals, a notion of the common good. The situation is illustrated from the debate about the constitution of Quebec. There may, however, be forms of liberalism which both call for the invariant defence of certain rights and allow for the integrity of particular cultures.

It may well be wrong to assume that 'difference-blind' liberalism can offer a neutral ground on which people of all cultures can meet and coexist. Liberalism cannot claim complete cultural neutrality. It is hard for us all to recognize the equal value and worth of different cultures, and to respect them equally. Can we presume the equal value of all human cultures? Even if we do, we need not finally decide after reflection that they are all of equal worth. This could be condescending and homogenizing. But we should be willing 'to be open to comparative cultural study of the kind that must displace our own horizons in the resulting fusions. What it requires of us is an admission that we are *very far away from that ultimate horizon* from which the relative worth of different cultures might become evident. This would mean breaking with an illusion that still holds many 'multiculturalists' – as well as their most bitter opponents – in its grip' (73).

Taylor's essay is written with beautiful clarity. The commentators draw out important consequences, summarized in the introduction. Habermas makes a useful distinction between culture, which need not be shared by all citizens, and a common political culture marked by mutual respect for rights. Appiah rejects group recognition as an ideal because it ties individuals too tightly to scripts over which they have no authorial control. There may be hope of a '*democratic citizenship* of equal liberties, opportunities, and responsibilities for individuals'.

It may be that 'this requirement of political recognition of cultural particularity – extended to all individuals – is compatible with a form of universalism that counts the culture and cultural context of individuals as among their basic interests' (5). But if 'supremacist' cultures should not be respected (though they must be tolerated), what are the moral limits for recognition of particularity? Susan Wolf argues for the fuller public recognition of women, Steven Rockefeller for the need to respect individuals as individuals, and Michael Waltzer for a democratic liberalism which, while respecting all citizens, need not be entirely neutral in choosing policies for the common good. In these matters, however, there are no easy answers. As Anthony Appiah concludes, 'Between the politics of recognition and the politics of compulsion, there is no bright line' (163).

Between a laissez faire individualism and a politics of compulsion we need a constructive tension which will require hard work. I am reminded here of an early comment by Martin Luther King:

> There is a dire need today for a liberalism which is truly liberal. What we are witnessing today in so many northern communities is a sort of quasi liberalism which is based on the principle of looking sympathetically on all sides. It is a liberalism so bent on seeing all sides that it fails to become committed to either side. It is a liberalism that is so objectively analytical that it is not subjectively committed. It is a liberalism which is neither hot nor cold, but lukewarm.[1]

There is a kind of discussion of culture which floats above the everyday world of political, social and economic reality, and may immunize us against the force of that reality. Like theology, culture too has had its blind alleys. But the presence of risks should not inhibit us from engaging with difficult issues.

Communicative Action and Democratic Process

We must demonstrate the viability of intercultural theology by doing it. Before turning to the praxis of intercultural theology there is, however, a further voice which we should hear on the relation between culture, politics and society, the voice of Juergen Habermas.

Bearing in mind that concepts of culture inevitably reflect the cultures of those who make the definitions, and that the constructive tensions described by Berlin and Bernstein may be more adequate to the apprehension of social reality than comprehensive theories of everything, how are we nevertheless to forge connections between different areas and dimensions of culture? It is important to remember that neither Berlin nor Bernstein, nor other thinkers whom we shall examine, such as Nussbaum, see an inevitable connection between cultural pluralism and cultural relativism. There is no straight choice between relativism and a comprehensive univocal theory of rationality. Nevertheless, it is extremely helpful to engage in dialogue with comprehensive theories of social reality at this point, and to turn to the social sciences.

The social sciences, not least through the work of Marx, Freud and Durkheim, have sought to give accounts of society and of cultural development which uncover their basic structures through tracing universal frameworks of interaction. Especially significant in twentieth-century Europe has been the work of Juergen Habermas. Most famously through his theory of communicative action, he has sought to give a rational account of society which sets out the tensions between political, social and cultural forces, unmasking manipulation and setting out the conditions for fruitful social interaction. His work has been criticized for concentrating on rationality rather than solidarity in action, and for privileging argument rather than conversation – features to which we shall return. But it does provide a challenging suggestion for attempts to connect and integrate without losing the value of diversity.

Habermas's earlier writings tended to take a rather negative view of religion, as a force operating more to disrupt than to integrate communication. But he has conceded that this need not be the case. His work has been used extensively in international relations theory, and is clearly of value in uncovering the springs of social interaction. For Habermas, rationality is not to be conceived on the Cartesian pattern of the isolated individual examining himself. Understanding occurs between human subjects, as mutual understanding. Through mutual interaction there arise units like the state and the economy, which refer to the natural world and also to the human world. These units are shaped to achieve certain goals, such as power and money. In turn these larger social units come back to affect the 'lifeworld' of interpersonal action from which they first arose. This result may then be challenged by social movements which defend an ideal of communicative reason in the life world, freed from the coercion of the system world, with its inequalities of power and influence.

Modern industrial societies have concentrated excessively on instrumental action, on doing whatever is necessary to attain given ends. They have paid too little attention to communicative action, to seek to understand and come to agreement with others.

Though this call for 'ideal speech situations' may seem impractical, it has stimulated notions of participation and transparency in international relations. Habermas has forcefully criticized modern technical and political systems in which powerful organizations can exploit or colonize people in order to realize their own narrow interests, not least in apparently liberal and pluralist frameworks, in which the most powerful often have the last word, perpetuating poverty through globalization. Precisely because of these dangers, Habermas (1996, 177) identifies 'transnational global spheres' as crucial areas for discussion of global issues. Argumentative rationality and communicative action may be helpful dialogue tools between opposing theories.

Habermas distinguishes between different aspects of what we regard as knowledge: work knowledge, which is centred on controlling our environment (most scientific knowledge), practical knowledge, which relates to social interaction, and emancipatory knowledge or self-reflection. This third, most important, knowledge is gained by self-emancipation leading to a transformation of perspective, and is related to the notion of a hermeneutic of suspicion. He is, as it were, salvaging the project of modernity, with its emphasis on reason, as a bridge to civilization, while adding the Marxist critique of economic exploitation, through which human beings are denied freedom. The social form of human life has at its basis a defining moment of communicative action.

> Communicative action can be understood as a circular process in which the actor is two things in one: *an initiator*, who masters situations through actions for which he is accountable, and a *product* of the transitions surrounding him, of groups whose cohesion is based on solidarity to which he belongs, and of processes of socialization in which he is reared. (Habermas, 1992, 135)

Of course this comprehensive theory has been subject to all sorts of criticism. Gadamer criticized the notion of obtaining 'objective' knowledge of the social realm which can overcome prejudices. Said saw the work as Eurocentric, with insufficient attention to political colonial exploitation. Lyotard noted that society's marginalized groups might remain excluded in a final consensus of the majority. Tracy has noted the absence of religion in the division of the intellectual world into the three spheres of the scientific, ethical and aesthetic. Yet Habermas's massive plea for communicative action remains an important pointer, both to the inadequacies of unreflected policies of globalization and to the basic need of human beings for self-reflective communication in genuine reciprocity. It relates law, basic rights and constitutional democracy to fundamental human needs, and maps out carefully the connections and differences between the public and private spheres in human life.

Habermas's work overlaps and differs in striking ways from the work of two of the most significant recent American writers on politics and the public sphere, Richard Rorty and John Rawls. Only a brief comment can be made here (Rawls and Habermas have been discussed in relation to theology elsewhere: see Newlands 1994,1997).

Like Habermas, Rorty also affirms and then expands the Enlightenment notion of the reflective self, extending this to an appreciation of all persons, including the strangers and the other, and does this not only through reason but through a feeling of solidarity. Solidarity and obligation, especially to exploited groups, is close to Habermas's communicative community. But, while for Habermas there is a human transcendent core of rationality which is the source of moral action, for Rorty such a universal category is more of an idea which is helpful but which can be seen to be the product of contingent historical circumstances, through the development of liberal democracy – a political arrangement which as a matter of fact works.

Rorty is more cautious than Habermas about universal categories, notably in speaking of human rights, which will be central to this study. Respect for human rights is, for Habermas, an essential element of communicative rationality, and has an essential liberal democratic content (Habermas, in Cronin and de Greiff, 1998; Habermas, 1996, 127). It is cosmopolitan and centred on individuals. Individuals as individuals have rights. For Rorty such respect is dependent on a societal conception of mutual respect between peoples and nation states. Habermas is more suspicious of state nationalism, which may inhibit rights.

In this volume we have stressed the need for theology and Church to relate to culture rather than to turn into a cult. We have underlined the importance of theology and Church at the margins of society as well as at the centre. It should not be thought, however, that any methodology will be infallible. In his *Achieving Our Country*, Richard Rorty has issued a well considered warning against the danger of turning politics into cultural politics, echoing Eagleton's point about culture being no substitute for politics. Rorty argues that preoccupation with minority issues may distract from the continuing need to address such fundamental social injustices as economic inequality and unemployment, and he warns against using mantras from Foucault, Jameson and other postmodern thinkers as an excuse to avoid the issues of executive authority and abdicate responsibility for social action, and retire to a 'critical spectatorship'. The vacuum could be filled by a deeply conservative backlash (Rorty, 1998, 90ff). The point is well taken.

Rorty's brand of pragmatism, emphasizing the value of the piecemeal progress of a liberal humanism as against the creation of vast theoretical visions, is consonant with the approach from teamwork and contribution which is central to this study. While I do not share the belief that religion has no place in the public square, I think that many of Rorty's criticisms of public religion are effective, not least his critique of the Christian Right.

My conclusion in considering Habermas in intercultural perspective is that his insights into the dynamics of modern industrial society, with their possibilities for human well-being and human coercion, are of real value for a theological assessment. His insistence on the permanent value of rational persuasion and democratic process is always relevant. However, I tend to agree with David Tracy, following my attention to the work of Bernstein and Berlin, that a model of dialogue which seeks for conversation may be in the end more useful than one which seeks to persuade by rational argument (cf. Tracy, in Browning and Fiorenza, 1992, 19ff, 22ff). As Robert Wuthnow has put it (ibid., 216), 'Does not expressive communication lose something of its very essence in having to be defended against critics in terms of some standard of rational argumentation, effectiveness, or consistent appeal to social conventions?'

This is particularly important for a theology which seeks to recognize the contribution of theologies at the margins of the classical consensus. It may indeed be that an intercultural theology itself, by raising ultimate questions about the technicized society, may be just such a vital emancipatory margin within a globalized society.

Though we shall not examine his work in detail here, we may note the importance also of John Rawls in the development of theories of democratic process. Rawls is more cautious than Habermas about universal categories, even if his whole work is driven by concern for justice and the common good – though with lower-case letters. He is offended by slavery and shocked by the darker side of religion. Personal dignity is fundamental. He is concerned for personal and civil liberties, and for basic political rights. This requires toleration and mutual respect, but not for violation of basic human rights. Freedom and equality take precedence over specific notions of the common good. Hope for humanity lies in the gradual spread (through emerging consensus) of liberal democratic societies.

Rawls has been much criticized from many sides, and has modified his work to take account of this. Perhaps particularly noteworthy from a human rights perspective is the observation by Martha Nussbaum (*The Chronicle*, 20 July 2001) that Rawls is working from a traditional social contract, in which citizens are treated as roughly equals, benefiting from cooperation because each needs things that others supply. But needs are often asymmetrical: 'The requirements of the cared-for must be met, and their self-respect preserved, without exploiting care-givers – who are often women.' Rawls works within the liberal tradition of the social contract, where citizens cooperate so that each needs things which the others can supply.

Public Culture and Theological Conversation

In considering reflection upon the public square from Taylor to Habermas we have opened up some of the issues with which a revised poetic of theological discourse must deal: the nature of humanity individual and corporate in the sight of God, the constraints of conversation and community, the shapes of freedom and democratic process. We now turn to the praxis of intercultural theology, and here we will concentrate on two central issues, the one Christology, the focal point of the Christian contribution to theology and the Christian response to basic human well-being, and the other human rights, a basic ethical and political issue with central Christological implications.

Note

1 'Prayer Pilgrimage for Freedom, 1957', in *A Testament of Hope*, (ed.) J.M. Washington, (San Francisco: Harper Collins 1986,12f).

II
FOCUSING INTERCULTURAL THEOLOGY: GOD, CHRISTOLOGY AND HUMAN RIGHTS

CHAPTER 6

Humane Praxis and the Distinctively Christian

What can an intercultural theology contribute to the development of specific issues? I select here some central and closely interlinked areas: Christology, human rights, ethics and transcendence.

Humane Praxis

Christian theology is based on the divine love of God in Jesus Christ. Often its face has been of singularly loveless religion, but the abuse does not take away the proper use. Generosity even as an eschatological concept may have a considerable impact on the present. Theology as partnership should benefit from, as well as contribute to, the dialogue which is essential to human flourishing, and to the new creation which is God's purpose for all his creatures. Liberation theology, it has sometimes been noted, has tended in recent years to lose some of its impetus. This is partly because it has often been ignored or subverted by conservative forces in the churches. But it may also be because the narrow base of oppression which is its great and enduring strength is also limited. Emancipatory theology needs to gain the confidence to participate in the widest human dialogue, reminding the human of the humane, in the name of God. In doing so it should be able to gain new imagination and impetus, at a conceptual and also at a practical level. The crucified Christ at the centre of faith is also the risen Christ, the source of transformation, renewal and new horizons. This is not always possible in a situation of oppression. But the Christian hope is of the overcoming of evil by good. An intercultural theology, as a theology of humane praxis, seeks to re-imagine the basic contours of Christian doctrine, to reflect a trace of the divine love in a modern way through its reshaping.

Human language is inadequate to give us anything like a technical description of God. Yet there is the phenomenon of faith, which considers that in building up a cumulative case for belief in God it is responding to a source of meaning and loving purpose in the universe. Out of fragments of data, experience and interpretation, faith has developed as a community tradition, a tradition with many gaps and disjunctions, in Christianity and in the major world religions.

God is neither the patriarchal figure of the Hebrew Bible nor the kyriarchal figure of Christian tradition nor the mirror image opposite of these. God includes relationship in Godself. The imagery of incarnation and

Trinity, through the Spirit of the crucified and risen Christ, reflects the concretion of this relationship. God cares about his creatures, and is the source of all generosity. God cares as humans care, as mothers, fathers, relatives and friends care. None of these images is privileged or excluded. But his care is perfect.[1]

God is concerned for the welfare of human society, as well as for non-human creatures and the cosmic environment. Divine love instantiates mutuality, reciprocity and inclusiveness. It creates forgiveness and reconciliation and the mending of brokenness. It includes justice and peace. Each of these spheres calls for infinite effort and infinite patience. Divine love restores the damaged and injured to new creation by solidarity and unconditional identification. That is the spontaneity of grace, which is at once the great asset and the great judgment upon the community of those who believe. God's action leads towards a goal of new creation, of participation in the perfect relationship of the divine society. Because this is a society of love, peace and justice, it is the signal of the direction in which all our social life is invited to move.

The Distinctively Christian

How do we characterize the elements which make intercultural theology distinctively Christian? Not every shape, not every culture, not every theological proposal will be appropriate to an intercultural Christian theology. The most obvious classic example of a theological criterion on the nature of partnership is the role of Christology in Christian discourse about God. Karl Barth, as we have seen, appealed successfully to Christology to correct the distortions of *Kulturprotestantismus* at the beginning of the twentieth century. There could of course, as Barth became aware, be an equivalent problem in any theological culture, an authoritarian Christomonism which equally subverted the grace of the gospel. How may we distinguish legitimate and illegitimate facilitation of conversation through Christology?

B.F. Westcott, in his *Christus Consummator*, laid emphasis on the Christian affirmation of the centrality of Jesus Christ to all things. In doing so he was affirming no less and no more than the tradition affirmed, from Athanasius to Schleiermacher and beyond. If theology is the queen of the sciences, then Christology is the centre of that theological enterprise. The particular branch of the Christological tradition of which Westcott was such a distinguished advocate had dimensions ranging from the meticulous interpretation of the patristic tradition to the appropriate strategy for mission in deprived areas of the East End of London. Westcott was concerned to explore the best theological interpretation of the person and work of Jesus Christ within the best intellectual paradigms of the day. He searched for the most appropriate interpretation of the patristic texts in which the doctrine was first articulated. He was also passionately interested in the *social implications* of the doctrine in particular sections of contemporary society. Here was intercultural theology, seeking explanation and expression within different cultural milieux, past and present. Here was contextual theology, immersed in the cultural norms and expectations of its time. Theology could do much worse than Westcott did, then as now.

Hegemony

Let us consider the problem of hegemony. We are now much more conscious than Westcott was of the cultural limitations of our own perspectives, though eminent Victorians were not always as insensitive to these matters as we like, in our superior way, to imagine. We know about the links between knowledge and interests, between description and domination, and we mourn our lost innocence. Suitably chastened, we may well be able to continue Westcott's enterprise with considerable success in the future. Yet other possibilities arise. The one I want to explore is the possibility that, for Christian faith, theology, and especially Christology, may be most effective, and perhaps most true to her natural role, when she plays in the game of further developing human values as a team player on a level playing field with the other players, as a contributor, partner and catalyst. This is not a call for a false humility. False humility comes naturally enough to theologians without further encouragement. It is rather a recommendation of a strategy for the more effective deployment of Christology in a world in which the voice of Christian faith is increasingly either silent or so shrill that it blends with other postmodern fundamentalisms as an option only for the determinedly irrational.

Christus est Dominus. So, legend has it, as Lindbeck reminded us, the Crusaders chanted as they broke the skulls of their Muslim opponents in the Middle Ages.[2] Sadly, conflicts involving Christians and other religions in modern society, not least in the Balkans and in Indonesia, mirror scenes of medieval horror in ways which polite modern society never anticipated. Is Christology always inimical to human rights? If there is a persistent track record of oppression in the name of the highest religious values, beginning with the tragic juxtaposition of the divine love and anti-Judaism in the Fourth gospel, can we undo the past and offer Christology as a catalyst for human rights?

We must note at once, too, that the negative side of Christological advocacy has not impinged only on non-Christian people. Those who have claimed the 'right' Christology have rarely hesitated to anticipate presumed divine displeasure in their treatment of those with whom they disagree. In the name of Christ all sorts of minority groups have been persecuted by majorities in every century. Christians have prided themselves on their responsibility for taking a tough line on the role of women, on divorcees, on criminals, on all manner of groups. They have found it less easy to combine such acknowledgment with repentance and attempts at reconciliation and redress.

We may say that, as Christians, we forgive those who have suffered at the hands of enthusiasts for Christ who were too wedded to the cultural norms of their day to listen to the challenge of the gospel. *But it is not ours to forgive*. Only the damaged and destroyed can forgive. We may speak of the need to replace the language of conflict in our liturgies and hymns with the language of compassion, mutuality and reciprocity. But the replacement of honest brutality with politically correct sentimentality can only accelerate nausea. The simple liberalism of a gentle Jesus, meek and mild, will not solve our problems either. At least, not by itself.

What has gone wrong? Certainly modern theology can scarcely be accused of failing to attend to the manifold dimensions of Christology. Nineteenth-century theology did not fail to learn from Schleiermacher and from Hegel the importance of Christ. But the religion of *Kulturprotestantismus* tended to blend the God of the nation state with the Christ of the individual heart. Political conservatism was the order of the day at home, and outside Europe non-white people were subordinated to the culture of the white Jesus. Sin was largely conceived within the world of convenient introspection, and the aggression of a hegemonic Christian commercial culture was mainly overlooked. Christian Europe practically committed suicide in 1914. The project of worldwide Christian mission was all but halted in its tracks.

With Karl Barth, the God of religion was replaced by Jesus Christ, the Lord of the universe. Culture was subordinated to Christian community, and a defensive repristination of classical Christian doctrine in the face of Weimar decadence and Nazi fascism was achieved. While in Europe church attendance began to collapse towards the end of the twentieth century, in America God was still reassuringly linked to patriotism, and we remained on his side.

The modern was succeeded by the postmodern and the postmodern in turn deconstructed. In the third millennium we are firmly in the metamodern, the postfoundational. That is to say, we are aware of a variety of intellectual sub-cultures, which concentrate on different paradigms of thought and action, some more fissiparous, some more holistic. Within these guilds scholars find niches of the like-minded, and live happily ever after. If there is any truth in this sketch, then we shall not expect to find any single Christological argument which will be universally acceptable. But we may still legitimately hope to make a contribution to continuing dialogue, a contribution offered to be handled differently by different dialogue partners. This is part of the risk of the contemporary debate. I shall also argue that *risk and resistance* are also, in a different but not totally disanalogous way, part of the Christological contribution to human rights.

Christology has been central to some of the most striking attempts to make any sense of talk of God in the modern world. How can we speak effectively – to ourselves and to others – about God today? The enormous modern industry of systematic theology has explored numerous approaches, experiential, kerugmatic, narrative and other. As the deconstruction of the modern has been followed by the deconstruction of the postmodern, some theologians begin to explore the postfoundational or the metamodern, seeking new combinations of epistemological and hermeneutical paradigms. Others return to more traditional paths, for example in patristic or medieval retrieval. There are things to be learned from all these strategies. My own concern here is to try, with the aid of just a few examples, to distinguish legitimate uses of Christological language in modern society.

There will be always be Christian theologians and communities which remain entirely content with the traditional language of Christology: incarnation and atonement, redemption and reconciliation, sacrifice and substitution. But there is an important constituency, especially in Northern Europe and in North America, which remains attracted to Christian faith but which finds some areas of its house of language increasingly unusable. I regard this constituency as important for theology today. If I look to theologians who address this problematic, I find valuable suggestions in the work of David Tracy. In Tracy we find both a profound apprehension of the value of tradition, in worship, thought and action, and at the same time a keen awareness of the need to *recast our language* about God in a postmodern framework in which fragments, mystery and silence are often more evocative of the God of Christian faith than the exhaustive schemata of much modern theology. It is with this perception of the plasticity and elasticity of the postmodern turn that I come back to the basis of what is, if I hear rightly, often asked for today – a non-kyriarchal but unsentimental Christology.

Not everyone needs a revisionist Christology. There are millions of Christians for whom traditional Christologies already provide effective and meaningful frameworks for their lives and their work. There is no need to follow some varieties of liberal thought in claiming finality and potential universality for a particular perspective. But there are people for whom, for various reasons, traditional frameworks no longer provide satisfactory explanations, and who need to begin again. There are others who have had no framework and for whom traditional frameworks do not appeal. A liberal Christology may hope to offer something at least to some members of both of these groups. It may also aspire to emphasize particular aspects of Christology in a historic liberal tradition, notably in relation to social justice issues. But it does not claim any sort of monopoly on these concerns. It is open to dialogue and reciprocity. It seeks to make a contribution to the concerns of all who share at least some aspects of its central structuring elements.

Among recent German Christologies, for Moltmann the key to understanding is solidarity with the oppressed, for Juengel it is the power of the self-authenticating Word, for Dalferth it is the proclamation of resurrection. The presence of this powerful, compelling narrative of solidarity and effective victory is at the heart of all Christology. Yet we are also called on to find reasons for the faith that is in us. It is only against the background of a cumulative rational case for talk of God as creator and reconciler that any of the kerugma makes sense. Faith is not there only to make sense of things, we immediately recall. But unless there is a minimal level of rationality, to enable us to cope with life in the world of everyday reality, faith alone will not help us. It may have done so in the past. It will do so no more.

Transformative Christology

Where in the overlapping sub-cultures of modern society may we expect to find a response to Christus transformator? Christians believe that the cosmic Christ is present in all human life. This presence is a hidden presence, not always easily articulated and acknowledged. The worship of the church will always remain a focus of recollection and recognition of the divine presence. As traditional structures break down, worship becomes an increasingly unfamiliar experience to most Europeans. But, as long as it continues, in an open structure as an invitation to the divine hospitality, it provides a vital fragment in the cluster of Christian meaning.

From communities of worship, and sometimes without formal worship but through a kind of theologically orientated living, there emerge communities of Christian service. Some are explicitly church-related, like Christian Aid. Others are largely operated by people with Christian beliefs, in Oxfam, Médecins sans Frontières and others. Yet others contribute Christian perspectives to ethical and political decision making in economic, scientific and business enterprises. In this way different fragments may function at different levels in complex cultures, overlapping and reinforcing each other in often random ways. Such a vision of the pervasive power of fragments of Christian engagement may be utopian. But it does indicate ways in which a non-hegemonic understanding of the influence of Christ in our culture may be developed and acted upon. None of these elements is infallible or free from the possibility of error. Bernstein spoke of an engaged fallibilistic pluralism in philosophy. We may perhaps see the above sketch as a social application of this model in action. The power which is made effective in this understanding of Church is dependent on constancy of commitment, rather than organizational hegemony within a given culture.

There are likely to be at least two other factors supportive of Christian goals in such a social context. Even in the most authoritarian or misguided Christian culture there are likely to be exceptions to the rule, and authentic faith and practice keep breaking through. Christians believe that non-Christians too will have important contributions to make to the discernment of God's will for his creation. Hence they will expect to learn from the otherness of other perspectives, and to share in the human dialogue of values which they believe God wishes to encourage in the direction of his purpose for human fulfilment. In the nature of the case, neither complacency nor panic is appropriate to the contemporary social reality. The grace of God remains prevenient within the created order.

In the first part of this book we noted Paul Knitter's reconstruction of Christology as a pluralist Christology, as part of a project to overcome the disadvantages of more traditional exclusive and inclusive models. In speaking of divine action I have used the metaphor, used extensively by Richard Niebuhr, David Tracy and others, of a Christomorphic trace in history. What does this mean? It was used by Niebuhr to distinguish the Christological dimension in history from a Christocentric approach. A Christomorphic perspective remains theocentric, but it understands the whole created order to be shaped, influenced and directed towards the shape of the divine love as instantiated in the events concerning Jesus Christ. A Christomorphic approach is modest, in that it does not simply substitute Christ for God. But it retains the decisive claim that the universe is shaped and directed towards that love of God which is Christlike in every way. In speaking of a Christomorphic trace I see this as a quality of action through the development of events, which enables us to have faith in the compassion of God working in creation and redemption.

Awareness of the culturally embedded nature of language should allow us to use traditional as well as novel imagery without the constraints and coercions which have historically accompanied such language. This freedom should allow us to avoid the minimalist and to explore the transformative. All theological language uses the whole range of linguistic expression, metaphor, myth and symbol, the literal and the non-literal, the analogical and the metaphysical. Some are more persuaded of the basic and foundational nature of their usage than others, but none of us is exempt from particularity. This problem has inhibited much liberal theology from using concepts of incarnation and Trinity, and has had an especially deadening impact on worship. Jesus Christ is the distinctive Christian contribution to conversation about the nature of God. Christological reflection has focused on relationality and self-differentiation within the divine nature and in relation to humanity. We cannot produce here a fully developed Christology, but we can look briefly at a single strand which may be especially productive for an intercultural theology, namely the area of Spirit Christology.

This emphasis on a Christomorphic theology may provide a complementary way of developing Christology as a truly intercultural theological motif. John Hick, Roger Haight and Perry Schmidt-Leukel have developed the pluralist Christology in ways which seek to preserve what is important in classical models while facilitating the possibility of a wider interreligious dialogue. One avenue, explored by Haight following Geoffrey Lampe, is to widen the horizon of a Spirit Christology.

A Spirit Christology may be seen not as a substitute for, but as a development of, the concerns of a logos Christology. (To introduce an intercultural analogy, we may think perhaps of the wave/particle paradox of quantum mechanics.) The spirit of Christlikeness affirms all that is said of particularity and embodiment in the logos tradition, and expands this to include Christ's solidarity with, though not identification and absorption with, all mediation of transcendence in the cosmos. (This widening of the scope of Christology was anticipated decades ago by Allan Galloway in his important but not widely cited *The Cosmic Christ.*) God as Spirit is at work throughout the cosmos, and the events concerning Jesus play a decisive role in revealing to us within the Christian tradition the character of this Spirit as Christlikeness. Other central religious figures mediate the divine love. Christians understand the events concerning Jesus as decisive for the future of all humanity, and bring this faith commitment to their continuing dialogue with other spiritual traditions.

It may be that something akin to what Valkenberg has described as a bifocal Christology opens up space for a further development in intercultural reflection. Incarnation in the logos tradition can be affirmed as signally the divine commitment to particularity in the history of Israel leading up to the life and death of Jesus. Inspiration is understood as the effect of resurrection, in which the divine Spirit, which Christians properly understand as the Spirit of Christlikeness, is made effective throughout the created order, not in a temporal sequence but in an eternal simultaneity. Resurrection moves us from the denouncing of oppression to the announcing of hope, as James Cone has put it. A Christomorphic Christology will not make an absolute choice between incarnational and inspirational Christologies, but use both, not in dichotomy but in polarity. A Christology without the dynamism of the Spirit would not adequately express the Christian vision. A Christology without a strong incarnational basis would not fully express God's commitment to the material world and its everyday realities as God's world. The process remains a paradox or mystery. One way of signalling the mystery is a reworking of the dynamics of Trinity, in which difference and identity, particularity and commonality are registered as a constantly creative tension in the life of God.

In his essay entitled 'Christ and the Spirit – towards a bifocal Christian theology of religions' (Merrigan and Haers, 2000, 121f), W.G.B.M. Valkenberg argues an interesting case for a dialogical approach to other religions. He suggests that Christology has to be complemented by the confession of the Spirit as a power from God working within but also beyond the boundaries of the Christian tradition. 'Because of the double focus of Christology and Pneumatology, this Christian theology of religions will be both inclusivist and pluralist' (125), in this way relating the uniqueness of Christ and the universality of the Spirit. Valkenberg's essay suggests that there is still much scope for refining and overcoming the traditional impasses of debate on Christian uniqueness. This volume offers a comprehensive survey of recent discussion of plurality in Christology.

Though Spirit Christologies have been associated with liberal theologies and incarnational Christologies with conservative frameworks, concepts can easily be deployed in different connections. Ralph Del Colle has shown how Spirit Christologies have been developed in very traditional Catholic frameworks, and process theologians have no difficulty with concepts of incarnation. Likewise Trinitarian concepts can be developed in numerous directions. Del Colle's work provides a useful reminder of the residual complexity of the mystery of God, balancing the Western tendency to conceive of God purely through the imagery of the life and death of Jesus. A liberal Christology will emphasize the metaphorical and imaginative elements in the tradition of speculative Trinitarian theology which is here developed, will stress the dialectical and fragmented nature of the relation between pneumatology and ecclesiology, and will see the Trinity as essentially an outward-facing rather than inward-looking construct.

It is always appropriate to develop the full range of the Christian tradition, at least where the development does not run counter to what the theologian will regard as the centre of the gospel. This can easily be demonstrated by picking out just a handful of examples. There may be value, as I have just indicated, in a process approach to some issues of intercultural theology, not least in Christology. The variety of process proposals makes it possible to see that its basic imaginative concepts can be used in rather different ways, without necessarily buying into a process metaphysics as a foundational framework. Once again, Berlin's angle on agonistic liberalism may open the door to new creative tension.

John Cobb's writing represents a combination of openness and commitment: 'Openness can be sustained only where it is grounded in a faith that justifies and requires it. But we can affirm Christian faith wholeheartedly today only insofar as it opens us to all truth and value' (Cobb, 1973, 14). In his *Christ in a Pluralistic Age* (1975), Cobb set out a decisively Christological approach to Christian theology which combined Christocentricity with pluralism. He sees Christ as God's agent of creative transformation in the future of the universe, as a decisive but not exclusive contribution to the human future: 'The thesis of this book is that faithfulness to Christ requires immersion in the secular and pluralistic consciousness and that it is precisely there that Christ now works, impeded by our failure to recognise him and by our continuing association of faith with past, particularised expressions of faith' (187).

A Christian perspective must help us to move beyond absolutism and relativism to transformation, through a postmodern reconstruction. For Cobb this takes the form of a 'Christocentric Catholic theology' (Cobb, 1999, 76f), which is precisely not a universal theology of religion, but a vital contribution to human well-being. Religions really are diverse, but may be brought into creative engagement:

> It would be arrogant to assert that the project of catholicity is one that all should pursue, and it would be biased to assert that the only way catholicity can be attained is by its Christocentrism. But it is not arrogant to explain that we as Christians are impelled towards catholicity, and to acknowledge that what impels us is our Christocentrism.

The content of reconstruction is specified in *Postmodernism and Public Policy* (Cobb, 2002):

> God's effective presence known in Jesus is Christ, and Christ transforms. … Christ works most immediately and directly in individuals. By working through many individuals, however, creative transformation can occur in historical movements, including the Christian one … we discern Christ also in political events such as the nearly bloodless transformation of the Union of South Africa into a democracy inclusive of all its people. (28–9)

This perspective closely complements the notion of a Christomorphic trace developed in this study. Though I have not approached these issues from a process perspective myself, I am glad to acknowledge the value of this philosophy in opening up the problems, as exemplified in Cobb's work.

It is worth remembering that this open theological perspective is common to more contemporary theologians than one might sometimes imagine. Eduard Schillebeeckx could observe that:

> Salvation from God comes about first of all in the secular reality of history and not primarily in the consciousness of believers who are aware of it … Where good is promoted and evil is fought against for the healing of humanity, this historical praxis in fact confirms the nature of God – God as salvation for men and women – the basic of universal hope – and people moreover receive God's salvation – in and through a love which is put into practice. (Schillebeeckx, 1987, 9)

The theological relation between universality and particularity in culture was well expressed by Marjorie Suchocki. 'In Christ God's universal aim towards the good for all stands revealed. However, we have emphasized again and again that the universal aim must be relativized in order to be made concrete' (Suchocki, 1982, 182). To speak of Christ in non-exclusive terms need not weaken the call to Christian commitment: 'Christians cannot speak of Christ as exclusive, but perhaps we can speak of commitment as exclusive. While we can recognize both the truth of other glimpses of the Divine and the power of other communities of faith, we cannot seriously be committed to multiple centres, much as we appreciate them' (Eck, 1993, 95). The proposal of Wesley Wildman (1998) for a 'modest' Christology rather than an absolutist Christology, defending the centrality of Christ while being open to dialogue with other religions, moves in the same direction as my intercultural project, and also draws inspiration from John Cobb.

Sally McFague has developed the implications of Christology for ecology:

> What is emerging then from ecological economic Christology is a different notion of the abundant life, not the abundance of consumer goods, but the possibility, the promise, of a new life in God for all. … insisting that the way to this new life will be difficult, painful, and sacrificial, especially for those who are taking more than their share and thus depriving other people and the earth of a good life. (McFague, 2001, 179)

This book is a timely reminder that projects for conceptual convergence will have no practical effect unless they are accompanied by a wider concern for justice, including economic justice, which has a decisive effect on the well-being of the world's population. See too Majorie Suchocki's call for justice as a necessary element of religious dialogue, in Hick and Knitter (1987).

In recent decades there has been an astonishing flow of Christological proposals. Diversity and argument have stimulated the debate. In shaping a metamodern proposal I regard it as vital to foreground the worldwide nature of Christologies. The enhancing imagery of the newer Christologies can show us ways out of the log jams of our traditions. The sheer diversity of the range of a truly intercultural theology is well illustrated in Volker Kuester's *The Many Faces of Jesus Christ* (2001). Kuester offers description and critical analysis, beginning from the typology of H.R. Niebuhr's *Christ and Culture*.

Kuester looks for 'commonalities, divergences and opportunities for ecumenical learning' among these models of contextual theology. Some of the theologies of inculturation are in danger of becoming a *theologia gloriae*, to which the theologies of the cross are an important corrective. Many of them are an 'option for the poor'. Kuester in conclusion suggested that there may be unexplored value for these theologies in St Paul, and especially in his doctrine of justification (187). Like Jesus's preaching of the kingdom of God, the Pauline understanding of justification also stresses human dignity under the leading of the Spirit.

Kuester's study is a valuable reminder that the Christological task is a continuing process, which is still very much ' in progress', and from which limiting conclusions should not be too easily drawn. Christology encompasses huge cultural diversity, while exhibiting in different contexts the hallmarks of the life, death and resurrection of Jesus: kenosis, vulnerability and identification. Here is a mystery greater than the philosophical dichotomies of traditional European thought, indeed of all our concepts. It becomes possible to combine critical interaction with diverse sub-cultures with the central structuring elements of the Christological tradition. Future Christologies will doubtless wish to embrace this wider horizon, not colonizing the cultures but contributing to dialogue.

Utilizing the full range of Christological resources will require a careful scrutiny of the structure of the language, especially in its layers of metaphors, stronger and weaker, thick and thin metaphors. It is important to grasp that conservative and liberal Christologies arise out of the same linguistic and cultural bases, and that none is more privileged than others in respect of the scope and limitations of language. To recognize the complexity of language need not dilute the claims to engagement with truth and reality which may be made. An excellent example of the imaginative use of Christological symbolism is Robert Neville's *Symbols of Jesus* (2001).

Neville's 'theology of symbolic engagement' is based on a theory of religious symbolism which reinterprets traditional discussions about the nature of metaphysics. He groups symbolic reflection on Jesus around the six categories of atonement, the cosmic Christ, the deity of Christ, incarnation in the historical Jesus, Jesus as friend and the eschatological saviour. These categories are finally related to the additional symbols of God as creator and Holy Spirit.

Neville understands interpretation to have a triadic character – signs, their objects and interpretations taking the signs to stand for objects in certain respects, and giving rise to a threefold problematic: the definition of symbols, the nature of reference and the significance of interpretive context. Context is important: 'The normative argument for a Christian theology in a global public thus requires the making of a case for the cultural, referential and contextual conditions under which the Christology is true' (17). How are the symbols to be understood? 'The rubric for understanding all these Christological symbol systems is how they help flesh out the reality Jesus Christ has had as an operative transformative agent within Christian churches that engage God by means of Christ' (22).

As he explains in an appendix, Neville understands the symbols to be brought to bear within Christian life through the Holy Spirit (257ff). This is not an infallible process, for we can misunderstand the symbols. But it creates the possibility of true and imaginative discipleship. Neville's understanding of the veridical but parabolic nature of Christological language is clearly a valuable way of avoiding the dangers of triumphalism and relativism.

For Christian theology, Jesus Christ is *the* central clue to the nature of God as the divine love. But though Christ is not less than God, for God's relationality includes his presence in Jesus, the divine is understood to be more complex than our faith through Jesus Christ enables us to grasp. God is creator of all that is and also the source of the renewal and reconciliation of what is waste and destructive in creation. This is the sense of a Trinitarian paradigm which may open up the possibility of a modest but authentically Christian contribution to the dialogue between world religions which does not prescribe completely the understanding of the divine. God is personal, but not a person. God is threefold, but not numerically three. God is relational, but not exhausted in relationality. However, when a particular Trinitarian shape is fixed as the authorized pattern, then the whole point of this fluid and dynamic understanding is subverted, and human relationality tends to deteriorate. This brings us to the relation between Christology and ethics, and the litmus test issue of human rights. Human rights have been violated throughout history in the name of the Trinity of the divine love.

How far does this tell against the truth of the Christological claim? It is appropriate that, in an intercultural framework, we should examine the reciprocity between Christology and ethics in what most people understand as 'the real world'.

We shall return to Christology again and again in seeking to integrate the various strands of an intercultural theology. For Christology is *the* distinctive Christian contribution to the human conversation about the human future. The notion of the Christomorphic trace is the preferred imagery in this study for this integrating element. There is nothing romantic or triumphalistic about such a trace, for it is traced through the suffering of the cross, and the suffering of humanity in all its enormity. Not every sort of rationality or relationality will do. Spirit Christology cannot be allowed to become an abstraction from the awkward particularities of the events concerning Jesus. The Spirit of Christ is in every dimension the spirit of the Christ who lived a life of solidarity with suffering and injustice, the Christ whose resurrection was the resurrection of the man crucifed under Pontius Pilate. This will be basic to our attempt to speak finally of the mystery of God.

We have observed in the modern explosion of cultural expressions of theology the ability of Christology to give a voice to those who were previously voiceless. In an intercultural perspective we may hope to encourage members of Christian communities to appreciate voices which are not their own. The next step, hugely difficult but utterly necessary, lies in moving from recognizing particularity to welcoming the particularity of difference for the common well-being of human society. This is a process which is well recognized but which has as yet hardly begun.

There is a pressing need for a progressive Christology which retrieves the rich resources of the Christian tradition for a spirituality which is renewed and transformative, and which reflects the shape of discipleship by remaining decisively committed at every level to justice issues, and to dialogue and reciprocity in the search for human well-being. One way to reinforce this intrinsic connection may be through constant attention to the intercultural dialogue between Christology and human rights, the area in which some of the sharpest challenges arise to Church and society today.

Christology, Culture and Morality

The shape of transformation raises again the question of the relationship of morality to religion. Christology inevitably raises questions of the ethical. Christology cannot solve all the ethical questions in moral philosophy, but it undoubtedly claims to add a distinctive contribution to discernment of the ethical. The time has long passed when it could be plausibly argued that only religious people are truly moral. We may think of the classical Christian virtues – love, patience, understanding, generosity, opposition to social and economic injustice – and find that these are often exhibited in the highest degree by non-Christians. At the same time, Christians would want to say that their faith informs and deepens their moral sense. A religion, or indeed a culture, which is ethically indifferent cannot be defended. They would add, too that the value of their religion is not exhausted by morality.

What has theology to do with morality? This is a highly complex issue, and clearly there are positive and negative aspects in the interconnection. Both conservative and liberal theologians have argued for the separation of morality from religion. This is clearly not the place for an extensive study of religion and morality. But the understanding of the relation of culture (or counter-culture) to theology is not ethically indifferent, above all in a theology which is centrally concerned about human rights.

From a conservative standpoint, theology is about God and transcendence, about a religious or spiritual dimension in life. Once it is related to politics and morality, it speedily descends into moralism and the transcendent and truly spiritual dimensions are lost. From a liberal standpoint it is argued that morality is best kept free from the doctrinal prejudices of religion. The track record of religious involvement is bad. The tendency to theocratic pretension is always dangerous. It is nonsense to imagine that religious people are more ethical in any way than others. *Let ethics be ethics*. Theology is about a religious perspective, a philosophical view of life involving transcendence. If it cannot be sustained on this basis, it cannot be sustained at all This state of affairs underlines the limited usefulness of traditional liberal/conservative polarizations; often the insights of different traditions are required.

It can be argued in the opposite direction that God has set down 'the maker's instructions' for the conduct of human life, both in prescriptive commands given by revelation and in natural orders of creation. To live as God intended is to obey these commands and mandates, and to disobey is to sin against God. From a liberal perspective the connections between theology and ethics can also be emphasized. Christian faith is about justice and human rights. God on the cross committed himself to solidarity with the marginalized. There is an intimate connection between the nature of God in Godself and human rights. This state of affairs highlights the limited usefulness of traditional distinctions between liberal and conservative theologies. The intercultural project needs at times the wisdom of both these traditions, difficult as it may be to bring them into dialogue.

Theology is concerned both with religion and with morality. The connections and disjunctions are equally important. Theology is concerned with religion and with transcendence. Theology arises from concern for the transcendent, appropriated in experience which is mediated in different ways, through texts, worship, reflection and action. In Christian theology this concern is articulated through faith in God and thinking about God. God is understood as the source of all that is, personal and communicative. Reflection upon God may take the form of a philosophy of religion and/or a systematic theology. Even in such variations as religionless Christianity and this worldly transcendence, Christian faith remains concerned with the search for authentic transcendence and authentic religion. This applies to avowedly non-metaphysical and non-foundational varieties of faith as much as to more traditional forms. God as the infinitely mysterious ground of being may be meditated upon through a variety of philosophical perspectives held in tension with each other.

But, for Christian faith, this transcendent source of being has a distinctive *ethical* character. There is a reciprocity between God's ethical nature and our ethical reflection. God's nature is understood as love, defined in different ways at different times. There may be incompatibilities between the understanding of love between different cultural groups, and indeed this may give rise to intolerance and even hatred. The concept of love may be overshadowed by other central concepts, such as of revenge or judgment. But the place of love, however understood, somewhere in any Christian understanding of God has perhaps rarely been challenged. There remains therefore the challenge of an appropriate linkage of religion to ethics.

Theologians have not always been happy with perceived relations between doctrine and ethics: 'There is a definite content to the promise *Eristis sicut Deus*, and to the concealed invitation to man to become the master of his own destiny. What the serpent has in mind is the establishment of ethics' (Karl Barth, CD 4.448.) In some respects Karl Barth and more liberal theologians have quite a lot in common. Barth, a great comfort of insecure churchmen and theologians of the 1990s, was much concerned to debunk most of the tradition of Christian ethics. Moral theology, like natural theology, was a product of human religiosity and of the dubious amalgam of things human and things divine. Not from nature nor from philosophy, but only from God in Jesus Christ could ethics become possible, as a gift of grace rather than an endowment of nature.

In contrast with Barth, let us consider a radical liberal text. Bishop Richard Holloway in his *Godless Morality* was equally concerned to dispense with traditional moral theology. But for him the solution was rather different. It is worth looking here at Holloway as a text in relation to the cultural shape of Christian ethics. First we must separate ethics from religion, from doctrine, from biblical commands. And then we shall we that theology has a different, more modest contribution to make to a common morality for a common humanity. Do we have to be religious to be moral? We do not.

Religions tend to associate God with particular phases of social development. Sin is essentially a religious idea: disobedience of God, Abraham and Isaac, Genesis 22. The idea of sin was part of a mechanism of force designed to secure compliance with authority. Redemption, then, rescues from sin. But Jesus was different. 'His attitude to sin was more congruent with present day understandings of morality than the religious systems based on external obedience.' Morality tries to base itself upon observed consequences, not on beliefs, superstitions or prejudices. Our search for basic moral principles will, if we are wise, always allow for situational variations. Pluralism is essential, infallibility is impossible. Hence we should look for '*a morality without God*'.

Holloway argued that, while religions have command ethics, taboos and demands for obedience, Jesus advocated an ethic of rational choice, which today would choose between different goods in a fallibilist pluralism. One might go on from both Barth and Holloway to suggest that a Christian ethic, an ethic of grace, must be prepared to act as a catalyst in the search for human ethical values, as a contributing partner in a mutual enterprise rather than as managing director. The ethic of Jesus Christ is an ethic of mutuality, identification and sharing in discovery. That would be a new role for Christian theology, and one which it might find it extremely hard to develop,

Intercultural Ethics

There is of course a constant dialogue between faith and philosophy in the history of Christianity, classically in Thomas Aquinas. For him natural theology was perfectly natural, and reason could lead on to faith. Revelation remained a higher form of wisdom, capable of completing and correcting. For Barth, on the other hand, natural theology is misleading and often dangerous, taking away from the uniqueness of faith alone. What I am suggesting is that revelation is indeed unique, but that it may often occur in the engagement between faith and reason, rather than as a unique formula which remains somehow free from embodiment within particular cultural expression. Faith exists as a unique strand *within* the cumulative rational process which contributes to the development of human society.

This is especially true of the dialogue between faith and philosophy. Here Iris Murdoch had imaginative things to say about the relation between morality and religion. Murdoch was highly critical of current philosophical orthodoxies. She stressed the important of the 'inner' life and the dangers of natural human egoism 'Faith' enables us to intuit the moral value of the good. The aesthetic, through imagination and images, is a gateway to awareness of transcendence. The concept of the good can have a necessary existence. *Moral values are a part of the real fabric of the world.* For her the good is impersonal but is at the heart of human meaning. Moral value has a religious element. In addition, a realist understanding of morality undergirds declarations of universal human rights. For Murdoch, *the good reveals itself in the religious life and in the quest for goodness a religious quality is revealed.* Fact/value dichotomies are shown to be wrong. The nature of moral value can be plausibly argued to be 'real'.

Even theologians who are close to Barth in a rejection of 'metaphysics' will usually use philosophical concepts in at least some areas of their work. For example, Reinhold Niebuhr, though he refused to develop a philosophical concept of God, used philosophical analyses of *power* and of human nature throughout much of his work.

Beyond philosophy, it is impossible to engage in theology without being indebted, formally or informally, to the humanities and often to the natural sciences in innumerable ways, through the use of literary analysis, historical criticism, legal background and so on. But instead of seeing all these disciplines as auxiliary disciplines subject ultimately to final theological judgment, it may be better to see them as equal partners in a process of human development in which Christian theology has a decisive interest, if not always a completely determining role.

There is after all a connection between ethics, truth, Christology and aesthetics. Pamela Dickey-Young expresses in a feminist tradition the centrality of Christ through categories of aesthetics:

> In the Christian tradition Jesus as the Christ re-presents or embodies rather than constitutes what is worthy of belief, action and enjoyment. That is, we have argued that truth, beauty and goodness are universal values, implicit in but accessible not only through the Christian value system and not only to Christians. (Dickey-Young, 1995, 143)

Moral good creates 'beauty', an inclusive value.

Christology, Ethics and Corporate Culture

Theologians are easily tempted to resort to romantic generalizations about individual freedoms and rights. Such values are important, but they cannot be seen in isolation from the economic and political shapes of the world in which we live.

We have concentrated in this chapter on Christology and ethics, but how far is the current Christological discussion even intelligible outside the academic guild? What would be the role of an unsentimental Christology in the normal conditions of the postmodern world? I have explored elsewhere the potentially transformative role of Christology in extreme conditions of discrimination. Such people will always be with us, and sadly they will continue to be within as well as outside the churches.

For the moment I want to consider the role of Christology in the working and social lives of European citizens. This may be thought too Eurocentric. Europe's interests do not always coincide with those of other continents – hence the tragic history of recent Africa. Yet Christology is a powerful reminder of the solidarity of all humanity: we are all neighbours in Christ.

European culture is dominated by commerce and industry, banking and technology. Ironically, just as we begin to see the relevance of the Black Christ in solidarity with the suffering inhabitant of the southern hemisphere, we are losing any sense of the meaning of Christology for the frequent flyer, the global business traveller. In so far as such people think of Christ, many apparently subscribe to a highly individualist and characteristically Protestant perspective which sees Christ as a kind of therapy, a stress-releasing agent for the busy executive. We have to respect the *particula veri* in all such reflection, yet the theologian will scarcely be satisfied with such a conclusion.

Because we all live simultaneously in a number of cultural worlds, for some people a particular confessional background will provide a Christological framework which the traveller will deploy in the context of the changing cultures in which he works. But are there common features of our modern commercial reality to which Christology may make a distinctive and unique contribution? Perhaps there may be possibilities for bridge building here after all.

Here I suspect we may be driven back to basic features of the concept of incarnation, but in an inclusive rather than an exclusive sense. Jesus came into a world which was riven, like ours, with the conflicts between cultures, the dominant and the dominated. Like ours, it was strongly oriented towards the cultivation of factors of esteem, wealth and status. Jesus made choices, which led to his death. Christians believe that. In some mysterious way, to which we shall only gain access eschatologically, God the creator of the universe was uniquely involved in this life and death, and brought an effective transformation out of death, which affected God, and the created order for ever after. Christian doctrine attempts to clothe this mystery in explanation, and is only partially successful. It is within this overall pattern of divine compassion that all life is lived, and according to which it is encouraged to move. Within this vision faith lives, and has hope. For faith, the conflicts of interest which characterize modern society are to be resolved with reference to this framework, this is the *cantus firmus*, not only of individual human life, but of the entire universe. What happens in the major religions and in all human thought and theoretical reflection is to be related to this point of reference, in order that the recollection of Christ may shed light on every aspect of the created order. But when this vision is to be imposed on society as an authoritarian template, it is entirely corrupted.

Leading observers of the religious scene in the past century have noted significant features, and have evaluated them in different ways. This must be an ongoing process. They have stressed the importance of religious experience, sometimes direct, sometimes indirect. Appeal to direct experience has the merit of intensity and urgency, and the disadvantage of a tendency to intolerance of those who do not share that intensity. Indirect experience is more accommodating of pluralist interpretation, but may fade into vagueness. Appeals to the Word, to narrative, to rationality, have their own pluses and minuses. Alasdair MacIntyre's Benedictine oases of spirituality may light up the world around them, and nurture faith, but they may not communicate beyond the magic circle. MacIntyre recognized this in looking for commonly agreed virtues. But these may not be imposed by the elect communities on the unelect; they need to be negotiated in a context of mutuality. Theology on the edge of these centres may be more open to dialogue and more humble, but it may also lose the central dimension of grace and descend into an intolerant moralism.

A contemporary intercultural theology which is concerned with generosity will be aware of the economic dimension of the Word. Generosity very often involves the availability and deployment of financial resources. This means that theology has to be aware of the spheres of economics, of politics and especially of business. Commercial interests have shaped the development of human society from earliest times, and no more so than in the present. A huge percentage of human energy is taken up in the practice of business. Where transcendence is understood as having social as well as individual implications, the structuring of the world through business becomes an important sphere of theological reflection. Economics plays a crucial role in the development of the encultured self. Economic decisions are themselves often inextricably bound up with political choices. Therefore theology also has a contribution to make to political decision, though history shows how careful it must be to avoid offering a theocratic validation to political theory.

The relation between theology and business studies is important. It is also subject to imbalance, in the ambiguous associations of forms of religion with forms of laissez faire capitalism. Business demands investment, and this raises issues of ethical investment. It involves employment, and raises issues of fair employment practice. It requires resources, and the choice of resources raises sharply environmental issues. Management requires the development of strategies to cope with change and to channel conflict constructively. Economists, politicians and political theorists often spend their lives discussing the merits of alternative frameworks of economic order. Here, too, is an opportunity for the development of interdisciplinarity in problem solving.

Much of human life is taken up in business environments. Here is scope for reflection and action on the best deployment of human resources in a just and harmonious co-humanity. How can a theological reflection on transcendence connect and interact with a modern business environment? If Christianity is purely a matter for use at home, and to be excluded entirely from the corporate workplace, then this is a curious situation for a faith that claims to provide a vital contribution to human flourishing.

We may react against this train of thought by regarding literature or art as more appropriate dialogue partners in a search for transcendence. Yet there can be little great art or great literature without an economic sub-structure – no Michelangelo, Shakespeare or Bach without patrons to commission. The self as encultured self is also the business-oriented self. The charts of the on-line traders may tell us as much about the potential and the fragility of the human as the paradigms of chaos theory or of postmodern hermeneutics.

We may also reflect that the connections between theology and business may be indirect. What is required is not so much a dialogue with the commercial environment as such, rather an influence on individual and private moral character of a more traditionally religious sort, such that this will influence public conduct. This may be partly true, yet it is important to reflect on a corporate business ethic, and to offer a perspective from the area of faith to this development. Such reflection is already present in the tradition, for example in the long reflection concerning usury, which hinges on just and equitable practice. Theological reflection on debt, already developed in relation to Third World debt, might be extended to consider the whole culture of the relationship between creditors and debtors. Questions of confidentiality also need to be balanced against issues of fairness, as the responsibility of the banking systems of the world for the disposal of Jewish assets from the Second World War has made abundantly clear. The issue of business collusion with totalitarian regimes likewise remains a difficult and unresolved problem.

In creating a theology related to the material world it can never be overlooked that economic policies provide one of the most powerful influences in the modern world, affecting the health and well-being of all human beings. Christian notions of justice and sharing, arising from the Christological centre, remain of vital importance to global welfare.

Theology and Worship

I have suggested that the way forward for theology will be increasingly in terms of interdisciplinarity and a shared quest for rationality. The engagement of theology with a wide variety of disciplines should enable theology to make an effective contribution to human flourishing in a multicultural future. This does not underestimate the continuing importance of autonomous study projects within all disciplines including theology. It would be unwise to envisage intercultural theology as the answer to all issues of faith, theology and community.

It seems clear, too, that an intercultural interdisciplinary engagement, in theory and in practice, can never take the place of worship as a mediating instrument in the transmission and facilitating of faith and service. Worship needs to be sensitive to intercultural concerns if it is to be meaningful, and this may mean massive rethinking. The practice of worship in a context which neglects human rights is clearly a deep distortion of the gospel. The singing of inane hymns will be an increasing barrier to wider participation. Worship may take many different forms, more and less formally expressed. But the sphere of worship contributes decisively to the formation of faith and its implementation in society.

Notes

1 I use male language for God, following the tradition but recognizing the problems. This study is committed to the huge importance of feminist contributions to theology.

2 This phrase has been discussed recently by George Lindbeck and by Bruce Marshall. It is hard not to underestimate the violence which has been committed in the name of Christ, and the levels of sophisticated justification which this has received. Cf., too, Bartlett (2001), who speaks of Christ as hope rising from the abyss.

CHAPTER 7

Human Rights, Theological Partnership

Human Rights in Intercultural Praxis

We have spoken of theology as leading to and advocating humane praxis, Here it is important to acknowledge again a debt, often a somewhat unfashionable debt, to the long tradition of *liberal values*. Liberalism is often criticized for being purely situation-oriented in its ethical dimension, for being unable to suggest common goods, and for being radically individualistic. It can be self-defeating, since the exercise of freedom by some can curtail freedom for others. There is no doubt that some kinds of liberalism are radically selfish, and myopic in their systematic reductionism, but the abuse does not take away the proper use, and liberal positions are capable of learning from critics.[1]

What distinctive contribution can Christian theology contribute to political and social practice, to civil society and human rights? Again there is no automatic benefit, for Christianity has often been used in support of radically selfish policies. But this need not be the case. Christian faith which most Christians would recognize as authentic is other-related, promoting the selfless rather than the selfish. God is characterized as self-giving, self-affirming love, instantiated in the incarnation in Jesus Christ, in solidarity with the oppressed to the point of death. Faith is always eschatologically open, open to correction. We do not yet have the final understanding of God and the world, and must be open to learning from other human beings in mutuality and reciprocity. Faith does not affirm complete relativism. It affirms the values of the Kingdom of God, as indicated, for example, in the Sermon on the Mount. These values are non-negotiable. At the same time, it distinguishes between faith and knowledge. There remains an important dimension of epistemological humility, which should lead to a humility of praxis.

Of course this openness has been capable of endless distortion. Indeed the hypostatization of cultural accidents into eternal verities remains a dangerous temptation. But to capitulate to failure would be a tribute to oppression and injustice. The struggle for the fruits of faith in love, peace and justice remains a continuing and vital task.

Theology must always engage with culture and with society in their overlappings and their diversities, their continuities and disjunctions. It must engage with intellectual constructs like civil society. But it must not forget the nuts and bolts of actual human interchange, biological, economic and environmental realities. Because grace is its *raison d'être*, it will be free to engage in constructive tension and dialogue with different and contrasting conceptual frameworks. But because its central categories are themselves given with particular cultural constructions, it will not be able to presume a hegemony over other contributions to the human dialogue. It will be a partner with a vital and distinctive contribution, but still a contribution which works within mutuality and reciprocity.

I am particularly interested in the role of theology in contributing to the dialogue of human values and to humanitarian action beyond the churches themselves. This leads inevitably to the role of theology in relation to human rights in society. There is of course a long-standing debate in both philosophy and law about the status and even the existence of human rights. When churches consider the status of the European declaration on Human Rights, for example, they tend to find theological objections. Are not the rights of the churches based on the gospel, which is above all merely human rights? The difficulty is of course that the historical track record of the churches on justice issues has often been, not better than, but below the standard of ordinary human rights.

Christians, it is often argued, ought not to use the language of rights. They may indeed be eligible for rights, but their Christian duty may lie in not exercising rights. Rights are individualistic, and do not make for an other-regarding community. It is one thing , however, for Christians to give up any claim to rights which they may possess. It is quite another to deny rights to others in the name of a higher scale of values. History does not lead us to have great confidence in those who have deployed this argument in the tradition. We may note that liberal theologians have often been quite as intolerant as conservatives in this respect. Nineteenth-century theological liberalism was often accompanied by social conservatism, notably in the opposition to women's rights. It would be good to think that conservative Christianity, with a more acute awareness of a doctrine of grace, was more sensitive to oppression, but that would not always seem to have been the case. A classic case is historical evangelical enthusiasm for the death penalty.

However, it is important in this discussion to keep in mind the big picture, as it were. There are important philosophical issues in the debates between liberal and communitarian positions, and there are serious conceptual differences to be argued in the debates between ethics based on a search for the common good and the ethics of human rights. But there are of course overlaps and commonalities in these searches. The common good includes human rights and human rights involve the common good. It is not necessary to conclude that one approach has necessarily all the right answers. Here we follow a liberal human rights approach, but recall that much illumination on human rights has been produced by other approaches, notably the work of John Langan (Hennelly and Langan, 1982).

Human Rights and Christian Tradition

Human rights has been one of the most powerful concepts in sociopolitical thinking in the last 50 years. Yet like other powerful concepts – freedom, God, justice – it has been and remains much contested. Lack of an agreed definition, or even agreement on the existence of human rights, has been a cause of much frustration among writers on the subject.[2] Different writers have emphasized civil and political, economic and social, individual and collective rights. Some have started from philosophical ideas of individual freedom, others from legal debates about state sovereignty. Alan Gewirth has sought to ground human rights in the necessary conditions of human action. John Rawls imagines a system of basic liberties which are necessary in a just society, and these include individual rights. There are problems about cultures which claim exemption from critical scrutiny from outside. Peter Jones asks pertinently why some systems of value should be open to critical examination yet others not. The intensity of debate is itself a token of the importance of the issues involved.

Perhaps the best brief account of the complex issue of rights is given in Peter Jones's *Rights* (1994). Beginning from Wesley Hohfeld's 1919 classification of four forms of rights, as claim-rights, liberty-rights, powers and immunities, Jones examined the morality of rights, natural and human rights, the justification of human rights, freedom, autonomy and rights, socioeconomic rights, democracy, groups and rights, and the difficulties inherent in rights language, including conflicts of rights. Morality may go beyond rights to include love, care and concern for others as individuals. Jones's conclusion is particularly germane to theological inquiry:

> In some philosophical circles, the moral and political thinking associated with rights has recently become unfashionable. In particular the aspiration to ascribe rights alike to all humanity is now viewed in some quarters with a mixture of hostility and derision. But before we join in these smug dismissals, we should remember why it is that people have taken up the idea of rights. Outside the cocooned world of the academy, people are still victims of torture, still subjected to genocide, still deprived of basic freedoms and still dying through starvation. We should remember these people before we decide to forget about rights. (227)

What does the Christian tradition in the past and in the present have to contribute to human rights? Judging by a plethora of recent interest, the churches might claim that the Christian tradition has always been an advocate of human rights. There has always been recognition of the creation of man as a creature in the image of God, with his own dignity before God. There have been pleas for religious tolerance in the early church (Lactantius) and the role of freedom of conscience (Augustine). Aquinas, following Aristotle, was much concerned with justice as central to the common good. Luther stressed justification by faith alone, and the freedom of the Christian man. Calvin followed Luther in supporting the individual judgment against the authority of church tradition. Many of the framers of the American Declaration of Independence and similar documents had strong Christian connections. In the biblical narratives God brought freedom from slavery to the children of Israel, and Christ dies in solidarity with the poor and the sinful.

But we have to wait for the legacy of the Enlightenment, in the French revolution and the American Declaration of Independence, before we find a serious reckoning with human rights in society. Why should this be? It must be remembered that society up to 1750 was largely an autocratic and feudal society, in which claims to individual rights were commonly suppressed. After the Constantinian settlement the churches turned from pleas for tolerance to zeal for prosecuting those in error. *Error has no rights*. Only God has rights, and all men are subject to God, sinners in acute danger of eternal damnation. They are called to a life of repentance and obedience.

The churches were prepared to recognize rulers and states as the God-given arbiters of affairs. Rulers and states are autonomous, and individuals have no rights over against them. The development of states in modern Europe gave new impetus to the rights of states. Individual freedoms were the internal affair of sovereign states. The law and the Church offered mutual support to state power. It would therefore be stretching credulity to see the Christian Church as a player in the vanguard of human rights issues. The Church dealt too with its internal conflicts in a firmly authoritarian manner.

The situation is not of course entirely clear-cut. We noted that there were people of Christian convictions involved in some of the American declarations of the eighteenth century, and there were Christians prominent in the anti-slavery campaigns, and in the early work of the Red Cross. But these were largely individual actions, based on Christian convictions but carried out outside the institutional churches. As often, the values of the kingdom were bought to the attention of the Church through agencies of the secular world.

Reflection on the Christomorphic shape of salvation suggests a further connection between the theological tradition and human rights. It is true that we have to wait for the Enlightenment for a considered focus on rights, and it is the case that human rights is a hugely powerful instrument for encouraging compassion in the politics of the modern world. Human rights as a subject comes late to the theological agenda (under 'Human Rights', the *Oxford Companion to Christian Thought*, published in 2000, refers the reader to articles on anti-Semitism, apartheid, democracy, justice and liberation theology). Yet there has always been, amid the failures of the churches, a witness to compassion and unconditional love as a thin line throughout the history of religion. For Christianity this is often focused on the notion of discipleship. This notion has its ambiguities and tendencies to triumphalism, yet it has also inspired selfless service to our fellow human beings in unconditional acceptance and devotion.

A classic but always relevant case is discipleship in the life and thought of Dietrich Bonhoeffer. In his later life and work he reflected often on the shape of 'the form of Christ in the world'. Christians have seen Bonhoeffer himself as a classic modern instance of that form. Bonhoeffer has been venerated. But it is not always noted that Bonhoeffer and his circle almost all met with violent deaths at the hands of fascism. Those who held back from this level of commitment largely survived into a new era in which they continued to flourish in Church and society. The Christomorphic shape is not something to be entertained lightly. There is a usually very high probability that it will lead to disaster within the prevailing culture, not least the ecclesiastical culture.[3]

Much rights reflection has in fact been carried on in reflection upon justice, and upon social justice in a theological context, especially in recent decades. This is a most important stream of tradition. But conscious focus on human rights concepts may provide alternative approaches to asking fundamental questions about the nature of humanity and the reconstruction of civil society, especially in the light of the all too frequent experience of seeing justice denied within a state justice system. Beyond the letter of the law and the culture of a given juristocracy there may be further issues of the nature of the shape of community to be examined.

The issue of rights is succinctly encapsulated in a brief comment from what I regard as a classic of judicious analysis of human rights issues in a particular case, Cornel West's *Race Matters*. It was said of America, but it applies in different tones to all our cultures: 'We simply cannot enter the twenty first century at each other's throats, even as we acknowledge the weighty forces of racism, patriarchy, economic inequality, homophobia and ecological abuse on our necks. … None of us alone can save the nation or world. But each of us can make a positive difference if we commit ourselves to do so' (West, 1994, 159).

Human rights remain central to discussion of citizenship in the modern world. From a Christian perspective they are grounded in a theological understanding of humanity as made in *the image of God*. As such, human beings deserve to be treated with dignity. This implies equality and specific basic rights. Christian faith understands humanity to be moving towards a fulfilment which is characterized through the love of God as shown in the events concerning Jesus Christ. Christian faith offers this understanding as a contribution to the continuing exploration of the nature of humanity and the development of society. Theology includes a basic eschatological dimension. It regards its basic themes as both reliable and provisional – reliable in their central structures, provisional in their modes of expression and articulation.

Rights and Ambiguity

Emphasis on human rights has brought and will continue to bring great benefits to society. This is all the more remarkable when we consider how real the problems are in defining and advocating rights. It is vital to be aware of these critical issues, and perhaps equally vital to be clear that the abuse does not take away the proper use. Let us look at some of the problem issues.

From a *philosophical* perspective, there is nothing 'given' about human rights. Indeed each decade highlights new dilemmas in the philosophical literature on the subject. Still perhaps the best overview is provided by Alan Gewirth (1982). He examined, for example, the nature of rights as claim rights, the question of whether rights are important even when they do not actually exist, the possibility and implications of absolute rights.

From a *political* viewpoint, rights can be seen as a two-edged weapon which is used and abused in international politics. David Forsythe has explored these issues in a series of books. Human rights was used in the Cold War as an instrument of policy by Presidents Carter and Bush, with rather different agendas. As Isaiah Berlin long ago demonstrated in his *Two Concepts of Liberty*, individual rights may conflict with social and economic rights. It is all too easy to emphasize the rhetoric of individual freedom and deny great sections of a population basic respect and the conditions for economic well-being.

From a *legal* perspective there are again positive and negative aspects. Human rights legislation has brought and continues to bring benefits to individuals and groups marginalized by unfair laws. At the same time it exposes conflicts of law, in which the interests of some groups inevitably conflict with those of others. Connor Gearty's *Understanding Human Rights* (Gearty and Tomkins, 1996) gives an excellent survey of these issues. But legislation is intimately connected with politics, and this may have controversial consequences. Legislation based on classical liberal views of individual freedom may conflict with ideals of social democracy, which stresses communitarian values.

From a *theological* perspective, there are at least as many different options and ambiguities. We noted that in issues of abortion and contraception theologians on both sides of the argument regularly appeal to natural law, human rights and human dignity. Churches on the one hand campaign, often very effectively, for the implementation of human rights in far-off countries. At the same time they may campaign, sometimes with more and sometimes with less justification, for *exemption* from human rights regulation in their own practices on religious grounds. Members of national churches invoke ancient legislation which concedes their autonomy under God. How far does this extend to the practices of every group, and how do we know what God intends for these churches in any case?

From a *cultural* perspective, there has to be the recognition of pluralism at many levels of social grouping. It will not do to pit Eastern values against

Western, capitalist against socialist, white against black and so on. A cosmopolitan perspective is much superior to relativism.

Rights and God

One of the earliest theological discussions of human rights is to be found in Alan Falconer's collection, *Understanding Human Rights* (1980). In an essay here on Christian faith and human rights, Moltmann sees the Reformed emphasis as being on human dignity through man's creation in the image of God, the Lutheran emphasis on a correspondence between Christian life in the sphere of faith and human rights in the sphere of the world, and the Roman Catholic emphasis on the analogy between nature and grace, in which grace illuminates the dignity of man in nature. Moltmann identifies another starting point in the experience of inhumanity, in a liberation theology context. Falconer concludes that Christians should be open to the needs of humankind as presented in conflict situations, in a theology of wayfarers.

In the present, the language of human rights is frequently used in the churches, usually on both sides of debates, for example on pro-Choice and Pro-Life. As in secular politics, conservative and liberal groups have become equally adept at seizing ownership of the language of human rights on behalf of their positions. Debates about love are polarized by such modifications as loving the sinner but not the sin. Debates about natural law and the common good may reach radically different conclusions from similar premises, as with the debates between Finnis and Nussbaum, both drawing on Aristotelian premises. The specific implications of human rights can be contested in numerous directions.

Arguments for the centrality of human rights would appear to be both complex and necessary – complex because of the range of different evaluations of rights, necessary because of the continued global violation of rights, especially of the most vulnerable. David Forsythe neatly sums up the history of the debate:

> We do not lack for differing theories about human rights. For Edmund Burke, the concept of human rights was a monstrous fiction. For Jeremy Bentham, it was absurd to base human rights on natural rights, because 'Natural rights is simple nonsense … nonsense upon stilts'. The contemporary philosopher Alasdair McIntyre tells us *there are no such things as human rights*; they are similar to witches and unicorns and other figments of the imagination. (Forsythe, 2000, 28)

Forsythe has examined the regional and global implications of human rights standards, the role of non-governmental organizations and the often unnoticed yet increasingly huge power and financial muscle of transnational corporations. He notes that 'Only six states have revenues larger than the nine largest TNC's. If we were to include transnational banks in this figure, the power of private for-profit enterprises would be much larger' (191). So, for example, the Mitsubishi and Mitsui corporations have each twice as much revenue as the Netherlands, the world's seventh most prosperous nation state. Reflecting on the politics of liberalism in a realist world, Forsythe traces in contemporary geopolitics an oscillation between liberalism and neo-liberalism, between romanticism and realism. He concludes that human rights activity on any level does make a tangible difference to the contemporary world, but that there is a very long way to go: 'The various levels of action for human rights – whether global, regional, national or sub-national – were not likely to wither away because of lack of human rights violations with which to deal. Pursuing liberalism in a realist world is no simple task' (236).

What has all this to do with theology, culture and intercultural theology? Not much, if theology is concerned only with abstract ideas and aesthetics without ethics. But since theology, and especially Christian theology, is committed to searching for truth and ultimate meaning in the universe, it cannot be done in isolation from these geopolitical realities. Behind the economic and political statistics lie equally important issues such as nutrition and health care. In the European Holocaust 6 million were murdered, and in the famine in China in 1958–62 30 million people perished. AIDS currently devastates Africa. Where were human rights considerations there, and where was God's action in all of this? A theology which is done in isolation from world affairs may be a coherent and academically satisfying enterprise, but it can hardly be an adequate Christian theology.

There is an integral connection between concern for human rights and concern for God, but it is not a simple or direct connection. God is not an interventionist God in the most literal sense, who may fix things in the world at will. But, equally, God is not entirely dependent on the cosmos. God remains creator and redeemer of the world, and may act in ways complex beyond our full understanding to encourage fulfilment in the universe along particular lines – lines consonant with God's own being and purpose as eternal compassionate love. This action may link with human action in more and in less direct ways.

The Enlightenment search for the common good, often without reference to God, may be understood by Christians as itself prompted by the divine love. This is not to suggest that agnostic thinkers were somehow anonymous Christians, but rather, from a Christian perspective, that all good action is a response to *the source of goodness who is God*. Enlightenment thinkers were correct in thinking that it is possible to seek for and to achieve a measure of the common good without appeal to God. But the quest need not exclude the question of God.

Ignatieff

Perhaps the best current analysis of human rights is Michael Ignatieff's *Human Rights as Politics and Idolatry* (2001). The purpose of human rights, he argues, is to protect human agency and therefore to protect human agents against abuse and oppression. Beyond this, rights do not claim to be morally comprehensive. Without rights people lack agency. To minimize controversy and allow for moral pluralism we should avoid foundational arguments like religious arguments. But this does not mean relativism. Rights are universal because they define the interests of the powerless. They involve a commitment to dialogue with people with whom we disagree. Human rights interventions will not always be successful, but must be done with consistency. We should not make a creed out of rights – that would be idolatry. They do imply non-negotiable concepts such as the rights of individuals: 'Relativism is the invariable alibi of tyranny' (74). Religious arguments cannot be privileged: 'We need to stop thinking of human rights as trumps and begin thinking of them as a language that creates the basis for deliberation' (95).

It seems to me that this essay is a model of sanity, but I would also like to think that an intercultural theology may contribute to this 'thin universalism' by bringing its tradition to the table not as a trump but as a contribution on equal terms to the conversation. In this way it is perhaps possible to see the compatibility of religion with what is a genuine rather than a privileged political liberalism, which will be open to conversation while retaining an intolerance of oppression.

Christians believe, as characterized in the incarnation of Jesus Christ. They bring the way of Jesus Christ, as an icon of humanity as God intends it, to the table for consideration. They believe that all human beings are created to be fulfilled in the image of God, and to be fulfilled with dignity and well-being. They do not wish to impose this vision on others, but they offer it in the belief that it has infinite value for the human future.

Schleiermacher held that all human beings have a sense, in their self-consciousness, of absolute dependence on a higher transcendent source, but this is often inhibited by a corruption of this sense through cultural and personal factors. As a matter of empirical observation, this is clearly not the case, and experience is notably deceptive. There is, however, an awareness in most societies that our humanity is largely shaped by our relationships with others, by the recognition of difference. This means that the formal possibility of relationship to a transcendent other is not unintelligible in human conversation. The concrete condition of this possibility is specified in particular religious traditions, and in Christianity through faith in God through Jesus Christ.

There are comprehensive discussions of the relation of religion to political liberalism in Dombrowski (2001) and in the collection edited by P.J. Weithman (1997), especially the essays by N. Wolterstorff, who criticizes the restrictions on religion often proposed by political liberalism, and T.P. Jackson, who brings a Christian 'civic agapism' to political discussion. In this debate it is important to be fair to both sides of the discussion. Wolterstorff is a good example of a conservative theologian who is committed to social issues and whose proposals could hardly be regarded as oppressive to non-Christians.

Nussbaum

In the search for a differentiated rationality in relation to rights, we may find in the writings of Martha Nussbaum an excellent dialogue partner for theology. In *Cultivating Humanity* (1997), she provides an exemplary retrieval of aspects of classical culture as a contribution to tackling pressing problems in the modern world, notably the understanding of citizenship. She identifies the dangers inherent both in modernist universalism and in postmodern particularity, and she invokes a Socratic model of rationality to steer an intelligent course between extremes. The argument is a development of her earlier *The Therapy of Desire* (1994), an examination of the theory and practice of Hellenistic ethics. In that volume, discussion of the debates between Aristotelian and Stoic ethicists led her to stress the continuing value of reason, in correction of Foucault's conclusion, based on *his* study of classical ethics, that reason is always the instrument of power and so is of very limited effectiveness.

In a chapter on narrative imagination she underscores the value of literature as a vehicle of the compassionate imagination. After charting the role of tragedy in encouraging us to identify with suffering, she notes the coincidence of the rise of the modern novel with the rise of modern democracy: 'In reading a realist novel with active participation, readers do all that tragic spectators do, and something more. They embrace the ordinary' (95). She recalls again the tradition of the Stoics: 'Marcus Aurelius made a further claim on behalf of the narrative imagination: he argued that it contributes to undoing retributive anger' (97). She identifies the danger of some forms of multiculturalism: 'The goal of producing world citizens is profoundly opposed to the spirit of identity politics, which holds that one's primary affiliation is with one's own local group, whether religious or ethnic or based on sexuality or gender' (110). A section on the study of non-Western cultures leads to reflection on the aims and limits of cross-cultural teaching. Students should become aware of their own ignorance, of other world cultures and to a great extent of their own.

Nussbaum then turns to African–American studies. Particularly effective is her account of her own lack of meaningful contact with black people through her life and teaching career. 'I see few black faces. I find things out mostly by teaching and imagining.' This is a severe challenge in 'an America nominally integrated but still consumed by bigotry' (185). The citizenship theme is in turn developed into the realm of women's studies.

(This was to be taken up soon in a further book.) Feminist thought led on logically to other areas in the study of human sexuality. Nussbaum highlights academic suspicion of the subject from her own experience. A delicate and difficult task, it should nevertheless be a central part of the curriculum. What of the role of religion in the search for citizenship? She maintains that love of the neighbour is a central value in all major American religions. 'These religions call us to a critical examination of our own selfishness and narrowness, urging more inclusive sympathy' (293). The 'new' liberal education will be not for an elite but for all humanity.

Against the objection that a search for *humanitas* is inevitably simply an exegesis of Western values, it is striking that in her *Women and Human Development* (2000) Nussbaum concentrates almost entirely on Indian traditions and culture, and demonstrates the continuing importance of the central values of humanity in this framework. Through the examination of legal, political and religious debates, law cases and practical outcomes, she shows that issues of rights and capabilities in India manifest in depth all the ambiguities and complexities which appear in other cultures. Much of the generalizing rhetoric surrounding the status of 'Western' and 'non-Western' perspectives will simply not stand up to close rational scrutiny.

A chapter, 'In Defense of Human Values', makes a valuable case for a balance between respecting cultural particularity and maintaining common values. It interprets human rights through a comprehensive model of human capabilities. She argues against cultural relativism:

> It has no bite in the modern world, where the ideas of every culture turn up inside every other, through the internet and the media. … Why should we follow local ideas, rather than the best ideas that we can find? … Finally, normative relativism is self-subverting: for, in asking us to defer to local norms, it asks us to defer to norms that in most cases are strongly non-relativistic. Most local traditions take themselves to be absolutely, or relatively true. So, in asking us to follow the local, rationality asks us not to follow relativism. (49)

Capabilities

Arguments from diversity and paternalism are equally weak. Nussbaum lists central human functional capabilities, vital to the dignity and well-being of each person. These include life, bodily health, bodily integrity, senses, imagination and thought, emotions, practical reason, relation to other species, play and control, political and material, over one's environment (80). These include basic capabilities, internal capabilities and combined capabilities. 'Citizens of repressive nondemocratic regimes have the internal but not the combined capability to exercise thought and speech in accordance with their consciences' (85).

Capabilities have a close relationship to human rights, to political and civil liberties and to economic and social rights. Combined capabilities are rights, and do not have the 'Western' tone of talk of rights, though rights language is still useful in drawing attention to the role of justification and the importance of liberty in argument for capabilities. This theoretical framework provides a basis for renewed attention to women's preferences and options in a world which has long systematically suppressed women.

Nussbaum turns to the role of religion in these debates. Religion may be but need not be, oppressive. She will argue here for frameworks of political rather than comprehensive liberalism, avoiding the tendency to exclude transcendence which is often a feature of secular liberal positions. The argument is illustrated from legal and religious argument in Indian court cases. Families are important to women, but the concept should not be allowed to become coercive: 'My approach, by contrast, begins by focusing on the capabilities and liberties of each person, and does not assume that any one affiliative group is prior or central in promoting these capabilities' (276). 'The fact is that justice and friendship are good allies: women who have dignity and self-respect can help to fashion types of community that are no less loving, and often quite a lot more loving, than those they have known before' (290).

'Women in much of the world lose out by being women' (298). The world community has been slow to address the problems of women, because it has lacked a consensus that sex-based inequality is an urgent issue of political justice. A capabilities approach 'can fairly claim to make a distinctive contribution to the practical pursuit of gender justice' (303).

Nussbaum's work provides an effective response to the problems of relativism and the charge that rights talk is always Western. As has been noted (see Chris Brown in Patman, 2000, 47), 'Part of this turn involves the use of classical notions of the 'virtues to construct the kind of account of what it is to be human that would not be vulnerable to the charge of cultural imperialism. The virtues as espoused by Aristotle and other Greek thinkers are frames of mind which orient one towards characteristic human experiences.' It is clear that concepts of human rights, like all concepts, are always open to further debate and modification. But it is all too easy for autocratic rulers to attack them in order to preserve their own coercive ideologies, in any part of the world.

The concept of human rights is central to the quest for humanity and citizenship. Theology may well wish to assert other concepts which are central to human flourishing – we have mentioned generosity. But rights may be an integral part of the realization of the purpose of a generous God for humanity.

In Part II we have sought to develop a conversation between theological and non-theological traditions in the exploration of Christology and of humane praxis. We shall explore further the nature of the intercultural in proposing an interdisciplinary approach to the mystery of God in Part III.

Notes

1 I have discussed debates between liberals and communitarians at length in *Generosity and the Christian Future*. On this issue see Fergusson (1998). On the relationship between political liberalism, economic theory and human rights issues, see now the very comprehensive discussion in Plant (2001), and the works which he cites, notably Larmore (1996) on political liberalism and Geras (1995) in defence of the notion of a universal sense of human solidarity. I am very sympathetic to Plant's plea for the need to struggle towards a common world of meaning and dialogue despite the difficulties. In my own view the tradition from Schleiermacher to Tracy may be seen as an appropriate balance to the tradition from Barth to Hauerwas. Narrative theologies tend to be embraced by conservative and radical theologians in an (in my view mistaken) anti-liberal solidarity. Narrative theologies have much to teach us, but they are not the only model for doing theology today.

2 There is of course an enormous modern literature on both human rights and on political liberalism. Apart from the views discussed here, on human rights there is a good survey of the theoretical issues in Beetham (1995), and of practical applications in Power (1981). The importance of human rights as collective, rather than purely individual, is brought out by Felice (1996) and by Kymlicka. For an excellent account of human rights from a tradition of seeking the common good, rather than a classical liberal approach, see Hennelly and Langan (1982). On political liberalism John Gray's many writings are instructive, for example the second edition of *Liberalism* (1995) and especially Gray (2000). In the latter, Gray seeks to develop liberalism as a *modus vivendi*. 'Modus vivendi continues the liberal search for peaceful coexistence; but it does so by giving up the belief that one way of life, or a single type of regime, could be best for all' (Gray, 2000, 139). A liberalism which includes this element of provisionality and openness to conversation is compatible with our emphasis on a fallibilistic Intercultural approach.

3 Sally McFague has highly pertinent observations on Bonhoeffer's witness in her recent environmental theology (McFague, 2001).

III
INTEGRATING INTERCULTURAL THEOLOGY: EMBODYING INTERDISCIPLINARITY

CHAPTER 8

Theology, Culture and the Humanities

Intercultural theology is by definition concerned to engage with different cultures and with other academic disciplines. It is always in danger of becoming infinitely diffuse. Yet it is also concerned by definition with integration. It is committed to exploring and creating connections between different modes of discourse and life world, not to create an artificial unity but to encourage dialogue and conversation. We shall begin to survey this field by considering the engagement of theology with the humanities. Though we readily associate the humanities with a natural enthusiasm for connections between culture and religion, this enthusiasm is by no means unqualified. At different times we find differing approaches to culture, and to the relationship between theology and culture. The project of an integrated interdisciplinary approach to intercultural theology will always be incomplete, but much can be learned from making the effort.

Literature, Culture and Theology: Eliot and Auden, Morrison

A critical theology has to engage with the academic discipline of systematic theology and with the Church. It is to the theological world, and from the Church, that those who write about and practise Christian faith turn for much of their inspiration. One of the most useful things an intercultural perspective can do is to remind and encourage theological readers simply to *listen* to other voices in their reflection on issues of theology and culture. A main purpose of Part III is to remind us of this prior need to listen, without which there is likely to be no real dialogue. Neither Eliot nor Auden would have written as they did without absorbing particular theological perspectives, for better or for worse, and without participating in particular sorts of Christian worship and practice.

It is also desirable for theology to engage in a wider dialogue with both the human and the natural sciences. In the first instance this is necessary in order to learn how the world is. But in a religion of incarnation there is also an imperative to a wider dialogue. Christian faith is given to be given away, not in triumphalism but, we have argued, as a contribution – Christians believe a vital contribution – to the search for common human values within the created order.

Love and justice, culture, literature and the liberal arts: these are enormous themes, and it is not easy to say anything worthwhile of a general nature. The more these themes are studied, the more clear it is that they are infinitely heterogeneous. Culture has infinite sub-divisions, often with very different characteristics. Cultural studies embraces an enormous variety of themes. The recognition of difference, and the importance of fragments, is one of the hallmarks of current thought. In the following chapters we shall look at some fragments. We shall not give up hope entirely of making connections, for without connections there can be no common search for values. But we shall try to avoid avenues in which all cats become grey in the night.

We have already spoken of the Christian commitment to human rights which grows out of incarnation and reconciliation. Within the vast literature on human rights there is a precise and specific Christian voice to be heard. This will not solve all the myriad legal and philosophical issues raised, but as part of the specific Christian contribution, it should not be neglected. Christians of course also differ on this issue, as they do on other things. Here we engage in dialogue with law and the social and political sciences.

Christianity and literature, as is often pointed out, were closely intertwined until comparatively recently. Christianity has had an enormous influence on human thought over the last 2000 years, and this impact will continue to reverberate, in different forms, some more, some less muted, through the next centuries.

A good example of the dialogue with literature is given by Karl-Josef Kuschel in *The Poet as Mirror: Human Nature, God and Jesus in Twentieth Century Literature* (1999). Kuschel is conscious of the current isolation of theology. 'One does not need to read the most recent demographic surveys to know how remote religious language has become from the reality of life. In religious language, a particular order of the church and society has become frozen, and if it is transferred to changed social conditions, it must often seem comical or ridiculous' (8). He affirms George Steiner's claim that human beings can experience transcendence in the encounter with a great work of art and notes that even Karl Barth could say that art could function as a parable of the reality of God. But 'not every experience of mystery as a result of a work of art is itself an experience of God' (18). Art contains only the possibility of truth, and can be subject to self-deception:

> For the ultimate verification of human products as signals of the truth lies with God himself. Works of art as places of the seeming true are symbolic illuminations of the mystery of human nature – that is my theological definition. For its part, Christian faith illuminates the human condition, the human mystery, in the light of the word of God, attested in holy scripture. (20)

Kuschel's comments on intercultural theology mesh closely with the concept of an intercultural theology advanced in this study. He comments that 'Sensitivity to language and awareness of the transcendental character of the great work of art make up the cultural competence of theology. Cultural competence is the expression of a truly intercultural theology. By contrast, in contemporary theology interculturality is understood in one-sidedly ethnic terms' (21). He notes that churchgoing Christians are losing contact with their living cultural environment. A new intercultural theology is then explored, illustrated from the work of Durrenmatt and others, and centred on a 'Christ-poetics'.

Among the diverse group of theologians who constituted the Christian realists in the late 1930s and 1940s were two notable literary figures, Eliot and Auden. At this stage we shall examine a selection of significant thinkers in the arts and in the humanities, not to press them into a Procrustean bed of theological hermeneutics, nor indeed to engage in a new literary study of their work. Instead we shall simply attempt, as far as possible, to listen to their own voices and be open to the agendas which they introduce, rather than the agendas which we might be inclined to design them into. Just to listen is not easy for the theologian.

Eliot was a friend of John Baillie, met him in Britain and America, and attended the Moot, that significant gathering of intellectual figures in England throughout the Second World War years. Along with Barth, Temple and others, Eliot contributed an essay to the collection on *Revelation*, edited by John Baillie and Hugh Martin (1936). Whatever we may think of it, it was a serious attempt by a leading poet at a piece of theologian's theology.

Baillie had left New York before Auden arrived in 1939. Auden was soon to become a close friend of Reinhold Niebuhr – a friendship eloquently testified to in their correspondence, published by Ursula Niebuhr in 1991. It would be hard to see any direct influence of Baillie on Eliot, though they were to keep in touch right up to Baillie's death in 1960. But Auden was to be deeply influenced by Niebuhr. In this section I want to look at at least two dimensions of the relationship of Christianity and literature through Eliot and Auden. I want first of all to see how much it matters for a literary figure *what sort of theology* and what sort of churchmanship he or she embraces. Then I want to examine the possible influence of the poet on the relationship between faith and culture. To do this effectively it will be necessary to consult scholars in the humanities: the tradition of the theologian as virtuoso is not always the best avenue.

Eliot

Eliot's essay on revelation is the first in the *Revelation* collection. Eliot begins with the observation that 'it is because I am not a theologian that I have been asked to contribute'. He goes on to add:

> I am concerned with the general differences between those who maintain a doctrine of revelation and those who reject all revelation … I take for granted that Christian revelation is the only full revelation; and that the fullness of Christian revelation consists in the essential fact of the incarnation, in relation to which all Christian revelation is to be understood. The division between those who accept, and those who deny, Christian revelation I take to be the most profound division between human beings.

He then considers the nature of secularism, attacking some contemporary writers – Gerald Heard, Herbert Read, Bertrand Russell, André Gide, Middleton Murry, at some length Irving Babbitt, and Aldous Huxley. The tone is fairly dismissive: 'M Gide's conversion to Communism has been presented as something involving an heroic sacrifice of his creative gifts. It might, of course, be retorted that possibly the exhaustion of M Gide's creative gifts had something to do with his conversion to Communism. There is a psychological mysticism which is not Christian.' He is more positive in his assessment of D.H. Lawrence. 'He was aware that religion is not, and can never survive as, simply a code of morals.'

Today we suffer from 'a strong and positive misdirection of the will'. Eliot turns to 'the principal characteristics of philosophies without revelation': instability, recurrence of ancient philosophies, tendency to evoke an opposite, and the production of immediate results. 'The whole tendency of education (in the widest sense – the forces playing on the common mind in the forms of "enlightenment") has been for a very long time to form minds more adapted to secularism, less and less equipped to apprehend the doctrine of revelation and its consequences.' He concludes:

> Any apologetic which presents the Christian faith as a preferable alternative to secular philosophy, which fights secularism on its own ground, is making a concession which is a preparation for defeat … Should we not first try to apprehend the meaning of Christianity as a whole, leading the mind to contemplate first the great gulf between the Christian mind and the secular habits of thought and feeling into which, so far as we fail to watch and pray, we all tend to fall? … What a discursive reading of secularism, over a number of years, leads me to believe, however, is that the religious sentiment – which can only be completely satisfied by the complete message of revelation – is simply suffering from a condition of repression painful for those in whom it is repressed, who yearn for the fulfillment of belief, though too ashamed of that yearning to allow it to come to consciousness.

Here we see Eliot in his conservative theological mode, sharing that disillusionment with liberal enlightenment, partly as a reaction to the apparent sterility of humanist philosophy, partly in response to the clouds of communism and fascism which were all too visible on the European horizon. In this reaction he was in good company, as the next essay, by Karl Barth, demonstrates. Eliot's stress on the incarnation was to lead to some of his most profound poetry. He understands the difficulty of the 'psychological mysticism' which will neither let the word be the world nor God be God. At the same time, we can have some sympathy with the verdict that this was by no means Eliot at his best. It was too dismissive of issues which need to be tackled, too undialectical to explore the constructive tensions in the culture. It was not perhaps uncharacteristic of Eliot who could be callous, supercilious, devout and humble by turns, and could often be extraordinarily insensitive to the human condition. On the positive side we may appreciate Eliot's brilliant use of Christian imagery in his poetry.

Today we would be much less enthusiastic about his elitism, not least in his conviction of the manifest superiority of Christendom.

Both Eliot and Auden were of course highly complex characters, and the complexities led to tensions which in their poetry and prose were often immensely creative. As with all of us, there were other occasions when the tensions were more destructive, or even when the tension was lost and they were (and we are) reduced to unreconstructed prejudice. Both Eliot and Auden had a firmly realist sense of the difference between the sacred and the profane. Neither was partial to 'psychological mysticism', though both were aware of the mystery of divine transcendence. Both were at one level prisoners of the theological and ecclesial perspectives which they inherited, largely by serendipitous means, as we all acquire knowledge which we have not studied in professional courses. Both turned these accidents to their craft with profound effect, and could produce work, at least on occasion, of the very highest order.

In his *Christianity and Modern European Literature* (1997), Daniel Murphy has a fascinating chapter on Eliot: 'Darkness of God: T.S. Eliot's Quest for Faith'. Eliot moved from humanism to religion, as he explained in an essay, 'Religion without Humanism', in 1931. He was especially fascinated by the *via negativa*, notably in the mysticism of St John of the Cross, but also in Buddhism. These come together particularly, Murphy notes, in 'The Fire Sermon' in *The Waste Land*. While much of Eliot's early poetry had been critical of religion, *The Waste Land* explores the tension between belief and unbelief. Murphy quotes a letter of Eliot to Charles Williams: 'We are, I know not how, double in ourselves, so that what we believe we disbelieve, and we cannot rid ourselves of what we condemn.' The way of darkness is ultimately the way of light, as in 'East Coker'. These religious themes are brought to a final resolution in *Little Gidding*. In faith, and in life beyond death, the symbol of suffering and the symbol of God's love are one.

> And all shall be well and
> All manner of thing shall be well
> When the tongues of flame are in-folded
> Into the crowned knot of fire
> And the fire and the rose are one.

Perhaps in some ways mirroring the mood of foreboding of the 1930s in much of Europe, there is more of the cross than of the incarnation or even the resurrection in much of Eliot's work. This gives it its power, but also a certain limitation. With Barth and Niebuhr, and also with Auden, Eliot drinks deep from the Augustinian tradition. To affirm the gospel as good news, as transformative within the created order, without either trivializing suffering or romanticizing the world, remains a difficult task. Bonhoeffer was to struggle towards this in his letters and papers. Auden was aware of the dilemma, but perhaps too steeped in Kierkegaard to be able to address it effectively.

Auden

I now turn to Auden, again to his theological connections. His correspondence with Ursula Niebuhr comments on the relations between Christianity and culture. She wrote (1991, 280):

> Wystan Auden was a close and dear friend to Reinhold, me and our children. He was always kind, interested and generous; we, as did other friends of his, gave him a strong family setting … He and I had shared the same sort of English and Edwardian childhood. We both had doctor fathers: both of us had devout mothers … Anglican liturgy had also interested us both.

She notes the influence of Kierkegaard on Auden, his use of the leap of faith and/or irony. She comments, 'We cherished this friend, his imagination, and what he saw and taught us about life, not only about the human situation but also about a certain vision of glory.'

The correspondence reveals remarkable daily snapshots of the way he related religion to culture:

> WA to UN 19 Dec 41 'It makes me a little sad to realize there is more indignation over the Japs than the Germans, because they are "little and yellow". The Hearst Publisher editorial the next day might have been written by Goebbels.' … I am still pegging away at my Christmas Oratorio, which will be immensely lay, and very theological. There are many theories about me, One party believes I am a starry eyed idealist, another that I am a crass materialist. One professor who is a fanatical Aristotelian met another professor in the corridor and said "I don't like to say anything malicious about another human being, but I hear that Auden is a Platonist!"
>
> 2 June 44 WA to UN Auden has just been to a wedding at Riverside Church. 'What has American Protestantism come to? Do you know what the organist played just before the wedding? The prelude to *Tristan*!'
>
> 14 Feb 46 WA to RN 'Kierkegaard as usual put his finger on the sore spot when he said that the task of the preacher is to preach Christ the contemporary offense to Christians.'
>
> 30 May 57 WA to UN Among other works have read Simone Weil's *La Pesanteur et la Grace*. Have you? Wildly exasperating, I think, but very important. An exposition of the via negativa carried to almost heretical lengths, i.e. for her it is not the Cross that is the stumbling block, but the Incarnation, or rather any of the references in the Gospel to Christ enjoying himself. However, it is more honest than any modern work I know about the characteristic experience of God in a sceptical schizophrenic age like ours.'

These snatches of correspondence signal much that is characteristic of Auden: his wide reading and concentrated reflection on theology, his always self-deprecating style. The medium also influences the nature of intercultural dialogue. The debate about the extent, if any, to which Auden's powers declined in his later years has probably much to be said on both sides. He did somehow lose focus on the larger canvas in concentrating on occasional pieces. His theological reflection never issued in the kind of archetypal religious poetry which his middle period promised. But he did consciously seek to develop an appreciation of private and individual space, as a kind of protest against the collectivization which he saw everywhere at work in modern society. Eliot, despite an exceedingly turbulent private life with his two mistresses, always succeeded in remaining a respectable icon of religious establishment, high-minded and High Church. In Auden there is an almost Kierkegaardian paradox between appearance and reality. He almost appeared to cultivate a reputation for dissolute character and lack of discipline, yet for most of his life he worked immensely hard for regular hours, and was consistent in his personal commitments.

Auden, like Eliot, *draws a clear line between the sacred and the secular*, at least in theory. Auden asserts that 'To a Christian, unfortunately, both art and science are secular activities, that is to say, small beer'. The artistic imagination is purely natural, and is liable to be moved by 'certain objects, beings, and events, to a feeling of sacred awe'. This smacks of pantheism. To the Christian, on the other hand, the truly sacred is not that which naturally arouses awe in the human imagination:

> The Incarnation, the coming of Christ in the form of a Servant who cannot be recognized by the eye of flesh and blood, but only by the eye of faith, puts an end to all claims of the imagination to be the faculty which decides what is truly sacred and what is profane. A pagan God can appear on earth in disguise but, so long as he wears his disguise, no man is expected to recognize nor can. But Christ appears looking just like any other man, yet claims that he is the Way, the Truth and the Life, and that no man can come to the father except through him. The contradiction between the profane appearance and the sacred assertion is impassible to the imagination. (Auden, 1948, 457)

There is an excellent discussion of Auden in the chapter, '*Credo ut Intelligam*: W.H. Auden's Vision of Christian Co-inherence' in Murphy (1997, 323f). He comments, 'The writings of Niebuhr, together with those of Willams and Søren Kierkegaard, were largely responsible for shaping the Christian vision that dominated Auden's poetry from 1940 till his death in 1977.' Murphy mentions especially Niebuhr's 'An Interpretation of Christian Ethics, Christianity and Power Politics', and the 'Nature and Destiny of Man'. From Kierkegaard Auden derived a conception of the ethical as a fulfilment of the radical freedom of individual consciousness, and the act of moral decision as a leap from the aesthetic to the ethical.

He sees truth as the product of a dialectical tension: 'The one infallible symptom of greatness is the gift of *double-focus*.' He can write, 'We, being divided, remembering, evolving beings, composed of a number of selves, each with its false conception of self-interest, sin in most that we do' (quoted by Murphy, 1997, 344). Following Kierkegaard, Auden stresses the inevitability of suffering, but this produces a resolution, for example in *The Enchafed Flood*:

> It is where we are wounded that is when He speaks
> Our creaturely cry, concluding his children
> In their mad unbelief to have mercy on them all
> As they wait unawares for His world to come.

Faith alone is what is required: 'Our redemption is no longer a question of pursuit but of surrender to Him who is always and everywhere present. Therefore at every moment we pray that, following him, we may depart from our anxiety unto his peace.' He adds, 'The course of history is predictable in the degree to which all men love themselves, and spontaneous in the degree to which each man loves God and through him his neighbour. Hope is founded on cross and resurrection.'

> Now, did he really break the seal
> And rise again? We dare not say;
> But conscious unbelievers feel
> Quite sure of Judgement Day.
> Meanwhile, a silence on the cross,
> As dead as we shall ever be,
> Speaks of some total gain or loss,
> And you and I are free
> To guess from his insulted face
> Just what Appearances he saves
> By suffering in a public place
> A death reserved for slaves.
> (*Friday's Child: In Memoriam Dietrich Bonhoeffer*)

Auden's Kierkegaardian perspective provides an instructive foil to Eliot's confidence in Christendom, and indeed to the implicit correlation of religion and culture which we see in the line from Schleiermacher to Tillich. We may think that an effective intercultural theology must take account of the interruptions as much as the continuities in the tradition, and of the existence of very diverse sub-cultures within the envelope of religion and culture.

Eliot and Auden were writing out of a traditional cultural elite, producing material which reflected the classical European theological tradition. In the light of what we have said about cultural diversity and the need to engage in dialogues in which all parties are as far as possible on a 'level playing field' – the only possibility for true dialogue without coercion – it is imperative to examine other sorts of voices. We find this *par excellence* in the writings of Toni Morrison. This celebrated Black American writer, winner of the Nobel

Prize for Literature in 1993, is writing out of another tradition. There was a long stream of Black American writing before she appeared on the scene, but that was often a tradition which was forced to make heavy concessions to the predominantly white public in order to be heard. Morrison seeks to reflect Black experience in her novels as it actually was – experience often harsh, brutal and unpleasant to remember, experience often silenced. She seeks to speak not for political grouping or social genres but for individuals, whose personal and private feelings have long been forgotten.

Morrison

Typical of this different voice is her best known novel. *Beloved* is not the easiest of novels to read. It is deliberately constructed of disjunctions and flashbacks, quick transitions between the living and the dead, allusions and understatements, explicit horrors and hints of greater oppressions. But the novel is its plot, and the narrative unfolds a tale of suffering in which religion plays various, often unpromising, roles.

The principal character, Sethe, is a slave, living with her three half-brothers, her husband Halle and a man called Sixo on a Farm called Home Sweet Home in Kentucky, in the years after the Civil War. At first their condition is marginally better than on other farms; the owner, Mr Garner, is benevolent. On his death the farm comes to his brother-in-law, ironically named Schoolteacher, who is the worst type of owner. After a failed escape attempt, three of the slaves are killed, another is placed in a chain gang where sexual abuse is rampant and eventually escapes. Sethe is raped and runs away with her children to Cincinnati. Schoolteacher comes to recapture Sethe, who kills one of her children to save her from a life of slavery, and is imprisoned.

Twenty years later Sethe and her daughter Denver are still shunned by the Black community because of her action. The baby's ghost is a malevolent presence in the house. A girl arrives and is accepted as the manifestation of the ghost, Beloved. One of the former slaves, Paul D, arrives, forms a relationship with Sethe and then leaves, horrified by the tale of the baby's death. Sethe goes into a decline. Eventually Beloved disappears and Paul D returns, to seek a better future for Sethe, Denver and himself.

This is a novel about the all-corroding effects of slavery. It explores the self, self-esteem and the destruction of the self in a culturally hostile environment. It raises the question of whether murder can ever be justified or understood. Against the sanitized stories of earlier Black writing it places the unacceptable face of slavery, corrupting all that it touches. Against the spiritualizing of suffering it chronicles the wounds in the flesh and in the minds of its characters. It highlights the rape of both sexes, bestiality and institutional violence. Damage is irretrievable and there can be no entirely happy endings.

Morrison's purpose is to 'fill in the blanks that the traditional slave narrative left', to combat the 'national amnesia' which she sees as surrounding the reality of slavery. As she explained in her essay, 'The Site of Memory', she chronicles the psychological damage inflicted on the men, and above all the pervasive exploitation of the women.

There is an undercurrent of religion in the novel but it is a dark and capricious religion. White religion does nothing to alleviate the suffering. Baby Suggs, mother of one of the slaves, becomes a lay preacher and offers hospitality, but her efforts fail in the face of the white man's power. There is a blurring of the veil between this life and the next, suggestive of indigenous African religion. But the horrors mock any attempt at lasting religious consolation. Beloved, with a New Testament name, is doomed to butchery and continuing mayhem. Here the denial of the standard of love and justice announced by religion serves to highlight the vital importance and the difficulty of achieving love in community, even as the institutions of religion themselves fail to deliver love and justice.

This is a very different world from that of Eliot and Auden, but in their entirely different ways Eliot, Auden and Morrison are doing what literature does best, seeking to offer a critically realist account of human life as it actually is, and, by showing their denial, highlighting values of love and justice. All are concerned with social issues and with the ultimate questions of human existence. By shedding light on darkness, or indeed by shedding darkness on light, each describes the contrasts between the actual and the desirable states of human community. A critical theology should be able to learn from these penetrating narratives of the human condition in seeking to make its own contribution to understanding God's engagement with humanity, so that the jagged fragments of human need and divine reality are brought again into some sort of serious conjunction.

To allow these different commentaries on human dignity to engage with each other on their own terms, while facilitating a genuine mutuality in a common recognition of mutual need, this is part of an intercultural theological venture which requires all the varieties of experience if it is to have any hope of success. The resources of any one tradition are simply too limited to be adequate, for human community is made up from fragments as diverse as the myriad cell types in the individual human brain. Only a pattern capable of assimilating, respecting and utilizing such a range of experience is likely to be effective. Monolithic theologies are unlikely to help us. It is perhaps no accident that the more successful historical theologies, of Augustine and Aquinas, are themselves constructed from diverse cultures, borrowings from East and West, from Islamic Christian and Jewish traditions. The diversities of the future will demand of us much greater efforts to think through difference, and yet to produce explanations and visions which will meet individual needs for coherent perspectives to live by.

Morrison's novel is loosely based on a court case involving a slave mother who killed her child in America in the nineteenth century. It is vital to note the difference. The novel is a novel, and the case is an attempt to establish facts and adjudge blame. Yet the issues involved in the one instance may help in our understanding of the other, provided that we do not allow our judgment to be unduly skewed by any particular line of interpretation. Only God can provide the grand perspective in which all the connections are properly recorded. The theologian's task is the more modest one of seeking to trace some of the threads of comparison and contrast which may help to provide a human perspective on the issues and the ways in which we can move forwards to a more humane society. Awareness that we are precisely not God may help us to avoid deifying partial aspects of this reality, as well as helping us to move towards God's preferred envelope of love, peace and justice for our actions. Neither Christendom nor exclusive whiteness nor blackness nor any other coercive concept will help.

One of the basic questions raised by these examples from literature and theology is the relationship of God to history. A spiritualizing approach which removes God and the question of God from the often unpleasant realities of history is clearly useless. An immersion in historical struggle which never shows any sense of transcendent presence within and through history is equally frustrating. Only a concept of God who can be reasonably believed to act in and through human history will engage the attention of serious seekers after common humanity and a God who is self-giving, self-affirming love. We have to be aware, too, of the limitations of a choice of examples far from our own domestic situation, which relieve us of the burden of pressing issues. Perhaps most commonly, occasions of vulnerability are tied in our modern world to poverty.

The search for an intercultural theology involves the search for transcendence. In this quest the European classical tradition of theology, despite its tendency on occasion to attempt to colonize the mind of God, still has much to contribute. However fallibly, it has at least produced important constructive efforts to understand our conceptions of God, while respecting the mystery. It has contributed too, in tandem with classical philosophy, to the search for universal ethical, political and social values. To this tradition the recent emancipatory theologies continue to make important modifications. In stressing the activity of God through the histories of alternative community they highlight the deficiencies of accounts which equally focused on Eurocentric community experience.

Philosophy, Culture and Theology: The Case of Wittgenstein

If we have learned one thing about culture in recent decades, it may be awareness of the infinite variety, sub-division and overlap of cultures. Yet there have been individuals who have had penetrating things to say about culture in general, and about culture in relation to theology and to faith. One of these was the philosopher Ludwig Wittgenstein. We shall have to consider again later the whole matter of philosophical warrants for a project in intercultural theology. I turn here in the first instance to the collection, *Culture and Value* (1980), as an instructive commentary on culture, often with a theological slant. Wittgenstein has been much commented upon by theologians, from Cupitt to Kerr and Phillips, who have put their own slant on his work. My purpose here is not to affirm or deny any of these interpretations, but to attempt to hear what Wittgenstein is actually saying.

Wittgenstein belongs to the same period as Eliot and Auden, a time when the spectre of fascism was growing over Europe, when romanticism became suspect and liberal thought appeared to call for correctives. Wittengenstein was looking for a new perspective in philosophy. Like Auden, he read Augustine and Kierkegaard, and was conscious of the power of suffering and evil. Like Auden, he developed an Augustinian introspective conscience which could be a burden. We may sometimes be tempted to think that theology matters only to theologians and perhaps the clergy, and has little influence beyond these circles. In Eliot, Auden and Wittgenstein we can see how the appropriation of a particular theological perspective can have deep implications for their work, positive and negative.

Culture and Value is in large measure a collection of aphorisms, some of which most of us will probably agree with, and some of which we may well disagree with. When he says that 'My ideal is a certain coolness. A temple providing a setting for the passions without meddling with them' (2e, 1929), most of us may find this at least interesting. When he says the following, we may think him strangely prejudiced: 'If it is true that Mahler's music is worthless, as I believe to be the case, then the question is what I think he ought to have done with his talent. For quite obviously it took a very rare set of talents to produce this bad music' (67e, 1948).

I want to list here some of Wittgenstein's aphorisms on culture and on theology in this volume. He always sounds sharper in German, but I shall quote the translation. 'I once said, perhaps rightly: The earlier culture will become a heap of rubble and finally a heap of ashes, but spirits will hover over the ashes' (3e, 1930).

> What would it feel not to have heard of Christ?
> Should we feel left alone in the dark?
> Do we escape such a feeling simply in the way a child escapes it when he knows there is someone in the room with him? (13e, 1931)

Wittgenstein was always aware of the value of tradition, not as a blanket which stifles fresh thought, but as a legacy which spurs to renewed effort. For him this tradition included Christ. It was on the one hand the Kierkegaardian Christ, present in living life and not in dogmatic formulas, Christ in the dialectic between faith and doubt as lived. On the other hand, it was the *cantus firmus* of the Catholic tradition as an underlying reality. 'Within Christianity it's as though God says to men: Don't act a tragedy, that's to say, Don't enact heaven and hell on earth. Heaven and hell are my affair' (14e, 1931).

Here Wittgenstein sounds like Barth (whom he could criticize), or indeed Auden, rather than the mystic which he is often depicted as being.

> Christianity is not a doctrine, not, I mean, a theory about what has happened and will happen to the human soul, but a description of something that actually takes place in human life. For 'consciousness of sin' is a real event. And so are despair and salvation through faith. (28e, 1937)
>
> The spring which flows gently and limpidly in the Gospels seems to have froth on it in St Paul's Epistles. Or that is how it seems to me. (30e, 1937)
>
> Why is this Scripture so unclear? … But who is to say that the scripture really is unclear? Isn't it possible that it was essential in this case to 'tell a riddle'? … The Spirit puts what is essential for your life, into these words. The point is that you are only SUPPOSED to see clearly what appears clearly even in this representation. (I am not sure how far all this is exactly in the spirit of Kierkegaard.) (32c, 1937)
>
> Christianity is not based on a historical truth; rather, it offers us a (historical) narrative and says: now believe! (32e, 1937)
>
> Perhaps we can say: only love can believe the resurrection. Or, It is love that believes the resurrection We might say: redeeming love believes even in the resurrection: holds fast even to the resurrection. What combats doubt is, as it were, redemption. … Holding fast to this must be holding fast to that belief. Then everything will be quite different, and it will be 'no wonder' that you can do things that you cannot do now. (33e, 1937)
>
> The Christian religion is only for the man who needs infinite help, solely, that is, for the man who experiences infinite torment. (46e, 1944)
>
> Religion is, as it were, the calm bottom of the sea at its deepest point, which remains calm however high the waves on the surface may be. (53e, 1946)
>
> An honest religious thinker is like a tightrope walker. He almost looks as if he were walking on nothing but air. His support is the slenderest imaginable. And yet it really is possible to walk on it. (73e, 1948)
>
> If Christianity is the truth then all the philosophy which is written about it is false. (83e, 1949)
>
> The words you utter or what you think as you utter them are not what matters, so much as the difference they make at various points in your life … A theology which insists on the use of certain particular words and phrases, and outlaws others, does not make anything clearer (Karl Barth). It gesticulates with words, one may say, because it wants to say something and does not know how to express it. Practice gives the words their sense. (85e, 1950)

> Life can educate one to a belief in God. And experiences too are what bring this about: but I don't mean visions and other forms of sense experience which show us the 'existence of this being', but e.g. sufferings of various sorts. (86e, 1950)

What are we to make of these fascinating examples of reflection on theology and faith within a particular cultural setting? Wittgenstein combined what are often the most acute observations with a life of very damaged, often tragic intensity, immensely vulnerable and immensely dominating by turns.

It should be noted that we cannot always be sure that in these aphorisms Wittgenstein is speaking of his own positions. When he speaks about an honest practitioner of religion being 'like a tightrope walker' he may see himself sometimes as inside this position, sometimes outside it, sometimes torn between the two. His *obiter dicta* on religion were so varied as to provide evidence for opposing views of his attitudes to religion. This may well reflect his tortured attitude to many things. Much of what he has to say is immensely acute, and some of it is nonsense. We must take him as we find him and be grateful for what is illuminating. It is remarkable that he was able to produce as much as he did.

There has been of course considerable theological interest in Wittgenstein, and scholars have found in his enigmatic works by and large what they have wanted to find. Radical Protestants like Don Cupitt have seen him as a base for postmodern interpretation of religion, while conservative Catholics like Professors Anscombe and Geach have happily combined him with Tridentine orthodoxy. W.D. Hudson and D.Z. Phillips have related him to the concept of forms of life, of the practice of individual and community, and have been roundly (but inaccurately) accused of Wittgensteinian fideism. D.Z. Phillips in an article, 'Religion in Wittgenstein's Mirror' (Phillips, 1994, 1135f) has suggested that Wittgenstein wanted simply to hold up a mirror to people's beliefs and practices, to enable them to see what they were doing and why, and to distinguish between religion and superstition. Frederick Sontag, in his 'Wittgenstein and the Mystical', stressed this side of Wittgenstein's thought, noting especially the influence of Tolstoy's *The Gospel in Brief.*

I have long thought that Wittgenstein's emphasis on the need for a little epistemological humility in matters of dogmatic theology was well made.

> Here again we get the same thing as in set theory: the form of expression we use seems to have been designed for a god, who knows what we cannot know … For us, of course, these forms of expression are like pontificals which we may put on, but cannot do much with, since we lack the effective power that would give these vestments meaning and purpose. In the actual use of expressions we make detours, we go by side roads. We see the straight highway before us, but of course we cannot use it, because it is permanently closed. (PI, 426)

Much has been written about Wittgenstein's famous line, 'Grammar tells us what kind of an object anything is' (theology as grammar). Kerr says well that, 'In effect, by remarking that theology is grammar, he is reminding us that it is only by listening to what we say about God (what has been said for many generations) and to how what is said about God ties in with what we say and do *in innumerable other connections*, that we have any chance of understanding what we mean when we speak of God' (Kerr, 1986, 148). This means that Wittgenstein was more interested in a realist philosophy of theology than in an idealist philosophy of religion of the traditional sort.

Wittgenstein, like Eliot and Auden, was interested in a realist understanding of faith which stressed the practical and the incarnational. Like Niebuhr and his circle of Christian realists, they were suspicious of making the wrong connections between the sacred and the secular. They looked to Augustine and to Kierkegaard, to a dialectic between faith and doubt, sin and salvation. But there the resemblance ended. For Wittgenstein and his friends, O'Drury, Rhees and the others, religion is essentially a private realm, though it may issue in public acts of devotion. This reflected the somewhat fragile private circle of acquaintance in which Wittgenstein moved. The connections between religion and philosophy are indirect. For Eliot and Auden there is a dialectical relationship between faith and literary activity. It is connected with the understanding of the self. Poets are not preachers, and to confuse the two would be disaster. For Niebuhr and his circle there is a more direct, though still dialectical, relationship between religion and the public square. Theology has a clear responsibility to be active in the realm of civic society.

The Augustinian, Kierkegaardian tradition has disadvantages, in its pessimism, its dualism between the soul and the body, its introspection, and these are all mirrored in the writers we have just been considering. There were also advantages, in a profound questioning of romantic optimism and any kind of superficiality in culture, coupled with a rigorous search for self-awareness. In each of the writers we see a struggle for balance. In Wittgenstein, this is the tightrope between Catholic piety and Scandinavian angst. It was after all in Norway that he was to spend months of agonizing on his own. In Eliot and Auden, there is an affirmation of this world, though not without scathing critique of its failures, along with affirmation of traditional faith in the gospel. Both Eliot and Auden are concerned to critique the public square, though Auden is also determined to protest for the importance of private space in the face of increasing globalization: he foresaw the downside of the Macdonaldization of the world.

Of the writers we have considered in this sample period around the 1930s, Reinhold Niebuhr had easily the greatest direct impact on a particular society during his lifetime. Yet the connections are all there, and together constitute a remarkable witness to a common search for human values in overlapping but different segments of modern culture, significant in their constructive tension. There is no substratum of a universal common culture. But there are *agreements between different strands* in which we see the characteristic impact of a Christian contribution to culture and from which we may learn, positively and negatively.

The Reconstruction of Intellectual History: Classics, Culture and Theology

Thus far we have examined the work of writers who flourished in the middle of the first half of the twentieth century. No period of human culture is totally isolated, however, from other periods. It construes itself partly in the light of previous cultures, and construes other cultures in its own light.

For better and for worse, the legacy of Greece and Rome has had an inestimable influence on European and American civilization, and beyond. It may be that the influence of the classical world is finally receding under the impact of modern capitalist society, but it is also possible that perspectives based on reflection on Christianity and classical culture, and the continuing revision of these perspectives, may still make an impact on the continuing human search for common values. It is not perhaps accidental that the culture of classical civilization has been the subject of recent sharp scrutiny, notably in the work of Alasdair Macintyre and Martha Nussbaum.

In much twentieth-century theology there was an unfortunate dichotomy between so-called Hebrew thought and Greek thought. Both tended to be classified as undifferentiated, opposed masses. Classical civilization was written off as essentially useless to Christianity. This approach, basing all on revelation in the Bible, tended to be associated with the thought of Karl Barth, but it had been anticipated, as often with these themes, in the thought of the previous wave of European theology. For Adolf von Harnack, classical Christianity was essentially the fruit of the Hellenization of the gospel. The task was to distil the centre of the faith from the Hellenized wrapping.

Going back a little further, the mid-nineteenth century brought admiration for a synthesis of the values of Christianity and the Classics, as in harmony and complementarity. The difficulty was that the harmony was often anticipated in the method of setting up the relationship. It is clear that the construct of 'the Classics' is as culturally relative as the construct of Christianity. In a theory of pure relativism, we are clearly incapable of any improvement on this position. But if we have some modest confidence in the ability of academic work to produce some tangible results, then we begin to see that classics, as construed by modern classical studies, is a much more fragmented and often, to us, alien culture than nineteenth-century scholars often imagined. The same may be said of Christianity. We are unlikely to find the same level of comprehensive synthesis, but at worst we may find some fragments which illuminate the search for both faith and humanity. We shall focus on the theme of discernment.

In his fine study, *An Ethic for Enemies*, Don Shriver traced the profound reflection on the tension between revenge and forgiveness in Greek tragedy.

The world of the *Iliad* and the tragedians is a savage world, in which there is little mercy. Readers of René Girard's studies on violence will scarcely be surprised by this observation. After all, such phenomena as the massacre of defeated prisoners on the battlefield has been not unusual practice right up to our own time, despite the Geneva Convention and the rest. The Gods are often vengeful and spiteful, and their will is done, as in heaven, so on earth.

We noted that the themes of revenge and redemption are at the centre of Simone Weil's famous essay, 'The *Iliad*: Poem of Might' (1957, 24f). 'Might is that which makes a thing of anybody who comes under its sway. When exercised to the full, it makes a thing of man in the most literal sense, for it makes him a corpse' (24); 'That a human being should be a thing is, from the point of view of logic, impossible, a contradiction; but when the impossible has become a reality, that contradiction is as a rent in the soul' (28). Only slightly less dire is the plight of the slave. 'One cannot lose more than the slave loses, he loses all inner life' (30). Weil chronicles the insensitivity of might. But against this she notes that 'the tradition of hospitality, carried through several generations, has ascendancy over the blindness of combat' (46). 'Thus I am for you a beloved guest in the land of Argos. Let us avoid one another's lances, even in the fray.'

Where much recent theology has contrasted the legacy of the Bible with that of the Greeks, Weil stressed the resemblances, and saw the Greek preoccupation with the nature of goodness as intimately related to the coming of Christian revelation. There was also no doubt a curious and unfortunate strain of anti-Semitism in Weil, but she reminds us of how much culture is a reading of previous culture. This growth of tradition and interruption is an unending and constantly changing development.

Greek Tragedy

Simone Weil is quoted at length in the preface to Louis Ruprecht's excellent *Tragic Posture and Tragic Vision* (1994). Here is another commentary of the classics which is firmly engaged with current theological and philosophical constructions. Along with *Afterwords* (Ruprecht, 1996), this is a powerful protest against the nostalgia, the tragic posture rather than the tragic vision which Ruprecht sees at the heart of a great deal of modern interpretation of the Greeks. He is also concerned with the effect of Macintyre's work on the issue of human rights. 'There are no such (natural human) rights), and belief in them is one with belief in witches and unicorns' (*After Virtue*, 69). Ruprecht sets out from the proposition that 'There is a subtle and pervasive pessimism that lies at the heart of most cultures that today call themselves "modern"' (12). He claims that 'tragedies do not necessarily end badly. They begin badly.' Christianity is a tragic faith (16). Against Steiner and Macintyre, he distinguishes tragic vision from tragic posture. Macintyre's narrative is a 'decline and fall' (21). But the Greeks were concerned with both the communal and the individual, and read tragedy as an essentially affirmative, non-apocalyptic genre.

Ruprecht stresses, as always, the importance of the tragedians as well as Plato in Greek culture, and Plato's own debt to tragedy. He then considers Hegel's tragic vision in his lectures on the philosophy of religion – Athens and Jerusalem. Hegel recognizes the gospels as true tragedy, tragedy that changes things. He goes on to Nietzsche's tragic vision, Dionysius against the crucified. He brings in Walter Benjamin on translatability, against Macintyre and Lindbeck, and asserts that Christianity simply cannot exist apart from the possibility of translation (165). It is of the nature of cultures to translate and to change. Cultures cannot simply be equated, as Lindbeck equates.

This remarkable study succeeds in bringing together Greek and Christian cultures in plastic and innovative interconnections. It takes up, in a modern context, important conversations between theology and the classical tradition which have been much neglected. It is courageous in challenging, with close readings of texts, received ideas in most areas of the subject. Once again we may note the significance of diversity and interruption as well as continuity in the interpretation of culture. Interpretations are given only to challenge further interpretation. Unless there are points of mutual engagement there can be no advance in interpretation. But the continuities cannot be allowed to dictate the course of future reflection. The canon of interpretability remains open.

The Use and Abuse of the Classics

Ruprecht's *Afterwords* continues the theme of the appropriation of Greek culture, in a sustained debate with Alasdair Macintyre and Stanley Hauerwas on the role of the re-appropriation of tradition. 'This is a book about the seductive power of *nostalgia*'(1). He claims Plato's Republic as an ally in the war against poetic nostalgia: 'These moralists, like Alasdair Macintyre, who wish to find in classical Greece a vision of moral community and harmony that escapes us in the modern world are simply ignoring the political and historical facts. They are looking in the right place, but for the wrong thing' (2). He goes on to argue that 'our modernity is neither as new and novel, nor as calamitous and disjunctive, as is customarily asserted' (6). Ruprecht reads classical culture and Christianity in a kind of intertextual dialogue. 'I will concentrate on what I take to be Christianity's central image – forgiveness.'

This brings Ruprecht to Christian texts – 'After Christendom?' – and the work of Hauerwas. 'The simplistic survey of this story he now calls "Christendom" lacks the very local color, the nuance, and the "thickness" he accuses modern stories of erasing' (129). As Macintyre went back to Aristotle, Hauerwas went back to a pre-Constantinian period of Early Christianity. He romanticizes the martyrs, and focuses on Augustine. In some ways he is similar to the fundamentalists. 'Where they are similar is in grounding their antimodern polemics in a nostalgic religious vision of a scriptural golden age' (160).

Is it possible to be unmodern without being anti-modern? We must recognize the continuities, and seek to go beyond both nostalgia and modernity. The final section is 'a post-mortem on post-modernity': 'Postmodernism is perhaps the most faddish of all the afterwords I have examined, and therefore the least compelling of the two forms of anti-modernism I have been discussing. It does not simply misread the past: it ignores it.' He reiterates that there is no myth more subversive than the myth of decadence. 'In a word, if there was no magical beginning – just a very, very good one – then we surely are not living "afterwards", at the end' (239). This is yet another valuable reminder that appeal to the postmodern can conceal as well as reveal.

Art and Music

In examining dialogue between theology and the humanities we have confined ourselves to the written word. But of course theology has been involved in numerous ways with the construction of the visual arts,[1] painting and sculpture, material artefacts in all sorts of media, precious metals, carpets, glass and porcelain, with architecture and landscape gardening, with particular foods at particular seasons, and, not least, with music. Again the engagement has sometimes been direct, as in the construction of religious objects from chalices to cathedrals, in paintings of the crucifixion or the Buddha. Sometimes it has been indirect, in the influence of Protestantism on Dutch painting or in American house construction, the convoluted spiritual dimensions of modern art, as in Francis Bacon. The whole range of the visual arts may signal transcendence in material forms in ways which resemble the theological construction of the sacramental, outward and visible signs of inward and invisible presence.

An intercultural theology would take notice, too, of the huge impact of music on religious perception and on contemplation of the transcendent, from the formal religious setting of Bach's cantatas to the evocation of transcendence in Mahler, in Javanese music or in Afro-American spirituals. This is a reflection still more developed in the practice of music than in the sphere of theory, despite a history stretching back to Plato and beyond. It is important not to colonize music as a promising source of religious apologetic. But it can be suggestive in a variety of interdisciplinary contexts – we may think of Arthur Peacocke's use of musical analogies to discuss divine action in a cosmological context. Here we can only notice a field open to much future development. We can scarcely imagine the fullness of creation to involve a silent world.

Faith may inspire the artist's imagination in countless ways. The work of art may strike the observer and evoke a religious response, a sense of shock, surprise or of peace. The world in which we live is constructed and drenched with the impact of many of these things: they help to form our world of experience and reflection. Studies have been done on the relationship between religious beliefs and practices and almost all of these items. They have contributed hugely to the formation and sustaining of faith, and to faith's reflection on God. Faith in turn has inspired much great art, in a continuing reciprocity. We shall not develop this area further here, but no intercultural theology can afford to neglect at least an awareness of this rich dimension of formative culture.

Eliot, Wittgenstein, the reading of the Classics, music and art, film and television – there is no end to the permutations of interaction between different cultures among themselves, including religious cultures. Cultures may involve ideas and customs. They may involve material artefacts. Theology may be engaged in these exchanges in different ways. From its own perspective, Christian theology has to decide *which* aspects of culture to relate to constructively, and on what basis. Here are opportunities for the effective communication, and also for the distortion, of faith. But if theology is too cautious and self-absorbed, its message will become more and more marginal to the lives of most human beings. To relate to debates about culture, which themselves are formative for culture, should be central to the theologian's task. The easier alternative, of remaining within the closed canon of official Church tradition, would be a serious failure of nerve. The same applies, as we shall now examine, in the relation between theology and the sciences.

Note

1 On the relation of theology to art, Nicholas Wolterstorff's *Art in Action* (1980) offers an instructive aesthetic of beauty. The ever-changing relation between philosophy and theology goes back of course to the pre-Socratic philosophers. For a snapshot of some recent paradigms, see Vesey (1989), Clark (1993) and Morris (1994).

CHAPTER 9

Intercultural Theology and the Sciences

Discovery, Research Culture and Diversity in Theology and the Sciences

For much of the history of Christian theology the humanities were at the centre of the universities and the focus of intellectual attention. More recently the social sciences appeared to hold more of the keys to human flourishing, but at present there is a significant concentration on the authority and the prestige of the natural sciences, not just as the ultimate source of consumer durables but as the focus of the scope and limits of knowledge.

If the obvious danger in dialogue between theology and the humanities is a tendency to be diffuse, in dialogue with the sciences it is perhaps the tendency to premature systematization. An obvious example is the popularity in Christian fundamentalist circles of creation science, and the rather optimistic dialogue between traditional Christian theology and cosmology.

The time has long since passed when theology could prescribe to science her sphere of interest, though postmodern fragmentation has produced revivals such as creationism, where science is controlled by biblical interpretation. We have passed, for the most part, too, the stage at which the laws of nature were thought to prescribe all that could be said of theology, though again the postmodern picture is varied – we may think of Richard Dawkins.

The natural sciences have long seemed to be the one clear instance of the truth of the modern paradigm: the same results are arrived at and understood all over the world, and without this science would simply not work. Yet postmodern philosophers of science have long noted the amenability of the same empirical data to different forms of explanation, since the theories are so often underdetermined by the facts. Many of the assured results of 'science' in the nineteenth century were overturned in the twentieth. They have observed, too, the effect of local cultures on scientific research This does not mean that the modern paradigm is discredited, only that it has to be treated with a measure of caution.

It becomes clear that the natural sciences are no more divorced from other dimensions of the culture in which they are conducted than other disciplines. Recent decades have seen an increasingly fruitful dialogue between theologians, often with a scientific background, and scientists. The areas of discussion have frequently included cosmology and the origins of life, but they have also covered environmental issues, a wide range of ethical concerns and the matter of the long-term human future. If we are to speak of intercultural theology, we should not neglect the scientific dimension. A discussion of theology and literature might well take account of technical scientific literature. Politics and power are also as germane to science as they are to other disciplines. In this dialogue there is a proper aim for scientific objectivity. Yet, as the results show, the outcomes of discussion very often reflect the ecclesial background of the scientist quite as much as his or her area of scientific expertise. This need not be a matter of regret, provided that the commitments are recognized and taken into account.

How may we conceive of intercultural dialogue between theology and the natural sciences? Again at several connected levels. There is a level of the scientific and theological imagination, in which the interplay of ideas may stimulate new perspectives from which to view data. There is a level of epistemology and hermeneutics in which readings of data and the standardization of criteria of judgment are critical. Here the turn to postfoundationalism may encourage dialogue between constellations of testimony in fragments. There is a level of ethical decision and its practical implementation in society, in which all disciplines have a potential input. We should not overestimate the extent of formally existing dialogue between theologians and natural scientists (only a small proportion are actively involved on either side, and far more among the theologians), but the facilitating capacity has considerable potential.

Such a view of dialogue could be dangerously elitist, government by an oligarchy of experts. Disciplines which understand their contribution in terms of reciprocity and equal partnership should be well placed to guard against this danger. Here again Christian theology may have a distinctive contribution to make. This is not to say that other theologies or world views may not also contribute; my concern here is with the responsibility and the particularity of Christian faith.

Much has been written about theology and cosmology, and theology and the meaning of life. The nature of divine action in the cosmos is clearly important for theology. It is, however, especially the dialogue between theology and the sciences as a social force with a considerable political dimension that I should like to highlight here. A considerable percentage of the earth's GDP is invested in the enterprises of natural and applied science, in technology. Much of it is spent in making profits for the northern hemisphere at the expense of the southern. In this way the natural sciences are harnessed to capitalist economic systems. It seems likely that there is no viable alternative to such methods of research and production, yet the result is often strikingly evident, for example in the lack of medicines in the South and their superabundance, at a price, in the North. The reverse is true of landmines, another product of science and technology. Theology here as facilitator may perhaps have a contribution to dialogue to make. It would not always be sufficient to fund congresses to discuss cosmology if the same scientific–technological complexes were systematically bankrupting the world's most impoverished nations. It is not helpful to draw naïve connections, but there are often important connections to be made. These are some of the connections drawn to our attention by emancipatory theologies. They are also the subject of much discussion and research among natural scientists themselves, for example in the development of 'green' chemistry. Again there is much scope for a theological contribution, if the theology is prepared to be a theology of risk.

Science in Society, Pure and Applied

Applied Science

As we have just seen, though the majority of studies of theology and science are directed at basic science, and even 'blue skies research', with a view to establishing comparisons between the basis of the natural sciences and the nature and action of God, the greatest changing impact of modern science on humanity has come through applied science. It is true that our continued physical existence depends on processes which have been active since the beginning of the universe, and our view of the relation of God the creator to and sustainer of life will naturally seek correlation with scientific theories in physics, cosmology and the life sciences. But our social existence within culture and society is heavily influenced by the effects of applied science on our day-to-day lives. Environmental issues, the impact of technology and global economic practices – these create much of the 'house of being' in which human lives are lived. While 'blue skies research' reflects on the further reaches of chaos theory, it is not without significance that the label 'blue yonder' is associated with the provision of high-speed Internet access.

It becomes desirable to reflect not only upon 'Big Bang versus Genesis' cosmologies, or on Darwin and Dawkins versus revelation scenarios, but more immediately upon the huge impact of natural science upon human life over the last half-millennium. The application of natural science as technology, it may be thought, has transformed our cultural environment in ways at least as significant as the impact of theoretical reflection on the sciences. Galileo and Newton, Darwin and Einstein have produced new frameworks which have changed our perception of our physical world. But in addition the development of the industrial society has altered the shape of society in fundamental ways. If the self is always an embodied and an inculturated self, then the situation of the self in new social locations has also revolutionized our lives.

The developments of the city, of agricultural and industrial revolution, of modern mass warfare, mass transport and capitalist global economies, of increasing literacy, and of the dot.com revolution have transformed self-perception and brought about huge benefits and huge losses. The benefits have been seen in increased global prosperity, which has created a sense of progress and a secular optimism. This has reinforced a common impression that natural science is *the* surviving modern paradigm, the bearer of truth, or as near an approximation to it as we can hope for. The losses, through global war and the exploitation of many economies, have dented optimism. But no viable alternative to a chastened scientific paradigm appears to be plausible.

How are we to understand the relationships of theology to applied science? Because the effects of applied science constitute an immensely varied and fragmented social phenomenon, there can be no single matching paradigm, no holistic response. From a Christian theological perspective, religion has to do with all aspects of the created order, and Christian faith has a particular contribution to make to the understanding and the development of the self as a social self. The freedom which is at the heart of human creativity as God's gift to creation is a freedom to live together with others in constructive and compassionate interaction. Societies and social processes which tend to maximize such compassionate interaction in freedom will be understood as moving in the direction which God intends for the created order. Societies which tend towards violence, exploitation and domination will be opposed, but not with matching violence. Strategies for dialogue will have to be evolved and put in place.

It would appear, then, that such developments as economic globalization and the spread of mass communication through Internet technology will be judged in their different manifestations differently, depending on whether or not they move in the direction of the love, peace and justice which is God's eschatological gift to humanity.[1] From architecture and town planning to healthcare provision, where new breakthroughs in scientific knowledge add to human welfare, this is to be welcomed without qualification. Where applied science leads to destructive consequences, this is to be avoided. Where there are ambiguous results, the good is to be maximized, as in all other areas of human thought and activity. Innovation is to be welcomed with enthusiasm, and with trust that we shall be given the strength to use our experience to avoid the pitfalls. It would be naïve to underestimate the scope for misuse provided by our common human failings of greed, envy and the like. But in principle the potential for human flourishing provided by applied science may be viewed as a gift of the creator to human beings.

The need to avoid misuse of the immense potential of applied science requires critical cultural analysis of the origins, motives and methods of its practitioners. It is pointless to sing hymns to justice and peace in one part of the world while financing disease and exploitation in another part. Theology will inevitably ask about the balance between commercial gain, ideological perspective and ethical responsibility. The mass destruction of the last century, entwined in the economics of capitalist and Marxist systems, is a salutary reminder of the urgency of this task. The ruin of much of Africa in very recent years demonstrates that nothing is to be taken for granted. Attention to the intercultural hermeneutics of applied science may be at least as important as reflection on pure science.

How science is applied in a given society will depend on political and economic decisions, and on public perceptions of the public good. Governments decide how to distribute resources for education among the various disciplines in universities. Companies seek to maximize profits from utilizing science in different geographical areas. They set price levels for drugs and other commodities, depending on what they think the market will stand. Despite the negative side of the use of science in warfare, there is a strong contemporary cultural perception that science is our best hope for the delivery of health and prosperity. This coincides with a lack of confidence in the humanities, as they themselves deconstruct Enlightenment notions of civilization. There are clearly important connections between the concerns of theology, the humanities and the applied sciences in seeking to develop and put into practice paradigms for enriching our lives. Technological innovation is a powerful tool for combating disease and hunger, and distributing resources more widely. The humanities play a vital role in encouraging self-critical reflection on our activities within their cultural milieu. Theology contributes convictions about the ultimate nature of goodness and justice which have direct consequences for commercial practice. In this sense the huge effort expended in the applied sciences is very much the concern of a theological engagement with culture.

Basic Science

It is within this context of a science-based society that we may return to other dimensions of the science/theology interaction. It would be convenient if we could operate with a clear distinction between philosophy of science, pure science and applied science. There are useful general ideas here to be explored: the theoretical but not empirically demonstrable, the realm of basic science, of basic experimental procedures which are in principle testable and repeatable, and then the area of applied technology. But there are no clear-cut distinctions between the three – all may involve aspects of the others. Theology has been concerned in the past mainly with the first and second areas.

Science and Theology

The debates which surrounded Galileo, Newton and Darwin in the past involved the physical shape and origins of the universe and the development of human life. They involved the apparent challenge of new theory and new experimental evidence to biblical authority. Theology lost, but in the interval it has become clear to philosophers of science that the connections between theories and facts are more complex than it seemed in the days of positivist science, and that the supposed hard data of experiment may be often interpreted in numerous different ways. More recently, large numbers of conservative Christians have used postmodern hermeneutical theory to justify Creationism, in modern repristinations of the biblical narratives. We can see that there are overlaps and divergences between the different constructions of reality which suggest the development of a more complex notion of rationality than the early protagonists of these debates imagined. At the same time, most 'mainstream' observers would conclude that the biblical narratives are, in important respects, culturally relative and limited by particular temporal constraints, and that scientific narratives are also open to diverse interpretation, though they do provide a reliable basic 'scientific' approach to problem solving.

One important result of continuing dialogue has been that theologians are increasingly able to accommodate theories in the natural sciences with faith perspectives, and scientists are able, should they wish to do so, to take on board a rational faith without having to abandon scientific rigour. We should not leave this discussion at a purely theoretical level. It may easily immunize us against practical consequences of applied science with which theology is committed to engage. From a theological perspective, it would be deeply ironic if large sums were raised to discuss faith and scientific theory from companies which are actively exploiting large numbers of people through applied scientific techniques. There has to be consistency between theory and practice in this field.

The constructive side of dialogue applies to theory in such areas as cosmology and the biological sciences. There is also the connected but distinguishable area of data discovered by modern science and their impact on faith. Our knowledge of the natural world is infinitely greater than it was in biblical times. This means that numerous biblical presuppositions, expectations and factual assertions have been superseded by greater knowledge. For some theologies, this remains a cause of irreconcilable conflict, but most theologians would regard revelation as a developing process which includes the correctives provided by human development as part of God's continuing gift of illumination. Hence there need be no inherent conflict between theology and basic science, though developments in both will stimulate dialogue, provided that both sides choose to remain open to discussion.

Indirectness

Much traditional debate on the relation between theology and science appears to have taken place on the assumption of a direct and immediate impact of science upon theology. It is worth highlighting here that much of the impact of applied science upon society is indirect and gradual. Take, for example the field of transport. The development of soil mechanics greatly influenced road construction, gradually providing an infrastructure which changes the shape of communities, making possible motorway networks and shopping malls, long bridges and airport runways. This affects patterns of social life on a regional and a global scale, as well as economic development, the delivery of food and medicine in emergencies and so on. This is typical of the ways in which applied science changes the environment in which we live. The results alter all logistics, from healthcare to warfare, but their relationship to the issues raised by theology is often tangential. The quality and characteristics of concrete used in construction work are crucial to the work, but arguably marginal to theology.

Biotechnology

We come to areas of applied science where there are directly controversial issues, such as biotechnology. Here some Christian traditions have severe problems, which come to light for example in the Roman Catholic tradition in Pro-Life movements, opposing various aspects of reproductive technology, such as abortion and artificial contraception, on ecclesiastical and biblical grounds. There is the development of cloning, where there are important ethical issues. In the past the churches were often able to impose their moral views on the communities of which they were a part. Increasingly they can only make a contribution to a current debate. Many of us would regard this as a much more appropriate stance in any case, since Christian values are not to be forced upon people. Here it is important to distinguish principles which should not easily be relinquished from absolutes. Guidelines are always desirable, since complex situations cannot always be approached *de novo*. But these guidelines should not be inflexible, since situations differ. In the face of these challenges theologians offer different solutions, inclusive or exclusive, depending on basic theological beliefs. My own preference is always to see theology as a contributor to a continuing dialogue, not as 'the answer' to every question.

Internet Technology

Another cluster of factors which are transforming society at different levels are exemplified by Internet technology. Here it is possible for information to be disseminated on a global basis to every home, and for communication on a hitherto unheard-of scale. In its drive to tap new markets, capitalism has an interest in widening the spread of the network as far as possible. Knowledge produces a measure of power and of freedom. On balance this is a hugely positive outcome of net technology. But this may be abused. Through the net interest groups of various sorts may find solidarity and support, for example, in combating human rights abuses. The net also supports numerous sites, where prejudices are inflamed and violence may be incited. The net may strengthen community in regional areas, through focus on local events and interests. It may also increase isolation, as individuals retreat into a virtual world of virtual reality. The net may enable persecuted groups to find a voice and connections, and it may also serve to monitor individuals and offer highly selective information. The Internet world is an example of the way in which society is changing at an ever-increasing pace through the application of scientific techniques. It is true that there may remain powerful similarities with past societies, with human needs, motivation and frailties remaining comparatively constant. But still the face of society and culture appears to alter at an exponential rate, and there is no reason to think that this trend will subside.

Vision in Science and Theology

It is within this world-wide culture of heavy reliance upon applied science that considerations of both theory and particular practice find their appropriate place. We should notice too that the current pre-eminence of the sciences over the humanities in education does not mean that scientists are uninterested in the humanities. On the contrary. Indeed, whereas nineteenth-century scholars viewed science as a small and almost secondary part of civilization (though they acknowledged the utility of the wealth provided by the Industrial Revolution), the predominant modern conception is to view the humanities as an important part of a science-based culture. Within this framework theology may also find a significant role, provided it is willing to act as a team player rather than as the conductor of the orchestra.

But when theology is given back a place at the table of dialogue, it is expected to make an equal contribution of its own. Apart from affirming the need for interdisciplinarity, what can it concretely contribute to the substance of the project? Theology contributes the vision that the source of all that is God, and that all is sustained in being by a divine agent whose nature is creative, self-giving love. To see everything within the hermeneutical envelope of the God of love, forgiveness, reconciliation and hope is to find a perspective which can enrich human life immeasurably. This is not to exclude other perspectives which may enrich life, religious and non-religious, but it is to claim that a theistic framework may (though it does not do this infallibly) bring a new depth of meaning and purpose to our lives in society.

This claim does not, however, entail the belief that all human activity can be perceived to have a direct religious meaning. Though it may all be understood in the light of God, *coram Deo*, it may be understood in its own light as human activity or natural process. I should be glad to affirm with Tillich that God is the ground of being, but I would not necessarily follow him in holding that all should be understood in terms of a religious a priori. Rather, I should see God's freedom as allowing human and created activity which may be understood in a secular as well as a religious sense. Thus there may be a secular as well as a religious meaning of transcendence, in which the created order is appreciated for its own sake, and human activity is seen as human action for its own sake, rather than divine activity, even though God is understood as the ultimate referent.

In other words, there is a measure of distance, mystery, respect and reciprocity as well as a convergence between divine and created action. It is in the dialectical tension between divine gift and creaturely response that human creativity develops in all its variety and spontaneity.

Within the core vision of God there is for Christian faith a further specification, defined in the affirmation that God became man, that the source of power became powerless, as the publicly identified victim of violence, and in so doing opened up a human dimension of God with eternal significance. This is an affirmation which Christian faith makes and at the same time confesses its inability to handle. This is a vision which is in its heart fragmented, a brilliant promise for which the available evidence of Christian charity is at best ambiguous. But it is at the centre of Christian theology in its intensity and with its danger. It is a hope that the future will be longer than the past, and that generosity will eventually prevail over animosity and parochialism. This hope arises within the Christian tradition, but its understanding of our common humanity under God generates in both theoretical and practical spheres a need for engagement with other religions and world views

It is sometimes suggested that the cosmos, though finite, may not actually have had a beginning in time. It is without boundaries. The dynamics of the same chaotic systems in the cosmos may lead to areas of unpredictability and areas of predictability, to random and also to determined behaviour at a quantum level. If there is anything in the so-called 'anthropic principle', then there may be curious connections between the conditions of the possibility of human life and the actual development of the cosmos. And, of course, there is perhaps nothing so complex yet known to us in the cosmos as the human brain, in which most of the complexity of being is mirrored. It is through strange combinations of the formation and then the collapse of frontiers that creative change takes place, at macrocosmic, microcosmic and human consciousness levels. We are significant because we are complex creatures, creatures with whom the creator has identified in incarnation, but we are part of a process which goes back into the distant past and looks into the far distant future.

Divine Action

We have looked at the implications of the sciences and the dialogue between science and theology, and we have noted the different dimensions of this debate with reference to the physical sciences, to pure science and to applied science. It has sometimes been noted that conservative Christian theologies are often more ready to engage in dialogue with the sciences than more liberal theologies, which, following Kant, tend to stress the interiority of faith and to be less comfortable with discussion of divine action in the external world. Though this study is consciously set in the progressive tradition, it is of the nature of an intercultural theology that it should pay attention to theology in different cultural modes, of which conservative Christian theologies are important examples. The nature of divine action is complex and mysterious. We may be in a position in later millennia to understand the complex forces involved, but for now we must do what we can with the data available, while maintaining due modesty about our conclusions.

What may be learned for the understanding of creation through dialogue with science? Faith is concerned with the response of the human consciousness to God. But consciousness is integrally related to neural activity, to the firing of millions of synapses in the brain. *The complexity of neural activity is often thought to be the most complex entity in the cosmos.* Within this activity the sustaining of faith may be seen as a decisive element of the manifestation of divine action in the cosmos, an action related to all other cosmic activity. Human consciousness is affected not only by immediate external stimuli but by habits of thought and action relating to cultural memory. It shares this facility in part with other animals, but develops it to an astonishing degree, enabling the development of imagination in a unique order of magnitude. It is in reflection on the tradition of the gospel and in response to its intimation of the presence of God that faith is formed and sustained.

Rudolf Bultmann, one of the most creative Christian minds of the twentieth century, famously affirmed that it was not possible to think of God in mythical imagery in a world of electric light bulbs, and was devastatingly criticized for narrowness and naïveté. In one sense he was right. We may find a constructive role for our mythology but we have to relate it rationally to the rest of our corpus of knowledge. However, this means that we cannot live in two unconnected worlds, the one of science and the other of faith. Bultmann was reluctant to articulate a positive relationship between science and faith. He feared the positivism which substituted knowledge for faith and in so doing detracted from the primacy of justification by faith alone, with no security except that of faith.

His sermons provided a moving illustration of the strength of such faith, not least in his opposition to National Socialism. Yet it ought to be possible to construct a paradigm of relationship between faith and science which respects the freedom of faith, refuses the reification of knowledge of God and is open to the divine mystery.

It is evident from the writings of many recent contributors to the religion/science debate, such as Peacocke, Hesse, Russell, Stoeger and Ward, that much scientific thinking has long since moved past the positivism which for Bultmann was a genuine barrier to dialogue. Faith may relate to a science which has embraced epistemological humility, which is aware of its limits and of the element of cultural relativity and interaction between the objective and the subjective in all its dimensions. It is clear, too, that faith retains a central shape of commitment and personal trust even for those who are inclined to support more conservative paradigms in the dialogue between theology and science.

Any serious discussion of divine action in an intercultural context must consider the impact of science on theories of divine action. One of the best ongoing discussions, characteristic of the dialogue, is in the series *Scientific Perspectives on Divine Action*, edited by Robert J. Russell and others. In *Chaos and Complexity* (Russel, Murphy and Peacocke, 1995) Russell offered a masterly survey of the central issues, in historical and contemporary perspective.[2]

The cosmological debate raises acutely in scientific form the traditional theological inquiry concerning the nature of divine action. Two of the most useful contributions to this discussion are also to be found in the *Chaos and Complexity* volume. Reflecting on 'Particular Providence and the God of the Gaps', and seeking a third way between deism and interventionism, Thomas Tracy argues that the structure of the universe is such that God is the creator of indeterministic gaps through which the world remains open to possibilities not exhaustively specified by its past. He uses the language of quantum indeterminacy rather than chaos unpredictability to suggest an open universe in which chance is built into what remains an ordered structure of divine action (ibid., 316ff). In this way we may imagine God acting to guide the direction of events without overriding the structures of nature which he has established. In this picture God may act in different ways at different times. Without determining the course of all events, God might determine enough quantum indeterminacies, acting in history, to guarantee that they will affect the course of events in the way that God intends (cf., too, Hebblethwaite, (1978, 223–36)). In his paper, Tracy finds quantum mechanics more helpful than chaos theory for his reconstruction of a view of divine action, but he notes that, in this dialogue,

> we must cope with the virtual certainty that scientific understandings of the world will change. There may be more gain than loss, however, in regarding our theological constructions as working proposals that must be continually rethought as we attempt both to remain faithful to the religious tradition that affirms God's action in the world and to appropriate fuller understandings of the world in which God acts. (324)

Nancey Murphy also has reservations about the value of chaos theory and its application to theology, though the notion of unpredictability is important: 'Top-down causation is not in itself an adequate account of divine action' (Russell, Murphy and Peacocke, 1995, 326). She strives for a new understanding of causation. She includes an unexpected Christological element in her programme. Divine complexity must show consistency:

> Thus if the paradigm of divine action for Christians is found in the story of Jesus, we should expect that same moral divine character to be manifested, analogously, in God's action within sub-human orders. I shall claim that the

> relevant feature of God's action in Christ, displayed analogously throughout the whole, is its non-coercive character. (330)

This means that God respects the entities which he has created, cooperating, not dominating. God acts in 'bottom-up' causation by means of his governance of the quantum events which constitute each macro-level event, usually through the structures of creation but occasionally through extraordinary events, through 'intentional orchestration of the vastly many micro-events' (346).

God's action can also be seen in a 'top-down' framework, influencing the underlying structures from above, say, influencing the human consciousness by stimulation of neurons, by 'bottom-up' causation from within to create religious experience (349). Against the objection of the apparent arbitrariness of divine action, Murphy argues that God cannot act regularly in extraordinary action without destroying human freedom, while admitting that the question why God might act at a sub-atomic level on some occasions and not on others remains unanswered.

Murphy's account succeeds remarkably in 'saving the phenomena' in the dialogue between natural science and religious belief. It works on the basis of a dialogue with a traditional understanding of theology and of biblical revelation. In a wider interdisciplinary framework these focal points might be widened to include the dimensions of religions and culture, politics and society. Here the model of God's direct converse with the individual, of the sort characterized in the Bible, would be correlated with the issue of God's impact on social and cultural change. This will in itself throw critical light on the primary biblical models, emphasizing the interlinked and interdependent nature of all our conceptuality, in a pattern of reciprocity resembling the divine reciprocity. In this way theology both contributes to and benefits from a maximally wide intercultural disciplinarity. The Christomorphic trace may be understood as both an endorsement and an enhancing of Murphy's guiding Christological model, while underlining that science, as we know it, is always science in society, clothed with all its economic, political and cultural connotations.[3]

Science and the Self

We have considered the basic intercultural theme of divine action and the sciences in relation to cosmology and evolutionary biology. Highly relevant to this discussion is the further scientific and theological question of the nature of the human person, and the relationship between mind and brain. In a dialogue between theology and the sciences, how are neurological and theological perspectives to be related? A useful snapshot of much contemporary thinking is provided in *The Human Person in Science and Theology* (Gregersen, Drees and Gorman, 2000). Gregersen notes the degree of social conditioning which is attached to the term 'person' through the ages, in its cultural and individual constructions, and looks to a theological dialogue with 'the bio-cultural paradigm'. He develops a notion of supervenience which allows for an efficacy of the mental, because mental properties are relational and not intrinsic to the brain. He sees here a complementarity with a theological construal of the eucharistic experience of God's transformation of the human mind by way of external words and signs with community: 'God's power to change minds is apparently not taking place in a disembodied setting, but in a specific bio-cultural environment' (182). Most of the contributors emphasize a 'many-maps' approach to the person. Hugo Lagercrantz argues that genetic determinism is not enough, noting that science has the potential to repair genetic defects: 'The complexity and plasticity of the brain encourages us to believe that there is substantial room for exercising a free will in shaping our cultural and social environments' (ibid., 14). The notion of the social and public self is stressed by Philip Hefner and Michael Welker, against Cartesian notions of the self in isolation.

Charles Taylor's justly famous *Sources of the Self* (1989) was a landmark in thinking about the social construction on selfhood. Gregersen and his colleagues develop the central thrust of Taylor's work into the mechanics of neurology, with the aid of current philosophical work on the mind–brain problem. If we are looking for images to articulate the action of the Christomorphic trace in history, then a theory of supervenience[4] may be one way of envisaging non-coercive divine action in the human mind, linking the macro and micro worlds of the physical sciences with cultural and political events. It would not necessarily be a repudiation of concepts of personal faith in the Schleiermacher tradition, but the development of a limiting paradigm into a transformational one, in which the uniqueness of individual consciousness is preserved but enhanced by the normative reference to other selves in relationship.

Here too, of course, there are problems and there is provisionality. A theology which is uncritically aligned to scientific paradigms may be ill-placed to criticize the use of scientific culture in ways which are contrary to faith's understanding of the purposes of a God of unconditional love. Attention to the fascinations of theological dialogue with cosmology or biology may mask from us unpleasant consequences of applied science which have affected the lives of millions of people: in the military science cultures of dictatorships in the twentieth century, sometimes in an unholy amalgam with religions, in the oppressive technology of totalitarianism and in the technological exploitation of poor countries by rich ones. While there is everything to be gained from a critical dialogue with science, there is nothing to be gained from an uncritical scientism.

The dialogue which has opened up in recent decades between theology and science is still at an early stage. Due caution is required, as hypotheses are constructed and discarded. It becomes clear that we are not in a position to uncover the 'causal joint' between the divine action which Christians believe to be at the heart of the universe and causal processes within the scope of scientific investigation. We are not God. Yet, if there are no demonstrable correspondences between God's action and action within the cosmic process, there may well be resemblances and complementarities which enable us to have a synoptic understanding of faith and scientific reason. Nothing in the physical sciences rules out divine action. Where faith believes in God's presence within a religious tradition, this faith may contribute to and enhance a holistic understanding of the universe. In a world largely dominated by scientific cultural paradigms, this dialogue is of obvious importance for Christian theology's contribution to the human future. A dialogue which respects the differences between scientific and theological arguments, while exploring the benefits of interdisciplinarity, is clearly of first importance.

In this whole section we may appear to have moved far away from the literary and historical issues with which we began. It is of the essence of my argument for an intercultural theology that there are not two cultures, the sciences and the arts, but rather there are many overlapping cultures and sub-cultures in human thought and action which require to be re-imagined in dialectical tension. This in some ways goes against the stream of the increasing specialization which was perhaps the most notable feature of twentieth century, though it also requires the particularities of specialist study to produce competent areas of dialogue.

We may reiterate the importance of the future. There is a tendency in thinking of cosmology and creation to concentrate on the past, on initial singularity or evolutionary development, but a theological understanding of the created order is concerned as much with the future as with the past. Ted Peters has said that 'the first thing God did with the cosmos was to give it a future. Without a future it would be nothing' (Peters, 1989, 87). I have tried to stress the significance of a conscious attention to the future elsewhere (Newlands, 1997). Here I only want to suggest that the main impetus of an intercultural theology is to concentrate our research programmes on thinking about the future as much as on the past.

Notes

1 Best known are the studies which have come from Hans Kung's globalization project. It is clear that globalization has advantages and disadvantages and can be viewed from many angles. Economies of scale, such as in food production, are balanced by an ever-widening gulf between the rich and the poor.

2 This project may be usefully compared with David Griffin's plea in many writings for the need to avoid mind/body dualism (cf. Griffin, 2000).

3 It is especially useful to examine this dialogue in the framework of intercultural theology in the light of the comparative neglect of the natural sciences in the hermeneutical tradition of Schleiermacher. It is important to try to bridge the gaps between the 'two cultures' of science and the humanities, however difficult that may be.

4 David Griffin (2000) has also extensively discussed theories of supervenience, in a process context.

CHAPTER 10

Theology in Metamodern Culture

Postfoundational Theory and Intercultural Theology in Dialogue

How do we use our theological resources within cultures in ways that are not just normative but transformative, sensitive to the creative possibilities in developing situations? Can we find coherent and generally applicable guidelines, to avoid ad hoc responses with an attendant general confusion of purpose? How do we develop a genuine interdisciplinarity? I find in Wentzel Van Huyssteen's (1999) account of rationality a helpful suggestion towards re-imagining the framework of an intercultural theology which is both interdisciplinary and genuinely integrative.

Van Huyssteen asks 'whether any form of interdisciplinary rationality can be credibly achieved – an interdisciplinary rationality that might finally support the claims by at least some in the theological epistemic community for a public voice in our complex, contemporary culture' (3). He seeks to develop a postfoundationalist notion of rationality which will

> first, fully acknowledge contextuality and the embeddedness of both theology and the sciences in the different domains of human culture;
> second, affirm the epistemically crucial role of interpreted experience and the way that tradition shapes the epistemic and non-epistemic values that inform our reflection about both God and our world;
> third, at the same time creatively point beyond the confines of the local community, group, or culture, toward plausible forms of transcommunal and interdisciplinary conversation. (8)

Accepting the demise of foundationalism, in explicit or implicit form, of the idea that there can be one overarching theory and structure of knowledge, and the advent of non-foundationalism, Van Huyssteen wants to avoid relativism, 'where incommensurability may finally stifle all meaningful cross-disciplinary dialogue' (11). Knowing has experiential and hermeneutical dimensions, leading to a postfoundationalist fusion of hermeneutics and epistemology. Rationality balances 'the way our beliefs are anchored in interpreted experience and the broader networks of belief in which our rationally compelling experiences are already embedded' (14). These networks include the 'research traditions' in which communities are embedded. These ideas are then developed systematically in dialogue with other writers in the field, notably with Calvin Schrag's notion of 'transversal rationality' and Susan Haack's concept of 'foundherentism'.

Haack is particularly germane to an intercultural project. Between foundationalism and nonfoundationalism (coherentism) she develops a third option of foundherentism. All our knowledge is indeed grounded in the foundation of experience, but is justified by nonfoundational means, appealing to a universal intent of human rationality. Our beliefs are justified by experience, but supported by other sorts of networks of belief. Personal experience is important, but must be related to other sorts of information: belief must be both experientially and theoretically satisfying. Experience comes in a wide spectrum, including sensory, introspective and memory experiences. What seems rational will have historical and even geographical variations. For Haack rational evidence is normally empirical evidence, thus leaving out the role of religion. There is, however, no rational ground for failing to include religious testimony.

Haack is concerned that her criteria of rational justification remain truth-indicative (Haack, 203f). She sums up her case effectively like this:

> Epistemology, as I conceive it, and its meta-theory, are integral parts of a whole web of theories about the world and ourselves, not underpinning but intermeshing with other parts. Standards of evidence are not hopelessly culture-bound, though judgements of justification are always perspectival. And we can have, not proof that our criteria of justification are truth-guaranteeing, but reasons for thinking that, if any truth indication is available to us, they are truth indicative …
>
> The old foundationalism aspired to a certitude impossible for fallible human inquirers: but the new conventionalism and the new tribalism surrender to a 'factitious despair'. Though we must settle for less reassurance than Descartes hoped to achieve, we need not give up the quest or the hope of truth itself. (Ibid., 222)

The consequences of this line of argument are these. Not only in theology but also in the sciences we relate to our worlds only through interpreted experiences. Even empirical scientific explanation is theoretically selected and interpreted, and functions only within the framework of these presupposed theories that constitute a specific reasoning strategy. If our beliefs are the result of our interpreted experiences, then the content of this belief can never be given immediately or directly in the experience itself. The distinguishing mark of religious experience is not simply in its subjective nature, but it is understood within a web of interpreted experiences which retain both subjective and objective elements.

There are important differences between theology and science, different forms of explanation, but they have a common rich resource of rationality. They share a search for a responsible epistemic pluralism, in a 'wide reflective equilibrium' (Van Huyssteen, 1999). What are the immediate implications for theology?

> In a postfoundationalist Christian theology the focus will always, however, in some ways be on a relentless criticism of our uncritically held crypto-foundationalist assumptions. … Precisely by allowing ourselves to freely and critically explore the experiential and interpretive roots of all our beliefs in our various domains of knowledge, we as theologians too are freed to speak and

> reflect publicly, but from within a personal faith commitment, and in this cross disciplinary conversation with those of other traditions and other disciplines, to discover patterns that may be consonant with or complementary to the Christian world view. (Ibid., 285)

Van Huyssteen is clear that evolutionary theory, and evolutionary epistemology in particular, may be welcomed by the theologian:

> The basic assumption of evolutionary epistemology is that we humans, like all other living beings, result from evolutionary processes and that, consequently, our mental capacities are constrained and shaped by the mechanisms of biological evolution. I will accept, at least in a minimalist sense, that all our knowledge, including our scientific and biological knowledge, is grounded in biological evolution … Evolutionary epistemology, rightly understood, will therefore furnish an interdisciplinary account of all our epistemic activities … I will argue, however, that though this may explain away deistic notions of God, it does not fully explain religious belief, and certainly not theism as such. (Van Huyssteen, 1998, 32–3)

It is always important to pay attention to objections to attractive theories, if real progress is to be made. We ought now to consider possible objections to such a construal. Richard Dawkins in a series of brilliant books, (*The Selfish Gene*, 1976; *The Blind Watchmaker*, 1986; *River out of Eden*, 1995; *Climbing Mount Improbable*, 1996) has argued that evolution explains everything and leaves no room for God. He makes a strong case for theories of natural selection and their consequences for religion, and, in *The Blind Watchmaker*, sums up his basic position in this way: 'This book is written in the conviction that our own existence once presented the greatest of all mysteries, but that it is a mystery no longer because it has been solved. Darwin and Wallace solved it, though we shall continue to add footnotes for a while yet' (Dawkins, 1986, preface). *The Blind Watchmaker* is a fascinating account of natural selection in evolutionary theory, in which Dawkins stressed the extremely random nature of genetic development.

Van Huyssteen argues that human beings are indeed determined by their genetic material, but not exhaustively so – they are also shaped by their ability to transfer information on a *cultural* level, to adapt their ecosystems to their needs, to think things through rationally. To quote Dawkins (1995):

> This is a world where DNA neither knows nor cares. DNA just is. And we dance to its music … If our genes do not completely determine our culture and our rational abilities, then it might be as reasonable to expect that our genes, our cultures and our rational abilities may not also completely determine the enduring and pervasive need of human beings for metaphysics, and ultimately, for life-transforming religious faith. (159)

Coming to Judgment

Can we find some way of negotiating the contrasting paradigms? Here, as often, I find help from Keith Ward, whose approach to theology I regard as very close to my own. The argument with Dawkins has been much developed by Keith Ward in his *God, Chance and Necessity* (1996) and in *God, Faith and the New Millennium* (2000):

> The Christian view is that one of the chief goals of creation and evolution is the emergence of beings that to some extent possess awareness, creative agency and powers of reactive and responsible relationship, with whom God can enter into personal fellowship. The universe is ordered from its beginning to the actualization of beings made in the image of the creator.
>
> Human beings, in this view, are *not accidental* by-products of blind cosmic processes. They are part of the envisaged and predestined goal of the evolutionary process. The existence of *consciousness*, purpose and moral agency is not some strange and temporary anomaly in a ceaseless recombination of atomic parts. It is that for the sake of which the whole material process has been laboriously and intricately constructed. (Ward, 2000, 123)

This, we might think, is not so far removed from Pannenberg's understanding of man as an historical being, whose sense of historicality comes from the experience of encounter with God, or even from Schleiermacher's stress on human consciousness as the key to transcendence. It could be objected that the postmodern dissolution of the subject has rendered talk of consciousness unintelligible. But another argument would be that the reflection of the self as an encultured self within an historical tradition strengthens the argument that cultural development is as important as genetic development in the construction of the human, and that this entire process may be understood by faith as response to the presence of God.

> It might even be that God's own nature, as love, is only fully realised by the creation of other conscious agents with whom God can share in fellowship, by giving, sharing and receiving a love that binds creator and creatures together in a community of spiritual being … The love of God might require that the fulfilment of creation is not only experienced by the one consciousness of God, but shared in a communion of love that God brings to completion. (Ibid., 215f)

In this conception, the gospel of the Christomorphic love of God as the key to human flourishing in community is the fulfilment of that same love which moves the stars. There is indeed a complementarity between theology and science and an interdisciplinary search for deeper meaning, in which the various human cultures, social, political and scientific, are the necessary discussion partners of an intercultural theology.

Comparative Theology

Keith Ward's work is especially illuminating for an intercultural theology in another way also, namely in the quest for a theology of world religions. This represents a crucial broadening of the discussion, in which the Christianity/science debate can be seen as part of a much wider reflection on divine action in the world. Once again, we have to try, however tentatively, to break out of the compartmentalization of so much of our thinking. Ward's tetralogy on religion breaks new ground in the quest for a comparative theology, drawing on the four major scriptural traditions of Judaism, Hinduism, Buddhism and Islam. He draws on the insights of religious studies while continuing to do theology, and produces a theology which is in some respects confessional, based on Christianity and within this the Anglican tradition, and in other respects non-confessional and pluralist. Such a project is very much complementary to intercultural theology. It concentrates on theology and religious writings in the world religions, while intercultural theology is focused more on interdisciplinarity. But a comprehensive intercultural theology would embrace the concerns also of comparative theology.

To see how the project would work we need look at only one of Ward's many examples, the Vedanta tradition on God in India, and the comparison of Vedanta with Christianity. The different historical situations of the Semitic and Indian traditions meant that there were many features of Semitic thought, such as the prophetic tradition, entirely lacking in India. But there are sages who hear the words of the eternal order, who know the causes of suffering and rebirth and the way to release from suffering (Ward, 1998, 137). The idea that there is a God who is totally other than the material universe is foreign to the tradition.

Ward's project is lucidly and succinctly summarized in his millennium study: 'The history of religions is partly a history of human ignorance and folly, and partly a story of the development of more adequate understandings of God and the way to the human goal, in response to new factual knowledge and wider human sensitivity' (Ward, 2000, 153). Adherents of different religions are likely to disagree, even among themselves, on major issues. It is therefore necessary to move towards a firm commitment to global pluralism, affirming, freedom of conscience, freedom of thought, a search for the welfare of all, a learning from others, a seeking for convergence where possible, a cooperation for good, and a common quest for reconciliation, peace and compassion (168).

Recent studies on the nature of rationality are as helpful to the present project as studies in the nature of culture. They underline the multifaceted nature of the postmodern and the postfoundational which characterizes modern life. They often remind us, too, that there are things of value to be learned from previous paradigms, and that it is often in the comparison and clash of paradigms that new ideas arise. The postmodern does not simply negate the values of the modern. Though we may regard postfoundational rationality and postmodern culture as the dominant models and the best available research traditions, we should not be deceived by an illusion of finality. It would be foolish to retreat to the premodern, but important not to regard the current state of discussion as set in stone. Theology has here the useful advantage of a strong sense of the eschatological limitation of all our language.

I shall not attempt here to create a comprehensive postfoundational framework for the interaction of theology and culture as such. This might be possible, but to have any chance of success it would be an immense undertaking well beyond the scope of this book. Instead I have suggested areas of the theory and practice of theology which would be compatible with such an endeavour. If we are successful, some hints of the more universal may be detectable from within the practice of the particular. I shall try to develop these suggestions with the aid of a device constructed for the purpose, the metamodern.

The Metamodern and its Predecessors

The attempt to find new perspectives on intellectual puzzles creates in every age its own jargon, and provokes renewed attempts to escape from the jargon. From 'the modern' has come the postmodern, the premodern, even the paleomodern. Foundationalism creates nonfoundationalism and postfoundationalism and even transfoundationalism, in seeking new ways to divide up theories and practices. I am going to offer another here, the *metamodern*, again with the object of suggesting a classification. This should be regarded purely as an imaginary and temporary envelope for the present purpose, and not as a candidate for another lasting piece of jargon. I now discover that the term has already been used, to a limited degree. It might have some affinities with Voegelin's use of *To Metaxu* (the between) to suggest the reality of intersubjectivity in dialogue, though I am concerned as much with the social as with the individual dimensions of dialogue.

The metaphor of the metamodern, as I would want to use it, signals postmodernity in an inclusive and transformative sense, rather than as a limiting and prescriptive mode. It underlines that the postmodern is in many respects very much part of the modern, and unthinkable without the modern, not only as its origin but also as a continuing force. The metamodern acknowledges both the advantages and the disadvantages of the traditional ontological categories of the European tradition. The metamodern underlines all that Bernstein and Berlin have had to say about engaged fallibilistic pluralism and agonistic liberalism. It is, then, not so much a category as a signal, indicating inclusivity and flexibility.[1]

There is a concise account of the varieties of postmodernism, and of postmodernism as viewed in the process tradition in David Griffin's Introduction to the SUNY series in Constructive Postmodern Thought:

> The postmodernism of this series can be called revisionary, constructive, or – perhaps best – reconstructive … It agrees with deconstructive postmodernists that a massive deconstruction of many received concepts is needed. But its deconstructive moment, carried out for the sake of the presuppositions of practice, does not result in self-referential inconsistency. It is also not so totalizing as to prevent reconstruction. … This reconstructive postmodernism involves a creative synthesis of modern and premodern truths and values. (Griffin, 2000, ixf)

Merold Westphal's essay, 'Appropriating postmodernism', and the collection it introduces give a comprehensive survey of current uses of postmodern philosophy in Christian Thought (Westphal, 1999).

Theology has had a long reign as 'queen of the sciences', but monarchy is no longer everywhere in fashion. And indeed it is not clear that kingship models are the best way of articulating a faith which is committed to solidarity with the poor and the outcast. Theological discourse, as many commentators have observed, is in danger of becoming isolated from dialogue with other disciplines and with reflection on the shape of society in the future. This situation may not be unwelcome to some members of the academic guild: it saves a great deal of tedious explanation and involvement with intractable issues. But if Christian theology is committed to the service of all humanity, then the interactive relationship of theology to culture remains of fundamental importance.

It may still of course be argued that theology, being reflection on God the creator will always be understood by faith as the highest layer in the hierarchy of the sciences. Nancey Murphy has persuasively argued this in her *Anglo-American Postmodernity*, using the model of top-down causation, against forms of reductionism (Murphy, 1997, 198). But in her explanation of supervenience, as a way of understanding the impact of layers of causation upon another, the internal integrity of each level is respected. God does not impose coercion on the structures which he has created. This picture will not support a notion of theology as somehow the arbiter of all human endeavour. Much more, it is another intimation of a non-coercive interaction of reciprocity and respect at the heart of things.[2]

How is theology to respond to cultural diversity? We may think that the attempt to relate multifaceted theologies to multifaceted culture is doomed to endless ambiguity and lack of precision. Better, perhaps, to accept that each sub-culture will quite legitimately appropriate theology in its own chosen way, and offer a distinctive theology to be retrieved in different ways. An example might be the way in which the very particular and largely self-contained theology of Karl Barth has been retrieved in particular theological traditions. Here is one way to retain specificity and focus. The universal always arises out of the particular. Theology makes its own substantive and intrinsic contribution.

Yet the need for a theology of correlation between the gospel and culture remains, not necessarily as an exclusive alternative but as another essential characteristic of a modern theology of engagement. It belongs to a theology of *grace* that is always oriented towards the other. It is not self-absorbed but other-related. It pays attention to different paradigms of knowledge at different times. Theology makes its contribution not simply in application to a context but in interaction. Such a theology of engagement we find, for example, in the writings of Eduard Schillebeeckx. Theology has a core and a unity, but that is an eschatological unity. Here God's presence to faith is through fragments, parables and icons of faith. There is ample recognition of this eschatological completeness together with residual mystery in all the classical theologians, though not perhaps so much in the more scholastic writings of some of their disciples.

From the side of culture, too, we noted a reluctance to be controlled by a hegemonic network of doctrine. What is welcome is participation, reciprocity, dialogue in which the course of the journey to be undertaken remains open. Participation requires listening as well as speaking, and a commitment to learning from the dialogue partners. The other side of this is a willingness to bring to the dialogue a distinctive contribution. In an authoritarian framework such an emphasis would be and is implicitly threatening, an attempt to pre-empt and control the direction of dialogue.

Facilitation: Theology as Partnership

To conceive the contemporary European social landscape as metamodern would seem to me to be at once a useful perspective and the source of a constructive vision. Of course within the metamodern there are different sorts of combination of modernity and postmodernity. There are huge chunks of the premodern (the monarchy in Britain is a complex combination of the premodern and the postmodern). The continuing flow and counter-flow of these clashing modalities create the sometimes random, sometimes chaotic and sometimes orderly vitality of our communities.

In this sketch of a thoroughly diverse sociality I want to reiterate the role of theology as facilitator. A facilitator seeks to encourage things to come to fruition, through word and action to advocate and bring about constructive new development. In the nature of the case it would be wrong to see theology as the only facilitator, for it, too, is constantly immersed in the force fields of the rest of society. Law and medicine, sociology and politics, engineering – there are many facilitators. It is as an equal partner with others that facilitation can best be achieved in a metamodern environment.

In the real world there are other facilitators, commercial special interests of all sorts, arms and drugs cartels, and the like. Christian theology believes it can and must participate as an equal partner in this process because it has resources to contribute, at an intellectual and a practical level. These resources have advantages and disadvantages: too much concentration on traditional doctrines may distract from specific local justice issues, too much stress on the particularity of oppression in one sphere may distract from other pressing matters. Faith believes that the resources are there, to be used effectively.

To act as a facilitator is not only to participate in a delivery system. Involvement as an equal partner is likely to affect the nature of what is delivered, and how. Theology understands God as a self-differentiated God for whom to be is to be in relationship and reciprocity. Facilitation is therefore an eminently suitable role for theology, though paradoxically it has very often adopted a hegemonic model. Again we are reminded of the dialectical nature of the theology–culture relationship. Partnership must reflect the character of the Christian God as self-giving love if it is not to be partnership in oppression and collusion. There is no escape from the risk of possible corruption of power. Intellectual and social paradigms can be equally coercive and prejudicial, as Gordon Allport demonstrated many decades ago. Where theology does not facilitate the love of God, it has no worthwhile role in society and is likely only to inflict damage.

Facilitation in turn suggests theology as partnership. Partnership implies a commonality of purpose, but not an automatic agreement. This concept invites further reflection on ways of harnessing the constructive tension between the hugely influential traditions of Barth and Schleiermacher in a metamodern frame.

Schleiermacher recognized that revelation in the Christian understanding of faith comes in, with and under human experience. He recognized that we are not in the nature of things granted anything like a blueprint of God, and that our faith and its theological articulation partake of the fallibility of human experience. His vision remained however a universalizing vision, and he did not see that the Enlightenment model of rationality was in some ways a mirror image of the paradigm which it replaced. It could become a totalizing vision which appealed to universally valid laws and truth. Like Aquinas, Schleiermacher still saw theology as the queen of the sciences, since the key to all that is the relation between creation and salvation, under the hand of God.

Barth was rightly suspicious of the ordering of the gospel under the universal categories of the human sciences. Faith is the result of the breaking in of unconditional grace, unpredictable and beyond our full comprehension. It has its own contribution to make to human flourishing, distinctive and life-giving. Unfortunately, however, Barth then went on to develop a system, centred on Christology, which was in many ways again as universalizing and schematic as the modern and medieval systems which he rejected. Here again was an autonomous paradigm which could re-articulate reality without the aid of the human sciences. Appeal to the human sciences appeared to offer only uncertainty and relativism, a danger which then became even more apparent in the development of postmodernism. However, theology was soon able to adapt and claim the postmodern as its own, locating its role in a special cultural–linguistic space in which ecclesiology could flourish, unencumbered by the compromises of modernity.

It seems probable that a theology which faces the challenges of the beginning of the third millennium will be likely to be a postfoundational theology, which relates constructively the tensions between the foundational and the non-foundational, the modern and the postmodern. For the further conclusions which I draw here I have to accept full personal responsibility. It seems to me that theology should consciously give up the claim, from Aquinas through Schleiermacher to Barth, to be the queen of the sciences, and to seek instead to be the servant of the sciences.

Such a proposal may seem to some to be a typical liberal capitulation to the spirit of the age. I do not agree. It seems to me that theology is best understood, not as the keystone of all knowledge, but as an ultimately indispensable partner, a contributor to the search for human flourishing which is understood by Christians as the fulfilment of the purpose for which God has created us. So understood, theology may often be the catalyst which enables change in the direction of God's purpose of reconciliation. It may inspire vision and enable transformation,

When theology seeks to produce a theocratic paradigm, either of thought or of action, it almost always fails in its purpose. For Christian faith, this role as partner rather than as controller is forever shaped by the pattern of incarnation, crucifixion and resurrection, in which the power of God is effective through the kenotic love of Jesus Christ.

A paradigm of theology as partnership will take different forms in different cultural situations. It will by necessity be a mode of intercultural theology. As contribution, partnership and suggestion, it will be significantly different from the classical patterns of theological construction of the past. It will of course have commonalities as well as differences, but it will expect to face uncharted waters and *to take risks*. A theology of partnership will include interdisciplinary engagement with the human and natural sciences. It will often appear as fragments, but these will be significant fragments, for they should reflect the indispensability of the theological tradition as a thread in a pattern, a trace in the programme. A Christian intercultural theology should articulate an understanding of unconditional grace as unconditional generosity, open to otherness and to recognition of particularity. It should be open to engagement in dialogue with other traditions, especially other religious and philosophical traditions. And it should relate intellectual effort to communicative practice in society, as the expression in overlapping cultures of differing traditions and lifestyles.

As we have seen, culture, like religion, can produce its own tyranny and triumphalism. In every situation there is need for critical analysis and dialectical tension in the dialogue between faith and culture. There needs to be concern for an even playing field, in every dialogue, and this applies especially to dialogues between majorities and minorities. Minorities may have to emphasize their distinctiveness in order to get a fair hearing in the first place. They must then take care not to produce minor tyrannies within their own cultures. This has particular relevance to the litmus test of the observance of human rights, which are regularly infringed by all absolutist theories, whether these derive from theology or from culture.

The theme of divine action provides a thread to connect the various dimensions of this study. In reflection on the natural sciences we have seen how cosmological theory may be seen as the setting for a concept of divine action as encouraging the physical development of the universe, through patterns of immense complexity and unpredictability, towards the central complexity of human consciousness. In considering politics and history we have sought to conceptualize what has been described as the Christomorphic trace, as a divine invitation to a particular shape of human action as response to the divine love. In emphasizing human rights we have suggested that this area is a kind of test and catalyst of the effectiveness of an appropriate response to God. In speaking of the nature of faith we have understood this as the recognition of pointers to transcendence in the tension between the tradition of the gospel and the way the world today is perceived to be. To go with the grain of the Christomorphic trace is to participate in the mystery of salvation. But this salvation is there for all creation, and points to the love of God present throughout creation, not least in other religions and in all human searching for transcendent compassion.

Diverse Partners

Schleiermacher's concept of the self as the subject of *religious consciousness* clearly stood in the line of Descartes and Kant. As such it focused on private identity and internal self-understanding. This made it extremely difficult for him to engage in any sort of intercultural dialogue with the natural sciences. We find this tradition reflected much later in the work of Bultmann and Ebeling. The concept of religious consciousness was a philosophical translation of Luther's central concept of justification by faith. Schleiermacher was well aware of the hazards of solitary belief, and countered the problems involved in his model of the self with a strong stress on the importance of Christian community, worship in community, and Christian involvement in society, in politics and government.

Karl Barth's theology of the word was much closer to Schleiermacher's concept of the self than is often allowed. Here the self-revelation of God is again mediated to the individual through the preaching of the Word. The relationship between Barth's doctrine of the Word and Kant's understanding of the self was clearly articulated many years ago by the extremely conservative but sharp neocalvinist theologian Cornelius van Til. It is sometimes argued that a radically postmodern approach to philosophy renders quite untenable modern concepts of the self. If that were the case, Barth's doctrine of revelation would become as vulnerable as Schleiermacher's notion of religious consciousness. Through the influence of Hegel, Barth was led to widen his concept of revelation to include the relationality of Trinity, and this openness to otherness has prompted fruitful comparison with Derrida. Yet the continuities between Barth and Schleiermacher remain important. Barth too, however, was interested in community, in Church dogmatics and in socialist politics. But his primary theological principle stood in the same line of tradition as that of Schleiermacher. What then were the decisive differences? Schleiermacher was concerned with a religious consciousness which would always be correlative to concepts worked out in the other human sciences. This was part of his conviction that God did not act by special divine interventions in the created order, but always in, with and under created causality. Barth, on the other hand, had learned from Kierkegaard the importance of the assertion that God is wholly other, and that all attempts at mediation between the divine and the human are human, save explicitly through the single mediative bridge of Jesus Christ.

Both the continuities and the discontinuities between theology and culture, and the dialectic between cultural dialogue and counter-cultural affirmation remain important. The liberal theological tradition, like the liberal tradition in politics, has enormous merits, but it tends to suffer from belief in its own finality, in the dialogues and interactions of the present moment as definitive. Both in theology and in politics, it can lead to the promotion of the elitist values of a particular group over the welfare of others. It may treat as foundational that which is at best only provisional, and reduce a rich complexity of tradition and argument to an attenuated single principle. It will speedily be recognized, however, that the neo-orthodox (and indeed the radical orthodox position in theology) suffers from mirror image defects. The liberal tradition failed, at least in part, through the experience of the two world wars of the first half of the twentieth century. Neo-orthodox theology has made little impact on the innumerable wars in the second half, and on the huge divides in terms of race, colour and economic privilege which have been solidified.

An intercultural metamodern theology has no reason to expect to be exempt from the problems which have continued to challenge all theology in the last two centuries. It has to hope to learn from all the leading traditions, and to deploy its own strengths, in seeking to relate through interdisciplinarity to a wide web of cumulative justifying warrants. It may benefit from critical reflection on the mediating theologies and on the kerugmatic theologies of the immediate past. It will be committed to a continuous process of hypothesis and revision, of trial and error. Confident of the reality of its ultimate eschatological significance for humanity, it will seek to be aware also of the reality of its eschatological limitations.

In human life there is no escape from ambiguity and provisionality, but there are rational options to be sought between the extremes of objectivity and subjectivity, foundationalism and non-foundationalism, however one seeks to define these. We have suggested that theology must cease to regard itself as more foundational than other disciplines, while remaining confident in its positive and distinctive contribution to future development. In the various spheres of intercultural reflection which we have examined there is the intellectual justification for a holistic understanding of reality and of Christian theology as a distinctive and indispensable partner in the quest for the human future.

An intercultural theology will seek to benefit equally from the traditions of Barth and Schleiermacher, not to mention the hugely flourishing Catholic and emancipatory traditions in the last 100 years. In doing so it will reach out beyond theology to philosophical, literary and scientific models in a continuing drive for a contributing and facilitating discipline which is at the same time central to human salvation.

It will not be able to limit itself to Christian and Western concerns, even if it is able only to signal awareness of the value of other relevant data. In this study we have concentrated specifically on Christian theology in dialogue with culture. This is not to minimize the important parallel dialogue among the world religions themselves, in which Christian theology will increasingly participate, and which is itself a condition for understanding diverse cultures.

It is clear that simply to speak about openness and love will not in itself bring about openness and love. There has to be a careful intellectual strategy, and an often painful exchange of memories, hopes and expectations. It cannot be assumed, either, that the experience of misunderstanding and marginalization will in itself lead to greater capacity for understanding, though it often does so. We may recall that, in the past, for example, some of the early Puritan communities tended to repeat the patterns of coercion from which they had just escaped. In the present, Marcella Althaus-Reid, in her account of liberation theology struggling against fascism in Latin America, *Indecent Theology* (2000) shows how liberation theologians have often themselves repeated and endorsed traditional patterns of domination. No research tradition, and certainly not intercultural theology, can safely regard itself as infallible.

The Metamodern and Truth

We have concentrated on interdisciplinarity and dialogue. But can we still speak of truth? What is it for a metamodern theology to speak of truth? How can we embrace cultural pluralism and still avoid a relativism which may conceal indifference and irresponsibility? In a Christian context we come to apprehend truth in community, through worship and service, through reflection on scripture.

In the various academic disciplines truth is perceived differently in different places and at different times. It is inculturated truth. Unpromising theories often produce areas of constructive dialogue where apparently promising theories run into serious problems. For example, we may instinctively suppose that realist theories will be more amenable to theological construction than non-realist theories. Yet major theologians (Duns Scotus and Luther) have produced important work in an anti-realist or nominalist tradition. We may think that anti-realism in philosophy inevitably leads to an attenuation of classical theology, yet in one modern scholar, Michael Dummett, we see that an epistemological commitment to anti-realism can be combined with affirmation of very traditional ontology and classical theology. The truth is complex, and the beauty is as much like fragments of stained glass as it is like one integrated picture.

Traditional theories of truth have usually alternated between correspondence and coherence theories. In the tradition of Kant's philosophy, coherence theories have been favoured, and are reflected in major theologians, for example, in Schleiermacher's account of religious experience as corresponding to the impact of the presence of God, and in Barth's stress on correspondence between the Word of God and the human response. Theologians are, as we have noted, attracted to realist accounts of truth, as correlative with the promise of God in revelation.

I have recommended a postfoundational approach to knowledge. This leads me to appreciate coherence and pluralist notions of truth rather than correspondence notions, though there can be foundational pillars within the web of connections. This perspective does not imply relativism. Theology retains basic house rules for the hospitality of dialogue, which remains open to change but not in the direction of violence or totalitarianism. This is part of the political dimension which Christian faith insists on as essential to truth. (It was under Pontius Pilate, the truth seeker, after all that Jesus Christ was crucified.) Within this model different philosophical theories can be appreciated in the continuing project to seek a better understanding. It has the ability and indeed the commitment to draw from paradigms of understanding in the humanities and the sciences, from traditional and emancipatory sources.

It might be thought that a postfoundational theory is in danger of gathering up all data into a theory of everything, in a holistic web of connection which precludes pluralism, or else simply reflects the theories of a particular sub-culture, without any reference to information outside this sub-culture. This can lead to a new crypto-foundationalism, as we have seen above, but it need not do so.

There is no escape from tradition, with its continuities and with its interruptions. Awareness of a web of postfoundational connections lends new credibility to some very traditional paths to the justification of theological discourse, notably the appeal to the threefold pattern of reason, revelation and experience, adding up to a form of cumulative case. Neither an appeal to pure experience nor an appeal to the form of life within a community of faith will be sufficient in itself. All apparently brute facts are open to multiple interpretation, yet there are matters of fact, for example in history, politics and economics, which no amount of cultural readjustment can smooth away. To subsume the complex grounds of a notion like truth under a single category, such as power, may also conceal as much as it reveals. We are left with the finding that on a huge hill truth stands, as Donne saw, and whoever seeks to cut the Gordian knot, to change the metaphor, is likely to be left with a simple but very limited form of reductionism.

In the field of philosophy of religion, Henk Vroom explored these issues thoroughly in his *Religions and the Truth* (1989), and came up with something like a cumulative case. After examining truth claims in philosophical and religious traditions, he concluded that religious theories are grounded in existentials, that is permanent, universal characteristics of human existence: basic needs, basic experiences, basic insights, the tradition, and specific beliefs (ibid., 344f).

In recent philosophy, Michael Lynch (1998) has argued that it is possible to combine theory which allows for a pluralist view of truth with what he terms a 'minimalist' realism (statements are made true by facts, which simply state what is the case, without any further ontology of facts) and avoids relativism (ibid., 136f): 'I've argued that the pluralist must retain a notion of truth that is stable across conceptual schemes if she is going to allow for cross-scheme evaluation. But a relative concept of truth is by definition unstable across schemes … Just because every truth is relative to a scheme, this does not imply that our concept of truth is "truth-for-C". All truths are relative, yes, but our concept of truth need not be a relative concept.' More recently concepts of functionality, warranted assertibility and superassertibility have been used to denote the conditions under which statements may be described as true (Lynch, 2001). Philosophers struggle to find precision where precision is hard to achieve. For Davidson, 'Truth is not a property of sentence; it is a relation between sentences, speakers and dates. To view it thus is … to relate language to the occasions of truth' (Davidson, 1994, 43f).

Yet there have always been alterative accounts, in the nominalist tradition as it were, which stresses the mystery of God, and in postmodern accounts of postfoundational truth. Typical was Nicholas Rescher's *The Coherence Theory of Truth*: 'In contrast to the foundationalist approach, the coherence theory dispenses with any basic, foundational truths of fact' (Rescher, 1973, 318). This allows for fallibility without falling into scepticism.

Of course the tradition of analytical philosophy is by no means the only contender for critical study of truth. For Nietzsche, truth is a word for 'a will to overcome that has no end in itself … a word for the will to power' (Nietzsche, 1967, 552) Truth is judged not by inherent qualities but by practical utility. There is no ultimate truth. For William James, truth is always to be related to practical life, but this does provide basic values. For Heidegger, truth is the unconcealing of the concealed nature of things. For Derrida, truth is signalled by recognition of difference. For Wittgenstein, the truth of a proposition hinges on its use.

For Foucault, '"Truth is no doubt a form of power" My problem is to see how men govern (themselves and others) by the production of truth. I would like in short to resituate the production of true and false at the heart of historical analysis and political critique' (Burchell *et al.*, 1991, 79).

After surveying the field, Barry Allen concluded that truth has no abstract value: 'Truth has no value apart from whatever is built, destroyed, sustained or impeded with what passes for true. Truth has no power of its own, no affinity for good, and will not make us free' (Allen, 1993).

What, then, has become of the traditional affirmation that God is the truth, and that Christ is the way, the truth and the life? Christians in community believe that in God's purpose for humanity Jesus Christ plays an indispensable and decisive role. This is a pointer to mystery, a Christomorphic mystery. It seems to me that all Christians can affirm gladly and doxologically their participation in the life of the triune God in faith. The eschatological element makes clear that all our theories are only pointers in the direction of the mystery of the divine love. The socio-historical dimension of faith, with its uncertainties and its cultural and temporal limitations creates the other side of this theory of truth. We do indeed participate in the life of God, but as pilgrims on the way to a mystery, a mystery which will reveal itself in all kinds of ways in the future. Christian truth is true, but it remains a suggestion, a pointer to the Christomorphic future.

It is no part of the theologian's task to adjudicate between the working hypotheses of colleagues in other disciplines, but it belongs to the intercultural project to attempt at least to be aware of research traditions which may shed light on theological concerns, and with which theological interests may engage in dialogue. The level of dialogue will inevitably depend on the level of familiarity or education in the particular discipline in question. But at least some limited awareness of the field involved should be possible, and that is always better than complete isolation.

Notes

1 Since writing this I have come to value the distinction which Cobb and Griffin frequently make between a postmodernism of construction, which seeks to relate the physical world to notions of Christian transformation, and a postmodernism of deconstruction, which tends to concentrate on individual self-understanding.

2 This also echoes the process stress on a non-dualist approach to divine action in the cosmos. I am inclined to view process concepts as a valuable toolkit for the imagination rather than a comprehensive world view.

CHAPTER 11

The Mystery of God

It is time to bring together the diverse strands of this project in intercultural theology.

Religion, Theology and the Geopolitical Future

A critical theology of transcendence may have a valuable and unique contribution to make to the human future. But to return finally to our basic question about the secular, does transcendence need religion, or indeed theology? It has sometimes been suggested that a 'this worldly transcendence', such as occurs when a piece of music, an amazing landscape or some other phenomenon evokes a sense of wonder and mystery, may be all the transcendence we need. It has also been suggested that a concept such as eternity may give us a sense of perspective, which may enable us to order our lives and our society in a more balanced manner. These sorts of proposals may be welcomed without qualification. Yet Christians, and indeed members of other religious faiths, have understood transcendence to be awareness of a response to something that is beyond us. For Christianity this is a response to the God of Jesus Christ.

We have noted throughout that religion is in many ways an ambiguous phenomenon, producing bad results as well as good in human life. We have seen how alliances of religion against humanism and communism in the 1930s could lead some (though by no means all) who took up this stance to sympathy with fascism. There is a clear link between certain sorts of religion and totalitarian regimes. To this extent Karl Barth in the Christian tradition was quite right to raise questions about the ambiguity of religion, questions later to be pursued by Dietrich Bonhoeffer. But in other hands religion could be used to subvert fascist tendencies from within, as in Paul Tillich's playing off of good German religion against bad. Karl Barth's solution, in choosing theology over religion, was in this case highly perceptive. But, theology too, could and did lead to another kind of theocratic authoritarianism. Even Christology, with its language of kenosis, is by no means immune to subversion. Foucault and others have taught us about the infinite complexity of power.

We cannot therefore guarantee the value of religion over against theology or vice versa. They may be equally subject to undemocratic transformation, and therefore may deny justice. In my view, however, there is not a stark choice between untenable perspectives and a perplexed silence. It is possible and indeed incumbent upon us to recommend appropriate religious and theological perspectives, because of their inherent enormous value for the human future. But we must offer these perspectives as recommendations, suggestions, as precious contributions for debate and development in a long-term future. In this way we can commend distinctive perspectives with enthusiasm, while seeking to avoid some of the triumphalism of the past. In the nature of the case the process will remain one of trial and error, but from a Christian perspective this should be no surprise. We expect that the Holy Spirit will guide humanity into all truth in unexpected ways which open up new and completely unanticipated futures – futures, however, which always and in every way reflect the future of the Christ, as an icon of unconditional love.

Simply having a religion or a theology, however well balanced and well informed, is after all pointless if it does not speak directly to the human condition in all and any of its circumstances. If Christ is not effectively recognizable to faith as the centre of human life and the search for ultimate meaning, the theological enterprise is simply irrelevant. If Christ is not perceived as the icon of unconditional love, the Christian contribution to the human dialogue is ineffective.

This implies critical theology and religion which embraces modernity in a critical manner, which looks forward rather than back, and which seeks the constructive among the global cultures in all their facets including their religious facets. It hopes that other religious and theological traditions will come to engage in a similar process, though the manner of that engagement will have to be worked out within each different culture.

This is by no means all that an intercultural theology has to accomplish. We have set out from the standpoint of systematic theology, with an emphasis on Christology. But systematic theology needs to be complemented by rigorous inquiry in the philosophy of religion, and by anthropological and other studies in religion, quite apart from the non-theological and non-religious dialogue partners. Any single proposal is a fragment, which gains value not only from its internal structure but from its reception. This too is part of the intercultural vision. An intercultural theology is unlikely to be adequately supported by any single strand of philosophical tradition. It requires the tension of difference in co-dependence. The temptation to cut the Gordian knot of mystery has to be resisted. Transcendence is not the prerogative of any particular intellectual or cultural framework. The further elucidation of the mystery through thinking, through conversation, through living is a central part of the Christian hope for our human future.

Integrating the Vision

What, then, are the central features of an intercultural theology? The sources may be seen first in the classical tradition of Christian faith, in the past and in the present. This includes the basic elements of reason, revelation and experience, as these develop through the past into the present, and as the present is moulded both by past tradition and by present experience. These elements go to produce religion. But theology is not fully categorized by the category of religion. Theology claims to seek to articulate a direct response in faith to the grace of God, though the invitation and the response are always indirect, always in, with and under human culture and religion. Faith is a religious category, but it understands itself as faith not in religion but in God.

The tradition is formative. It is the tradition of the gospel. Without it there can be no real development. The tradition of the gospel includes the scriptures of the Hebrew Bible and the New Testament. Without these we should have no shape in which to articulate the experience of faith, the presence in absence of God. The shape of God is given in the tradition of scripture as a shape of power in weakness, though it has often been distorted to be a shape of power in triumph, or even a manipulation through humility. It is a shape whose form will change though the content remains the content of unconditional love.

Theology remains an attempt to give reasonable grounds for faith. It is a conceptual process employing resources built up through a long and invaluable history. But it may also benefit from the conceptuality of the present, in complementing imagery derived from past cultures with the cultural and political experience, an increasingly multiform experience, of the present. But the sources of an intercultural theology reach beyond the tradition of pure theology. They include dialogue with and interaction with many of the disciplines already explored.

This includes, from the start, philosophical theology, but also the whole range of the humanities and the sciences. Intercultural theology must be prepared to learn from, must actively seek to learn from, the whole range of human scientific endeavour, and from the whole range of religious questing in human society. This is, perhaps, a continuing task for Christian theology over the next millennium.

Academic theology is important. There is an argument that what matters is a rational philosophical analysis which is not insensitive to everyday states of affairs but whose strength is in abstracting from these to pursue analytic research. A good example might be the strength in Boethius's work *On the Consolations of Philosophy*, written under the shadow of torture and execution but scarcely bearing a trace of these external circumstances. Philosophical philosophy may be the best means of throwing light not only on technical and abstract issues but upon the horrors of evil and the problems of injustice. Beyond the academic environment, however, theology may also benefit from attention to mass communications media, such as newspapers, film and television. It may be reflected that theology has always been done in 'the real world' – even medieval monasteries were constantly involved with the conflicts raised by ordinary human passions –

as Umberto Eco's *The Name of the Rose* strikingly demonstrated. Film media can highlight issues in unique and dramatic ways, for example in bringing problems of suffering, through disaster, poverty or genocide, to our direct attention. Newspapers both provide critical insight and, by the nature of their coverage, often warn us against uncritical acceptance of spin and manipulation. All of these factors are relevant to a modern intercultural theology.

What of the methods of such a project? These need not be fundamentally different from the methods of traditional theology. The new element will be the inclusion in dialogue and concept building of much non-traditional material, which will materially affect the outcomes. The aim must be theology which faces squarely the present realities of a society which is both multicultural and characterized by parallel, often mutually ignoring, cultures. There will not be a formal pattern of procedure to which all intercultural theology must subscribe, and theologies will continue to be more intercultural or less intercultural. But there will be the shape of a *research programme*, a shape determined by the search for dialogue, reciprocity and willingness to rethink and re-engage with changing cultures.

The norms of such a project will be determined by the Christomorphic shape which is the hallmark of all Christian theology and the catalysing contribution to human dialogue about the most serious issues facing humanity. Such norms are crucially inclusive. They are sensitive to cultural and political marginality, to the dialogue of world religions, to humanist projects of various sorts. But they are not infinitely inclusive. Faith remains decisively opposed to evil in all forms, to contempt for human rights and human life. But to take an extreme but still all-too-common issue, where there is genocide dialogue would often take the form only of appeasement, and be open to manipulation. On a more domestic scale, there is need for law enforcement in civil society. Sometimes, as Reinhold Niebuhr famously noted, there is no escape from using the lesser evil of coercion to prevent greater evils occurring to the most vulnerable groups of people. This is part of the fractured nature of the world as we know it.

Intercultural theology is not new but it is in urgent need of renewal. We noted that Augustine was in one sense a classically intercultural theologian, engaging in dialogue implicit and explicit with the cultures around him. But his was also a hegemonic theology, of a sort inevitable in the period. It is concerned to find a master thread which will bring everything into a Christian order of Christendom. More recent and more open intercultural theologies must include Troeltsch and Tillich. In many ways their projects, critically re-examined and developed, remain exemplary for a modern theology. A major question mark, both decisive and radically misleading, was raised by the counter-cultural theology of Karl Barth. Not all assimilation with culture will do. But equally, there is no theology which stands above culture and remains 'pure' (as Barth himself would on occasion acknowledge). The work of Troeltsch and Tillich has been out of fashion, in part because they consciously dialogued with contemporary sources which themselves immediately developed. Their weaknesses are not an invitation to build some new metaphysical bypass, but to concentrate on their legacy with renewed vigour and critical sensitivity. In many ways the work of David Tracy, with its powerful combination of critical dialogue and Christian vision, is perhaps the best modern example.

If we were to imagine a comprehensive, full-scale intercultural theology, this would be encyclopaedic in scale, would be constantly upgraded and would occupy a research institute. It would correlate Christian faith with all areas of culture, with the humanities and law, the physical and the life sciences, with applied science, the social sciences, political and economic issues in modern society and developments in the major world religions. It would run comparative dialogue with past cultures and traditions, and it would take account of the perspectives and interests of many different sub-cultures within the major cultures. Clearly such a project cannot easily be realized.

However, it is entirely possible to engage with intercultural dialogue in relation to a limited field, while maintaining a lively awareness that the intercultural may take other shapes in relation to significantly different dialogue partners. Thus, for example, a dialogue involving religion and literature may differ in important respects from, and overlap in other respects with, a dialogue involving the insights of Black theology. Both the commonalities and the specific differences, and the relationship between these, are essential to the process. In this way, an intercultural study should be a vehicle for a maximally critically reflective theology.

I have stressed the connection between the quest for transcendence and the quest for human rights. What happens when universal human rights are realized? Simply because human rights have been achieved in a given area this does not solve the question of transcendence. The Christomorphic shape of faith points to a continuing invitation to reflect on the mystery of God and of the human future in its various cultural dimensions. But the clearing away of injustice is an integral element of the Christian vision, not least where the vision has been clouded by human rights violations in the name of religion. It is not easy to attend to theological dimensions in life in a situation where basic human issues appear to be being ignored. Here Christian theology must learn a measure of humility from groups which advocate human rights in the teeth of continuing religious bigotry, and emancipatory theology has tried to build on these insights. Equally, human rights violations are of course as common among non religious groups as among the religious – witness the mass murders in Stalin's Russia and Mao's China. Here the dimension of the transcendent suggests a limit to the uses of ideology, and the trace of unconditional love gives a sharp refusal to the failure to respect individuals as precious to their creator. An intercultural theology will *prioritize* the most defenceless, but will continue to engage in constructive dialogue in every area of society.

God, Transcendence and Human Flourishing

Religion is not exhausted by morality. Christians are not more moral than others. If we were to reach a position in which all the goals of personal and social justice were achieved, faith would still have a central role to play in Christian life. Faith, Christian and other, is concerned with transcendence. A belief in transcendence will not in itself make for humane praxis or human flourishing. The world is full of religious bigots who have an unshakable faith in divine transcendence, in Christian cases linked to the figure of Jesus Christ, and there are other bigots who do not believe in divine transcendence. Metaphysical and logical categories may be morally neutral, but they are essential for creating the frameworks by which we think about and act towards the world in which we live.

Christian theology is committed to transcendence. It asserts the reality of a unique being who has created the cosmos and sustains it in being. God is the source of all that is is beyond human culture, yet is apprehended in, with and under human cultural activity and culture-based thinking. The culture in which we think transcendence influences, though it need not entirely determine, the way in which we imagine transcendence. It becomes important to develop a critical frame of mind, a research programme with a built in hermeneutic of suspicion, in order to evaluate and, if appropriate, embrace new ideas. This will include awareness of the cultural history of such notions, together with a constant critical appraisal of the plausibility criteria of particular cultures. Christianity has its own distinctive contribution to understanding transcendence and immanence.

The hard-won achievements of a humane society are not to be squandered lightly. When this happens, we see the results in holocaust. Respect for persons and for human rights, fought for and argued for from Aristotle to the Enlightenment and beyond, are among the most valuable of human accomplishments. Yet for Christian faith there remains also the importance of transcendence, of that which is beyond, the goal of life in the purpose of the God creator. A sense of transcendence is certainly not sufficient for human flourishing. Many of those in human history who have been most certainly conscious of transcendence have also been extremely narrow-minded, self-centred and prejudiced. Yet taking account of transcendence is necessary to the Christian understanding of the world as a gift, which comes from God and which belongs to God. How in an intercultural context can we develop a critical theology of transcendence?

From Human Rights to Divine Transcendence

This dilemma is profoundly articulated by Charles Taylor in *A Catholic Modernity* (1999) and in his response to comments on that paper. The argument goes like this: redemption happens through incarnation, the weaving of God's life into human lives, but these human lives are different. Complementarity and identity will both be part of our ultimate oneness. Our great historical temptation has been to forget the *complementarity*, to go straight for the sameness, making as many people as possible into 'good Catholics', and in the process failing catholicity. Taylor tries to look at the Enlightenment as Matteo Ricci looked at Chinese civilization in the sixteenth century: 'The view I'd like to defend, if I can put it in a nutshell, is that in modern, secularist culture there are mingled both authentic developments of the Gospel, of an Incarnational mode of life, and also a closing off to God that negates the Gospel' (16). The problem is in the project of Christendom, the attempt to marry the faith with a form of culture and a mode of society.

> The first danger that threatens an exclusive humanism, which wipes out the transcendent beyond life, is that it provokes as reaction an immanent negation of life. The point of things isn't exhausted by life. Suffering and death help us to affirm something that matters beyond life. We may lose 'the crucial nuance'. The Christian conscience experiences a mixture of humility and unease: the humility in realizing that the break with Christendom was necessary for this great extension of gospel-inspired actions; the unease in the sense that the denial of transcendence places this action under threat. (26)

There is a revolt against the modern affirmation of life in Nietzsche. This is a turn to violence, which may perhaps only be escaped by a turn to transcendence. We make very high demands for universal solidarity today, but how do we manage it? Self-worth has limitations. Philanthropy may turn to coercion, unless there is unconditional love of the beneficiaries (33). Christian spirituality points in faith to a way out 'either as a love or compassion that is unconditional, or as one based on what you are most profoundly, a being in the image of God. 'Our being in the image of God is also our standing among others in the stream of love, which is that facet of God's life we try to grasp, very inadequately, in speaking of the Trinity' (35).

Taylor responds in a later chapter to reflections given upon his lecture. He speaks of the insufficiency of human flourishing as the unique focus of our lives. But he appreciates also the affirmation of ordinary life, the new forms of inwardness and the 'rights culture'. Much modern philosophy has been 'monological'. But the goods discovered in community, 'together-goods', are important (113). It is important to strive for complementarity, and not to be content with incommensurability, as in Foucault's 'completely solo operation'. In a rights culture, the good of solidarity may be neglected. We may then look for moral sources, and find the importance of the love of God.

It is important to struggle for transcendence, and not to take its characterization for granted in the contemporary world (a similar plea for a contemporary understanding of transcendence was articulated in Ronald Gregor Smith's neglected but valuable last book, *The Doctrine of God*, in 1970). But such a search will not cut ice in contemporary society unless it shows full awareness of the triumphalism of much ecclesiastical practice, as much in the present as in the past. No writer has shown a more keen awareness of this than Mary Grey, not least in her reflection on the Church, *Beyond the Dark Night*.

It is important to put people rather than structure at the heart of the church, not least when there is fragmentation everywhere in culture and society. Rudolfo Cardenal spoke of 'the crucified peoples'; Grey stresses the importance of 'gathering the fragments'. She recalls Etty Hillesum, who wanted to be the 'thinking heart of the concentration camp'(Grey, 1997, 17), and invokes Christ who 'gathers the fragments'.

Grey reflects on M.K. Taylor's *Remembering Esperanza* (1990). This is by any account an important text for an intercultural theology. There are three dimensions of postmodern theology which need a theological response: these – which he calls a postmodern trilemma – are a sense of tradition, the celebration of plurality, and resistance to domination. Communal following of Christ presents one counter-cultural challenge to the ethics of individualism and competitive materialism (ibid., 40). Grey repeats the kabbalistic story of sin, expressed by the broken fragments of creation. Redemption, conversely, is seen as gathering the fragments, as *tikkun olam*, the process of mending and healing (ibid., 42).

Theology will bring to the table the admission that it too has had and still has oppressive structures. The issue of a strategy to combat structures of oppression from within is tackled effectively by Mark Taylor. (1990, esp. 111f, 157f). Taylor writes powerfully of the Christ of emancipatory reconciliation and of 'refiguring Christ for today's Christopraxis'. Christianity mirrors discontinuity as well as continuity. This is powerfully argued by Anthony Bartlett in his *Cross Purposes* (2001, 259).

> It is discontinuity that is at the heart of Christianity, the abysmal isolation of Jesus where the time-shattering possibility of love, of absolute gift, is generated. From the discontinuity of Christ arises the gift of continuity for all others by his breath, his spirit, his bottomless gift of life.

Intercultural may on occasion mean counter-cultural: For Mary Grey 'The passion for justice-making which is at the heart of the process of transformation is of its essence counter-cultural' (Grey, 1997, 93). Breaking the deadlock will demand new models of authority and leadership in the Church. 'It is here that the darkest hour of the long Dark Night is experienced' (ibid., 116).

Miriam and the many women who have gone before her as leaders have been 'not just un-remembered, but dismembered' (ibid., 121). Jesus is the kenosis of patriarchy (ibid., 124). The way forward is through dimensions of ecclesia in journeying, dwelling, traditioning, transforming and dreaming (ibid., 132). She cites Karl Rahner: to be fully human is to be oriented to the mystery of transcendent being (ibid., 135). It is Christ, transformer of culture, who blazes the trail (ibid., 136).

After the dark night, and the night which Eli Wiesel so starkly documented, it might be thought that there can be no return to transcendence. Invocation of transcendence is simply too dangerous for human beings. It is right that we should remain aware of the capacity for the catastrophic, but the abuse does not take away the proper use. Once we have made the critical effort to discount the negative, there is no reason, either, why we should not continue to learn from such classic theologians of transcendence as Augustine and Aquinas. There is some chance that we may see where they are not to be followed. It is much harder to see where we ourselves go wrong.

In a Christian contribution to understanding of transcendence, the Christological matrix of love, peace and justice, of vulnerability and generosity, leads us to construe goodness in the created order as the goodness of self-giving, self-affirming love, and evil as its negation and denial. Seeing human beings through the image of God in Jesus Christ, we may see occasions for self-giving love in human relations as pointers to transcendence.

Transcendence is not characterized as difference from human love, but as its source, inspiration and ground. As human beings experience this sense of the givenness of what is good in their lives and in the lives of fellow human beings, they affirm the active presence of the transcendent God. They do this in correlating rationality and experience with the tradition and narratives of the Christian community. They offer this construal as a contribution to a wider, intercultural, understanding of transcendence. They believe that it faithfully conveys what is at the heart of ultimate reality.

A critical intercultural theology of transcendence will affirm the presence of the Christian God in such a way as always to acknowledge other understandings of transcendence, and to respect these as far as they share in rejection of violence, coercion and domination. It will insist that the transcendence of God has nothing to do with violence and coercion. It will encourage a generous and pluriform manifestation of human community, unfettered by prescribed forms of religious conformity. It will see this freedom as a gift of the free grace of God.

Such a sense of transcendence may on occasion be counter-cultural. It is common for some forms of exclusive traditional Christianity to stress that their action is counter-cultural, while at the same time identifying closely with commercial and media interests which are a typical manifestation of a late capitalist culture. It is important that such notions as cultural and counter-cultural are subject to critical examination. Our intuitive notions may turn out to be misplaced.

How are we to recognize the dimension of transcendence and respond to it appropriately? Sometimes it may be at crisis points in the lives of individuals and societies that openness to transcendence occurs. Yet there is much value in the biblical metaphor of the still small voice. We like our religious notions and practices to manifest certainty and decisiveness, yet we know from historical appearances that such apparently unambiguous occasions and events are often deceptive. The presence of God is not in our power to command. It is always there, in the ways in which God through the various religious traditions has promised to be present, for Christians as the presence of self-giving, self-affirming love in our world. A vision which is not strident, dominating or controlling may still be an immensely persistent, persuasive and effective vision for the future of human flourishing. Such a vision may be an effective means of delivering basic rights, understood as the standards the God of self-giving love promises to all his creatures, for it will not be deflected by unusual events or by unexpected obstacles. It will expect just to continue to be there.

Human Actions/Divine Action

It would be unwise to suggest that, because human rights has become a focal issue of political ethics in recent years, it must therefore be *the* key entry point to questions of transcendence and of God. These are both different and related issues. It is true that the Christian tradition, along with other religious traditions, has usually envisaged God as making his existence and presence known through acting in history, prompting response through particular clusters of events. The difficulty is to find adequate grounds to justify the connection. The history of claims of divine action through particular ideas, religious bodies or political parties scarcely inspires confidence.

Christianity, again along with other religions, has always understood God as involved with the created order at many levels. Continuing with due caution, I propose an approach to transcendence and to talk of God which will connect directly with the importance of human rights as part of a movement towards the fulfilment of God's purpose for creation. In almost every generation there are new challenges to any sort of talk of God. Talk of God is multifaceted, and always needs to be developed over a broad range of issues. This discussion will focus on the issues raised by our study of religion and culture.

Systematic theology at the beginning of the twenty-first century is a fragmented discipline. There are clusters of interest around terms which loosely denote traditional allegiances, notably neo-orthodoxy in the wake of Barth, radical orthodoxy in the steps of Milbank, combinations of philosophy with conservative theology in the thinking of Alston, Helm, Swinburne and others. There are other, much less prominent groupings, including a new progressive tradition, to which this study owes most affinity. All of these groups have useful, often directly contradictory, points to make, and these need to be taken into account in any new proposal.

God in Christian reflection is the creator and reconciler of the universe, origin and sustainer of all that is, complex in Godself as Father, Son and Holy Spirit, incarnate in Jesus Christ, participating in crucifixion and death under Pontius Pilate and in resurrection, creating faith, destroying evil and effecting human transformation through love towards an eschatological fulfilment. As such, God is to be trusted, worshipped and looked to as the source and ground of human flourishing, personal and social, political and economic. God is self-giving, self-affirming love, acting in unconditional generosity. This would include the whole area of human rights. I think that there are grounds to affirm this complex image of God. But these grounds are anything but self-evident, and need to be re-imagined in every generation.

I concentrate here on the interface between human and divine action, especially in relation to human rights. But, since being and action are inextricably linked, something should be said here of divine being.

God is. God is s/he who is. God's existence is not exactly like human existence, but is, the Christian tradition tells us, analogous to human existence. The nature of the analogy remains mysterious to us, but it is there. God's being, as Aquinas appreciated, is act in being. It is also, as more recent theology emphasizes, being in action. The paradigm of being in action for the Christian tradition is incarnation. Christian theology is Christomorphic, but it is Christomorphic in an inclusive rather than an exclusive sense, for it is concerned with God's presence in all human history, from the narratives of the Hebrew Bible to the present.

God's being is as the one who is present in all human history as a mysterious hidden presence, and, for Christians, Jesus Christ is the clue to recognizing such presence. In this matter Peter Hodgson's comments in *God in History* (1989) remain instructive.

> My thesis is that God is efficaciously present in the world, not as an individual agent performing observable acts, nor as a uniform inspiration or lure, nor as an abstract ideal, nor in the metaphorical role of companion or friend. Rather, God is present in specific shapes or patterns of praxis that have a configuring, transformative power within historical praxis, moving the process in a determinate direction, that of the creative unification of multiplicities of elements into new wholes, into creative syntheses that build human solidarity, enhance freedom, break systemic oppression, heal the injured and broken, and care for the natural. … What God 'does' in history is not simply to 'be there' as God, but to 'shape' – to shape a multifaceted transfigurative praxis. … These metaphorical *Gestalten* are not empirically visible but they have a power to shape the world in which human beings dwell. (205)

This characterization of divine action seems to me to be persuasive, much more so than the rather speculative reflection on Hegelian Trinitarianism which precedes it. The interpretation is itself a faith interpretation, yet faith needs to be correlated with rational argument. Here I find the recent discussion of divine action in cosmological study apposite (Russell *et al.*,

1995). It is possible to conceive personal indirect divine action in ways which are neither interventionist nor purely naturalistic. In this way the impasse between existential, faith-centred interpretations which bypass dialogue with modern science and more traditional, providence-centred interpretations which welcome correlation with the physical sciences may perhaps be overcome. God may be understood as active throughout the macrocosm of the physical cosmos and also in the microcosm of human life. The creator is also the persuader of human political action.

What has all this to do with human rights, the first of our applications of intercultural theology? Have we now moved away from the practical instantiation of the gospel? Hodgson goes on to say this of shapes, Gestalten:

> At the overt, conscious level they serve as the actual shapes in which what we think, do and say appears in the world. The civil rights struggle in the 1960's produced such a gestalt, which initially functioned overtly as the guiding ideal of the participants in the movement, but which has become woven into the American public consciousness in such a way that later attempts to subvert the gains of that struggle by packing the Supreme Court, for example, have proved unsuccessful. (Hodgson, 1989, 206).[1]

It is not the case that we can attribute specific acts in political and ethical action to direct divine intervention. Nor is it the case that God's action is entirely impersonal, as a kind of master act in which everything is equally the result of divine permission. Rather, God has created the universe, and participated in his creation, in such a way that there are areas where divine and human action may tend to merge in attention to the embodiment of specific purposes, the purposes of self-giving, self-affirming love. The expressions of this love at cosmic and at anthropic levels will differ appropriately, but there will be an intrinsic correlation. The tensions between faith and reason, revelation and the mystery of faith are both real and complementary.

The position is complicated by the presence of catastrophic natural disasters and horrendous evils caused by human action. The resultant levels of unpredictability and destructive energy produce situations in which the divine purpose is frustrated. Faith believes that in these circumstances God will continue to act in love and that the divine love will eventually prevail. There is no 'answer' to the negative sides of creation. The transforming shape of divine compassion in the universe is vulnerable and is not coercive.

When we attend to human rights we are not automatically responding to the divine love. Our interpretations of appropriate Christian action do not suddenly become infallible because we use this vocabulary. But the popularity of the phrase and the debates surrounding human rights should not in my view disguise the tremendous significance of the notion, both for civil society in general and for Christian vocation within society. Ideas of freedom and liberty, we may reflect, were and are equally ambivalent. Yet notions of liberty were and are of huge significance for social development. What they need is continuing analysis, refinement and application. The same, I believe, holds for human rights. We may expect such a process to take a considerable time to evolve. But it is important that there should be a theological contribution to the discussion and a theological participation in the action.

It also becomes clear that discussion of human rights in theological perspective leads us once again to fundamental questions about the existence and the knowledge of God. It is not possible to demonstrate the existence of God by a priori deduction from rational principles. It is not possible to defend a reasoned faith simply by reference to confessional narratives. Christian faith arises from and is nurtured by attention to confessional narratives in the light of everything else that confronts us in our daily lives: experience of the physical world and of human interaction. Faith which is received and perceived as a gift from beyond ourselves leads us to include transcendence in our search for understanding. The quest for social interaction and for citizenship leads us to seek for common values and for common goods. Within the matrix of these searches focus on human rights from a Christian perspective may help us to imagine a powerful constructive relationship between ethics and transcendence, in which the one may reinforce the understanding of the other.

Not Every Shape: Christomorphic Correlation

In examining this relationship we note two features. First, attention to human rights is not of course necessary for the creation and sustaining of faith. There has been a living tradition of faith long before human rights were conceived. But secondly, the urgent modern concern for human rights, coupled with a large degree of agnosticism about the relationship if any between ethics and transcendence, provides an important opportunity for a distinctively Christian contribution to this debate. The shape of human rights is immeasurably deepened by the shape of Christ as the shape of the divine purpose for creation. Hodgson speaks of 'the shaping of ever new, fragile yet creative cultural syntheses out of the disparate elements of historical life' (1989, 207). God appears in the world in a specific though complex shape, the shape of love in freedom. The shape is formed by a conjunction of the three elements of the kingdom, the cross and the resurrection of Christ.

The Christomorphic paradigm is sharply relevant to all discussion of ethics, religion and politics. It sets the priorities as always related to those at the greatest point of need. This is especially apposite in a political context in which there is often a huge gulf between appearance and reality. For example, readers of the debate conducted in lofty tones between liberal and communitarian observers of American political theory would find it hard to imagine there the actuality of local gerrymandering and dimpled chads which appear to have characterized the 2000 presidential election. It is not enough to reflect on the need to have more Black or poor representation. It is also necessary to devise strategies for delivering a greater participation in political and social action on the part of the disadvantaged. In principle the churches, with their wide coverage of the social and political spectrum, should be able to be vehicles of conscientization at every level. There is clearly a serious danger that disenchantment may lead in time to new forms of authoritarian movements. Abuse of democracy does not take away its proper use.

Here we come back to the Christian awareness that faith is sometimes effective despite the appearance of things. Most of the time we can see only fragments, sometimes hardly a trace, of a Christomorphic element in the complexities of society. The situation could hardly be further removed from the triumphalism which has often characterized Christianity, liberal and conservative alike. Yet it is the Christian vision which 'traces the rainbow through the rain' and may provide an antidote to indifference, lethargy and despair. This is a *trace* which, from a Christian perspective, we may recognize in other religions and in humanist action, where we recognize the lineaments of the signature of the divine love. Such lineaments are, however, more likely to be found in concrete and coordinated instances of attention to grinding poverty than in sentimental reflection.

I have suggested that generosity may be understood in a wider framework than economic generosity. This is not to suggest, however, that economics is not vitally important as a lever of action in our capitalist society. By facilitating economic independence and economic power in marginalized groups, we may do something to redress balances and necessary equality: people are all too often forced into poverty and then despised for being poor, a fate allotted to non-white peoples for centuries. This is in the nature of the case a difficult task. In the case of Judaism, the economic muscle of a marginalized community was turned into a fresh excuse for hate. But, as we saw in the case of transnational corporations, economic power is a resource for change, good or bad, which is not to be underestimated. It has consequences, too, for a wide range of important environmental considerations.

The notion of a divine shaping of history was, as Peter Hodgson has well demonstrated, central to the theology of Ernst Troeltsch. Why, then, has it not been developed more effectively? Part of an answer lies in the fact that the idea of a divine shaping was developed all too effectively in ideologies associated with National Socialism, and indeed with Marxist determinism. Not every shape will do. That is why there is insistence here on a divine shaping, not as an exclusive constraint, but as paradigmatic of a quality of loving concern which can be recognized and welcomed elsewhere.

It is through a conception of divine action, for Christian faith through a sense of the Christomorphic shape in history, social, political and personal, that an intercultural theology comes to speak most readily of God. In the intercultural interaction of theology with the arts there is a puzzle about the mysterious nature of transcendence, which can be construed in different ways, but which Christian faith relates to a personal God. In relation to politics and human rights, in the experience of minority and marginalized peoples, issues of transcendence arise and are pointers for faith to God. In relation to the natural sciences, especially cosmology, issues of ultimate significance on a cosmic and on a human level are again related to divine action. In the theology of religions and in dialogue with secularization, in all these areas an intercultural theology points to a re-imagined concept of God.

This is not to say that more traditional theologies may not also assist in the apprehension of God in a contemporary culture, both in themselves and as part of a wider intercultural interaction. But for many thinking people in the twenty-first century an intercultural understanding of God becomes increasingly attractive and indeed imperative, if they are to sustain faith in the modern world. In such an intercultural theology a Christian understanding of God as self-giving love may also be helpful to those who do not share fully in the Christian vision, either from secular or alternative religious perspectives, as a profound dimension of understanding of both our corporate human condition and the nature of transcendence. At the same time, the Christian perspective may be enriched, critiqued and deepened by dialogue in reciprocity with other angles on transcendence. What is envisioned here is not a mixture, amalgam or reduction, but an agonistic and constructive mutual search for understanding. This is not an easy task, and is one littered with the wrecks of previous ventures. It is a project whose aims are fairly constant, but whose realization calls for fresh perspectives at regular intervals.

William Pitt famously called the New World into being to redress the balance of the Old. It may be through the reciprocal interaction of classical structures and postmodern issues that we can struggle through to a model of transformative Christian faith. We shall not succeed by reiterating ancient cultural stereotypes. We shall not produce an integrative framework, either, by concentrating alone on minorities, however necessary our attention to the margins may be. It is through the catalytic interaction of the traditional mainstream with new forms of the quest for faith that we are most likely to find a form of Christian life which is both catholic in its sympathies and alert to the special needs of marginalized groups within our churches and our society. It is a time, in other words, to keep our nerve and avoid apocalyptic solutions. The apocalyptic can be immensely instructive, as Catherine Keller (1996) has reminded us. But we must also seek to keep the faith by patient and single-minded persistence. God, after all, is Christlike, and we are called to find and to encourage the likeness of Christ in each of our fellow human beings. Historical experience shows that neither a minimal Christology nor a maximal Christology will necessarily help us with this task. It is only through reciprocity and mutuality in dialogue that we are likely to find

Christlikeness in difference, the differences which are constitutive of effective relationality.

'Give me someone I can trust.' Much postmodern thought has focused so much on theory that it has difficulty in relating to the life world of real communities, and the task of supporting open and energetic progressive Christian communities. Trust arises in different ways in different contexts, sometimes by a process of trial and error. In the search for a deeper understanding of the Spirit of Christlikeness, we have to examine the biblical material relating to the events concerning Jesus within the cultural mix in which it arises, and against the background of the tradition from which we ourselves work. We must listen to interpreters of this material and its significance in cultures other than our own, including non-Christian cultures. And then we must make an assessment. What has changed is the need to cast the net of material ever more widely, and to become self-aware about our methods and their implications for results. What we regard as Christlikeness will still be determined by our view of the resurrection, the death and the life of Jesus. We shall still need to reinterpret the major symbols of Christological interpretation: new creation, atonement, cosmic redemption, sacrifice and reconciliation, not least through the experience of the traditionally marginalized. Our view of the life of Jesus will be given deeper perspective by being related to lives in some ways very different from our own, and our view of the particularity of biblical imagery will be changed by awareness of its impact on cultures different from our own. The actualization of friendship, solidarity, compassion and commitment – all the elements of human love and generosity – may be deepened through intercultural exchange. In a conversation which includes the well-being of all humanity, this may be the exchange which responds to the 'wonderful exchange' of God's love in Christ.

The Mystery of the Divine Love

Intercultural theology is necessarily drawn to render an account of its relation to culture in its numerous varieties and sub-divisions. It must also render an account of traditional imagery concerning the nature of God. What contribution can it make to traditional talk of God as Trinity, and of the divine attributes? What can it say of the traditional doctrines of creation and salvation, and of the problem of evil?

Of course intercultural Christian theology itself arises out of the classical theological tradition, which itself mirrors the expression of faith through changing cultures. Though intercultural theology is especially focused on the variety of contemporary expression, it must always be prepared for genuine dialogue with communities which adhere to older and more closely defined expressions of belief, with conservative believers of every sort. It will also engage directly with cultural dialogues in the past, understanding tradition as *transformative* as well as interpretative, illuminating through rupture as well as continuity.

God in Christian understanding is a mystery whose content is transcendent self-giving, self-affirming love. This love is shaped by the matrix of generosity and vulnerability, by a quest for justice and solidarity with the marginalized. The vital role of the margins in a Christian framework has perhaps always been implicit in faith, but has been underscored in the emancipatory tradition, not least in the light of the apocalyptic scale of the evils of the twentieth century (though of course the last century also saw huge steps for human welfare).

The divine mystery has been centrally characterized in Christianity by the image of the Trinity. There has been emphasis on personhood, selfhood in relationship and community, in the various forms of the doctrine. All of this can be taken up and welcomed in an intercultural context, but with the critical gloss, learned from the experience of cultural hegemony, that the community is a community which can embrace diversity, in which there are no marginalized persons, but only a complementarity. This conception is basic to classical Trinitarian doctrine, but its implications have been often overlooked.

We may not extrapolate from our preferred political patterns to the nature of God, to envisage a social democratic triumvirate to all eternity. Yet a God whose nature and actions are less sensitive to the human condition than the best of human thought and action can be neither respected nor worshipped by intelligent beings; for Christian faith, the Christomorphic paradigm is the icon of God's unconditional generosity. This generosity is God's nature. It is both self-subsisting and self-relating. How this is so remains the divine mystery.

The triune pattern expresses God's responsible care for all that is in the cosmos. An intercultural doctrine of creation will situate the biblical creation narratives, as with all biblical imagery, in their cultural context and then seek to re-imagine them, in a process of demythologizing and remythologizing. Creative transcendence points to God from within artistic transcendence, from within cosmological complexity, from within the mystery of suffering and reconciliation in the emancipatory quest. This does not mean that all creation necessarily point to God: clearly not, for the theodicy problem, and especially omnipresence of luck, good and bad, and random evil, raises a question mark against all romanticism. But the Christomorphic trace enables those who recognize it to cope with the created order and see it as not totally inconsistent with the divine love.

At one level, intercultural theology takes away some of the edge of the problem of evil, for it does not expect instant solutions from divine intervention in particular instances of evil. But it re-imagines the infinite sorrow of the unconditionally loving God in the face of the inevitable inequities caused by the random factors in the created order and the frequent abuse of freedom through human wickedness. None of this pain is a matter of indifference to God.

Read from an intercultural perspective, the traditional attributes of God undergo subtle but significant change. Here the emancipatory vision of feminist theology is particularly apposite. The attributes have traditionally been read in terms of cultural patriarchy, thus reinforcing the patriarchal imagery of the biblical narratives. In this way a spin has been given to Christian theology which has disadvantaged all but the dominating groups in every society in which it has functioned as a powerful ideology.

An intercultural theology will open up the tensions inherent in narratives of victory in human development, by listening to the voices of the voiceless in every age. Faith points to the shallowness of a reading of humanity in terms of the survival of the fittest. It meditates on God's eschatological recapitulation of salvation for the losers in history. In the re-reading of the history and development of doctrine the dimension of comparative theology, in which the creation and salvation narratives of the world religions are read together with the Christian tradition, may be increasingly productive. This need not bring assimilation, but should produce a deepening of perspective.

Reflection on creation as the fulfilment of God's good purpose for the flourishing of the cosmos and of humanity inevitably raises the question of evil, random and deliberate. The traditional narratives of sin and fall attempt, sometimes movingly in powerful interpretations, to cope with these issues. Yet their attempt to compensate for chaos by focusing on an elect remnant of humanity inevitably tends to the marginalization of the remainder. Karl Barth's imaginative strategy of concentrating all election on Jesus Christ, and potentially of all humanity through him, represents a profound attempt to face the problems while saving the narratives. Yet, however wrapped in expressions of humility, it is always in danger of exclusivity and elitism.

We come then to the goal of cosmic and human fulfilment, to the doctrine of salvation. According to St Paul we are saved, being saved and to be saved. There is already salvation because God has encompassed the cosmos and all humanity in his creative will which is simultaneously salvific, to bring all that is to a goal of love, peace and justice. We are being saved because that purpose is being worked out in every generation. The trace of unconditional love is there in every context, often hidden but still present. We are to be saved because the process is to be continued at different levels in the future. This will not shed direct light on scientific cosmologies of unpleasant cosmic endings, but it offers an invaluable sense of direction. The trace of love is not there for a culmination without meaning.

In an intercultural perspective, there emerges something of value in each of the traditional approaches to Christology in a pluralist culture. There is a *particula veri* in the exclusivist option. For Christian theology the presence of Christ is an indispensable and unique element in human and cosmic salvation. Only he could do what he did. *Remoto Christo*, there is incalculable loss. There is something too in an inclusivist perspective. Other figures have been and are inspired by God to act towards the final salvific purpose. These are depicted in the world religions and in wider human endeavour. There is something in a pluralist perspective. The perspectives of those at the margins of traditional structures may produce new insights for all. This is not a question of reduction or assimilation, but of genuine dialogue in openness and reciprocity.

In a Christian theology the death and resurrection of Jesus Christ are not the end of the story of salvation. The spirit of *Christlikeness* is released throughout the cosmos and brings a transformative dimension to everything that it touches. This understanding of spirit may be related in dialogue with spiritual dimensions in the major world religions and cannot be arbitrarily restricted. In Christian worship the presence of the spirit is understood as presence focused in word and sacrament. David Tracy has spoken of the mystical and the prophetic dimensions of the divine mystery. This encapsulates well the need for worship coupled with political and social witness. This remains basic, but may be open to communication with other worship centres. It is generous but not without definition: it cannot be correlated with forms of spirituality which run counter to the shape of unconditional love. It is committed to community but not to every spirit, every religion, every form of spirituality.

In human terms, the spirit of God is always seeking to create community, but only the unforced community of the divine love. Since human community usually appears to require a measure of coercion in order to function effectively (national law and international law, for example), there will always be an inherent tension between the divine spirit and our efforts at community, not least spiritual community. But this tension is also an opportunity for growth, and a source of unexpected grace. Within human community there is inevitably endless plurality – of religious communities, political and national communities, interest groups of innumerable kinds. It is not the role of religion to construct one great and definitive community, but to encourage the fruitful interaction, again in very different ways, of communities reflecting widely differing cultural patterns

There remains a fundamental correlation between our understanding of divine transcendence and of human flourishing in community. This relationship requires a continuing search for deeper understanding at every level. It is a search which a responsible theology is always bound to pursue as a constructive contribution to God's future for creation.

An intercultural theology will be a welcoming theology which seeks to find community and commonality across a broad spectrum of human endeavour. But it will not be an undiscriminating theology. Unconditional love remains opposed to all injustice, violence and coercion. There will be strong and explicit disagreement with communities which practise coercion and with theories which justify violence, not least when this is done in the name of religion. There may be times when dialogue is just not possible without compromising truth: a classic example is Barth's clear opposition to the Nazis. But it belongs to the nature of intercultural theology that it seeks to engage in constructive argument wherever possible, that it does not write off people as utterly incapable of discussion. It knows that it is not infallible, and that not everyone can be expected to share the intercultural perspective. It remembers the triumphalism which has dogged so much of even the most well meaning Christian theology through the ages.

It may be objected that opposition to triumphalism can go too far. When God disappears in the kenosis of kenosis much that is of enduring value goes too, and may be lost in an undifferentiated mysticism. We have to be aware that even the best concepts have their advantages and disadvantages. Concentration on the divine humility may simply mask oppressive features, while concentration on the negation of negation may turn into a new kind of logical tyranny. There is no escape from the need to justify beliefs with reasonable argument, while preserving a sane awareness that different things may seem reasonable to different people. The spirit of love makes possible the transformation of kenosis into faith.[2]

The Quest for God

The centre of Christian theology remains faith's quest for understanding God. What shape does the classical doctrine of God take in the perspective of intercultural theology? The development of a comparative theology, in which the imagery of other religions is examined to illustrate contrast and challenge traditional patterns, is an important addition. In a similar way the emancipatory perspectives call for critical revision of the traditional images of dominant groups, and underline the limits of anthropomorphic language. When we speak of the being and action of God we are always free to use the imagery which speaks most directly to us, but we may not consider our own imagery to have exclusive rights over alternative perspectives. Above all, we may be able to learn the difficult task of engaging with cultures and ideas strange to us without colonizing them for our predetermined schemas. We must make our own selections, but we should be able to alter our hypotheses to accommodate new truth, and to respect the mystery of God.

God's being is the ground of the being of the universe and of ourselves. God's being is the shape of divine love. As unconditional love it is able to communicate at levels which are personal, and encompasses selfhood and personality in Godself. How this is so, and how this self-differentiating personhood relates to the total divine mystery we do not know. The Christian tradition has produced voluminous reflection on the triune being of God, reflecting biblical pointers to God as creator, reconciler and sanctifying spirit. Much of this writing helps Christians to understand their faith, but it is only an *eschatological symbol*, not a mirror image of God.

In this conception God not only exists but is active at various levels within the cosmos, which is understood as his creation. Once again no single paradigm of divine action will suffice. On a human level people may act in different ways at different times, and even at the same time. God's action would appear to be infinitely more multifaceted. An intercultural theology may provide a natural barrier to our common tendency to try to comprehend divine action in one particular pattern. This can lead to our distrust of new developments in human discovery, which we may regard as contrary to God's will. We look back to a long theological past, rarely reflecting that we may be only at the beginning of a longer theological future. An intercultural theology looks back in order to look forward to a long-term future.

Central to a Christian intercultural theology is the Christological dimension. The shape of theology is inseparably related to the man Jesus of Nazareth. It is through the particular, culturally determinate life of this individual that the decisive clue to the Christian understanding of humanity and of God is given. There is a recognizable content and a recognizable form. But the form of Christ in the world may be etched in different cultures in different ways. This is an inclusive rather than an exclusive form, an open invitation to an open dialogue. Premature attempts to foreclose the sphere of Christomorphic dialogue are contrary to the nature of its subject. In this sense an intercultural theology inherits basic elements of the liberal theological paradigm. It maintains a critical as well as a constructive relationship with the concerns of modernity.

An intercultural theology is a theology of the spirit. It stresses the active transforming presence of God to every situation, however promising or bleak that situation may be. But it does not endorse or underwrite every spirit. The spirit named in Christian theology is without exception the spirit of Christlikeness, a spirit of compassion, generosity and reconciliation. As such an intercultural theology may be equally critical of appeals to spiritual and to secular values. All depends on the specification of the appeal to spirit. The spirit of Christlikeness may be understood in dialogue and reciprocity with other spiritual traditions in the world religions. It is a spirit which is open to engagement, though intolerant of evil and persecution. As such it constitutes a challenge to what is often seen as spiritual, both in Christianity and in other religious traditions. As a spirit of truth, it does not confuse a genuine search for mutual understanding with indifferent acceptance of unexamined disagreement.

As concerned with a spirit of mutuality, an intercultural theology is committed to the building of community. It is not simply concerned with the floating of intellectual frameworks for the amusement of a handful of theological professionals. This community is a community whose texture is open to overlappings and differences between sub-groups at many levels. It is especially sensitive to the dangers of holistic and totalitarian ideologies, and the inevitable dualisms which they produce. It respects the beliefs of sub-groups along the whole religious spectrum, while retaining a preference for dialogue and interactive participation. In addition to religious groupings, it sees the strengthening of community and the development of civil society as steps in the direction of the fulfilment of the divine purpose for humanity.

Christian community is concerned with the maintenance of loving relationships, both internally and externally, but it is also concerned with the worship of God, traditionally focused on the medium of word and sacrament. In reflecting on the shape of the worshipping community and on the nature of worship, an intercultural theology will be an ecumenical theology which celebrates unity in diversity. This will involve both respecting denominational traditions and cultures, from the margins of the *ecumene* as well as from the large traditional denominations, and seeking common commitment in ways which go beyond simply living side by side in parallel cultures.

In such a reflection distinctive Christian beliefs may be re-imagined and developed through dialogue with the worshipping traditions of other religions and the cultural analysis of a variety of disciplines. The role of such dialogue would not be to weaken the distinctiveness of Christian worship and community, but to make it more genuinely open and to enable it to deepen its own self-understanding. Both the invitation of the gospel through preaching and the invitation to the hospitality of the eucharist will remain integral to a mature intercultural theology, as icons of the invitation and the hospitality of God within the whole created order. Eucharist is always an offer of hospitality, never a demand for attention. Concentration on the deepening of faith and concentration on engagement with a variety of human cultural activities are not competing but complementary Christian tasks. In this way an intercultural theology may serve humanity by being what it is, not a sociological or cultural analysis as such but a Christian theological perspective on God and God's loving purposes for creation.

A Christian intercultural theology has a distinctive, dialogical shape. Central to it are the structuring elements of Christian faith, but it does not have a fixed structure, a fractal pattern in all its dimensions. It emphatically does not seek to grasp elements of culture here and there in order to rebaptize them for its hegemonic purposes. It is not another intellectual spin-off from a Christendom ideal. The nature of the dialogue with different cultures and with different disciplines may also vary widely, be more direct or much more indirect. It may be more than 'only connect', but it remains vital to preserve an alert awareness of the connections.

This study has concentrated on the cultural dialogues between different disciplines and sub-cultures within a mainly Christian environment, rather than on the intercultural theology of world religions. It is sometimes easier for Christians to think of dialogue with partners further away, in conceptual terms, than those at hand, and we have deliberately chosen to focus on the latter. But the intercultural dialogue between the world religions, the major and the minor, remains an urgent task. The task of comparative theology, whether or not from a distinctively Christian perspective, remains an essential part of the wider intercultural project. It is not confined to the religious dimension but has its own links to other disciplines in the humanities and the sciences. There is scope here for a constantly evolving reflection.

There is one further area of dialogue in intercultural theology which should be mentioned here. That is the intercultural dialogue which the religions conduct within themselves, as they are exposed to different cultures. For Christian theology this means the dialogue with its own tradition, and the debate and interaction between theologies in different schools and in different places. This debate begins within the scriptures, in the numerous different and often conflicting perspectives in the Hebrew Bible and in the New Testament. It may be illustrated in the history of the interpretation of scripture. It continues in Alexandria and the Chalcedonian disputes, in the debates between Eastern and Western Christianity, between the schools in Paris in the thirteenth century, the Reformation and Enlightenment debates, the modern, anti-modern and postmodern theologies. Precisely in emphasizing their own uniqueness and authority, the various parties to debate underline the continuing variety of theological perspective. To this we must add the interaction of different denominations and traditions, and the impact of geographical separation, such as the impact of European theology on the rest of the world and vice versa. While most groups can find like-minded Christians in most parts of the world, it is important to recognize and to respect that diversity which, though it has its own disadvantages, appears to correspond more to the open invitation of the gospel than any universal framework is likely to do.

Intercultural theology has a unique and distinctive role to play in helping to build the human future, but in order to be effective it has to be entirely frank about its own limitation. Theology, churches and religious groups have much to give. The Christian gospel of unconditional love is understood by faith to be at the centre of human flourishing, and to be literally the force that moves the stars. Yet the track record of religious bodies in manifesting such love is highly ambiguous, with clusters of shining examples and clusters of appallingly bad cases. It will not do to say that the instances of lack of love are generally in the past. There is no more certainty of linear progression in religious history than there is in secular history.

If we look at the history of recent theology and religious community, with its swift changes of fashion, its often bitter divisions and frequently reactionary directions, there may appear to be little chance that this stream of human reflection and practice can offer much of enduring value to humanity. But on a cosmic scale, or even the scale of human history to date, it becomes important to look to a much longer term future, in which many of the current impasses and blind alleys may be overcome. If we were to see theology as in its infancy rather than at its peak, then things might look very different. Christian theology is based on the tradition of the love of God in Jesus Christ, and its vision for the future is a vision of fulfilment of the love, peace and justice of God. This is a vision which remains of infinite worth, even in places and at times where it may not appear to exist in concrete form. As such it is eminently worth struggling for in the ambiguities and provisionalities of the present. As the research tradition of the quest for God it remains central to human endeavour, precisely in its critical search for a deeper understanding – *fides quaerens intellectum*.

Notes

1 I note that John Cobb has independently noted some of the same events as signs of the work of the Spirit.

2 This was brilliantly spelled out by Ernst Kaesemann in his short study, *Jesus Means Freedom*.

Bibliography

Allen, B. (1993), *Truth in Philosophy*, Cambridge, Mass.: Harvard University Press.

Althans-Reid, Marcella (2000), *Indecent Theology*, London: Routledge.

Auden, W.H. (1948), *The Dyer's Hand*, London: Faber and Faber.

Badham, P. (1995), *The Contemporary Challenge of Modernist Theology*, Cardiff: University of Wales Press.

Baillie, J. and Martin, H. (1936), *Revelation*, New York: Macmillan.

Bartlett, A.W. (2001), *Cross Purposes*, Harrisburg, Penn.: Trinity Press International.

Bayer, Charles (1996), *The Babylonian Captivity of the Mainline Church,* St Louis, Mo.: Chalice Press.

Beetham, D. (ed.) (1995), *Politics and Human Rights*, Oxford: Blackwell.

Berlin, I. (1969), *Four Essays on Liberty*, Oxford: Oxford University Press.

Bernstein, Richard J. (1971), *Praxis and Action*, Philadelphia: University of Pennsylvania Press.

Bernstein, R.J, (ed.) (1985), *Habermas and Modernity*, Cambridge, Mass.: MIT Press.

Bernstein, R.J. (1992), *The New Constellation*, Cambridge,Mass.: MIT Press.

Boesak, A. (1984), *Black and Reformed*, Maryknoll, New York: Orbis.

Brown, D., Davaney, S. and Tanner, K. (eds) (2001), *Converging on Culture*, Oxford: Oxford University Press.

Browning, D.S. and Fiorenza, F.S. (eds) (1992), *Habermas, Modernity and Public Theology*, New York: Crossroad.

Bruce, Steve (1996), *Religion in the Modern World*, Oxford: Oxford University Press.

Burchell, G. *et al.* (ed.) (1991), *The Foucault Effect: Studies in Governmentality*, London: Harvester Wheatsheaf.

Chan, Mark L.Y. (2001), *Christology from Within and Ahead*, Leiden: Brill.

Clark, K.J. (ed.) (1993), *Philosophers who Believe*, Downers Grove, Ill.: IVP.

Coalter, M., Mulder J. and Weeks, J. (1996), *Vital Signs – The Promise of Mainstream Protestantism*, Grand Rapids: Eerdmans.

Cobb, J.B. Jr (1973), *Liberal Christianity at the Crossroads*, Philadelphia: Westminster Press.

Cobb, J.B. Jr (1975), *Christ in a Pluralistic Age*, Philadelphia: Westminster Press.

Cobb, J.B. Jr (1999), *Transforming Christianity and the World*, Maryknoll, New York: Orbis.

Cobb, J.B. Jr (2002), *Postmodernism and Public Policy*, Albany: SUNY.

Cone, J. (1969), *Black Theology and Black Power*, New York: Seabury Press.

Cronin, C and de Greiff, P. (eds) (1998), *The Inclusion of the Other*, Cambridge, Mass.: MIT Press.

Cunningham, M.K. (1995), *What is Theological Exegesis?*, Philadelphia: TPI.

Davidson, D. (1994), *Inquiries into Truth and Interpretation*, Oxford: Oxford University Press.
Davis, S.T. (ed.) (1988), *Encountering Jesus*, Atlanta: John Knox Press.
Dawkins, Richard (1986), *The Blind Watchmaker*, New York: W.W. Norton.
Dawkins, Richard (1995), *River Out of Eden*, New York: Basic Books.
Del Colle, R. (1994), *Christ and the Spirit*, Oxford: Oxford University Press.
Desmond, W. (2001), *Ethics and the Between*, New York: SUNY.
Dickey-Young, P. (1995), *Christ in a Post-Christian World*, Minneapolis: Fortress.
Dombrowski, D.A. (2001), *Rawls and Religion*, New York: SUNY.
Douglass, R.B. (ed.) (1990), *Liberalism and the Good*, London: Routledge.
Drinan, R.F. (2001), *The Mobilization of Shame*, New Haven: Yale University Press.
Eagleton, T. (2000), *The Idea of Culture*, Oxford: Blackwell.
Eck, D.L. (1993), *Encountering God*, Boston: Beacon Press.
Falconer, A. (ed.) (1980), *Understanding Human Rights*, Dublin: Irish School of Ecumenics.
Farley, W. (1996), *Eros for the Other*, University Park: Pennsylvania State University Press
Felice, W. (1996), *Taking Suffering Seriously: The Importance of Collective Human Rights*, New York: SUNY.
Fergusson, D. (1992), *Rudolf Bultmann*, London: Chapman.
Fergusson, D. (1997), *Community, Liberalism and Christian Ethics*, Cambridge: Cambridge University Press.
Forsythe, D. (2000), *Human Rights in International Relations*, Cambridge: Cambridge University Press.
Gascoigne, R. (2001), *The Public Forum and Christian Ethics*, Cambridge: Cambridge University Press.
Gearty, C. and Tomkins, A. (1996), *Understanding Human Rights*, London: Mansell.
Geertz, C. (1983), *Local Knowledge*, New York: Basic Books.
Geertz, C. (1973), *The Interpretation of Cultures*, New York: Basic Books.
Geertz, C. (2000), *Available Light*, Princeton: Princeton University Press.
Geras, N. (1995), *Solidarity in the Conversation of Humankind*, London/New York: Verso.
Gerloff, R. (1992), *A Plea for British Black Theologies*, Frankfurt/New York: Peter Lang.
Gewirth, A. (1982), *Human Rights*, Chicago: University of Chicago Press.
Geyer, A. (1997), *Ideology in America*, Louisville: Westminster John Knox Press.
Gray, J. (1995), *Liberalism*, Buckingham: Open University Press.
Gray, J. (2000), *Two Faces of Liberalism*, NewYork: The New Press.
Grey, M. (1997), *Beyond the Dark Night*, New York: Continuum.
Gregersen, N., Drees, H. and Gorman, W. (2000), *The Human Person in Science and Theology*, Edinburgh: T&T Clark.
Griffin, D. (1998), *Unsnarling the World Knot*, Berkeley: University of California Press.
Griffin, D. (2000), *Religion and Scientific Naturalism*, New York: SUNY.
Griffiths, P. (ed.) (1991), *Wittgenstein Centenary Essays*, Cambridge: Cambridge University Press.
Gutmann, A. (ed.) (1994), *Multiculturalism: Examining the Politics of Recognition*, Princeton: Princeton University Press.

Haack, S. (1993), *Evidence and Inquiry: Towards Reconstruction in Epistemology*, Oxford: Blackwell.
Habermas, J. (1981), *The Theory of Communicative Action*, Boston: Beacon Press.
Habermas, J. (1992), *Moral Consciousness and Communicative Action*, Cambridge: MIT Press.
Habermas, J. (1996), *Between Facts and Norms*, Cambridge, Mass.: MIT Press.
Haight, R. (1999), *Jesus, Symbol of God*, Maryknoll, New York: Orbis Books.
Harvey, A. (ed.) (1989), *Faith in the City*, London: SPCK.
Hebblethwaite, B. (1978), 'Providence and Divine Action', *Religious Studies*, 14/2, 223–36.
Hennelly, A. and Langan, J. (1982), *Human Rights in the Americas*, Washington, DC: Georgetown University Press.
Hick, J. and Knitter, P. (1987), *The Myth of Christian Uniqueness*, London: SCM Press.
Hodgson, P. (1989), *God in History*, Nashville: Abingdon Press.
Hodgson, P. (1994), *Winds of the Spirit*, Louisville: Westminster John Knox Press.
Holloway, R. (1999), *Godless Morality*, Edinburgh: Canongate Press.
Hoy, T. (1988), *Praxis, Truth and Liberation*, New York: University Press of America.
Hyman,G. (2001), *The Predicament of Postmodern Theology*, Louisville: Westminster John Knox Press
Ignatieff, M. (2001), *Human Rights as Politics and Idolatry*, Princeton: Princeton University Press.
Jasper, D. (1993), *Rhetoric, Power and Community*, London: Macmillan.
Jones, Peter (1994), *Rights*, New York: St Martin's Press.
Kaeseman, E. (1969), *Jesus Mears Freedom*, London: SCM Press.
Kay, J.F. (1994), *Christus Praesens*, Grand Rapids: Eerdmans.
Keller, C. (1996), *Apocalypse Now and Then*, Boston: Beacon Press.
Kerr, F. (1986), *Theology after Wittgenstein*, Oxford: Blackwell.
Knitter, P. (1996), *Jesus and Other Names*, Maryknoll, New York: Orbis.
Kuester, V. (2001), *The Many Faces of Jesus Christ*, London: SCM Press.
Kuschel, K.J. (1999), *The Poet as Mirror: Human Nature, God and Jesus in Twentieth-Century Literature*, London: SCM Press.
Lakeland, P. (1997), *Postmodernity*, Minneapolis: Fortress.
Larmore, C. (1996), *The Morals of Modernity*. Cambridge: Cambridge University Press.
Lawlor, L. (1992), *Imagination and Chance*, New York: SUNY.
Lee, Jung Young (1995), *Marginality*, Minneapolis: Fortress.
Lehmann, P. (1995), *The Decalogue and a Human Future*, Grand Rapids: Eerdmans.
Lynch, M.P. (1998), *Truth in Context*, Cambridge, Mass.: MIT Press
Lynch, M.P. (2001), *The Nature of Truth*, Cambridge, Mass: MIT Press
McFague, S. (2001), *Life Abundant*, Minneapolis: Fortress.
Machin, G.I.T. (1998), *The Churches and Social Issues in Twentieth-Century Britain*, Oxford: Clarendon Press.
Mackey, J.P. (1994), *Power and Christian Ethics*, Cambridge: Cambridge University Press.
Marshall, B.D. (2000), *Trinity and Truth*, Cambridge: Cambridge University Press.

Merrigan, T. and Haers, J. (eds) (2000), *The Myriad Christ. Plurality and the Quest for Unity in Modern Christology*, Louvain: Leuven University Press/Peeters.
Min, A.K. (1989), *Dialectic of Salvation*, New York: SUNY.
Morris, T.V. (ed.) (1994), *God and the Philosophers*, Oxford: Oxford University Press.
Murphy, D. (1997), *Christianity and Modern European Literature*, Dublin: Four Courts Press.
Murphy, N. (1997), *Anglo-American Postmodernity*, Boulder, CO: Westview Press.
Neville, R. (2001), *Symbols of Jesus*, Cambridge: Cambridge University Press.
Newlands, G. (1994), *God in Christian Perspective*, Edinburgh: T&T Clark.
Newlands G. (1997), *Generosity and the Christian Future*, London: SPCK.
Newlands, G. (2002), *John and Donald Baillie – Transatlantic Theology*, New York: Peter Lang.
Niebuhr, H.R. (1996), *Theology, History and Culture*, New Haven: Yale University Press.
Niebuhr, U. (1991), *Remembering Reinhold Niebuhr*, San Francisco: Harper.
Nietzsche, F. (1967), *The Will to Power*, New York: Vintage Books.
Nussbaum, M. (1997), *Cultivating Humanity*, Cambridge, Mass.: Harvard University Press.
Nussbaum, M. (2000), *Women and Human Development*, Cambridge: Cambridge University Press.
Nussbaum, M. (2001), *Upheavals of Thought*, Cambridge: Cambridge University Press.
Patel, Roy (ed.) (1990), *A Time to Speak. Perspectives of Black Christians*, Birmingham: CRRU/ICCRS.
Patman, R.G. (ed.) (2000), *Universal Human Rights?*, New York: St Martin's Press.
Peacocke, A.R. (1996), *God and Science*, London: SCM Press.
Peters, T. (1989), *Cosmos as Creation*, Nashville: Abingdon Press.
Phillips, D. (1994), *Wittgenstein and Religion*, New York: St Martin's Press.
Plant, Raymond (2001), *Politics, Theology and History*, Cambridge: Cambridge University Press.
Power, J. (1981), *Amnesty International, The Human Rights Story*, New York: McGraw-Hill.
Rawls, J. (1999), *The Law of Peoples*. Cambridge, Mass.: Harvard University Press.
Rescher, N. (1973), *The Coherence Theory of Truth*, Oxford: Clarendon Press.
Richardson, W.M. and Wildman,W.J. (1996), *Religion and Science*, New York: Routledge.
Ricoeur, P. (1979), *The Rule of Metaphor*, Toronto: Toronto University Press.
Ricoeur, P. (1981), *Hermeneutics and the Human Sciences*, Cambridge: Cambridge University Press.
Ricoeur, P. (1992), *Oneself as Another*, Chicago: University of Chicago Press.
Rorty, Richard (1998), *Achieving our Country*, Cambridge, Mass.: Harvard University Press.
Ruprecht, L. (1994), *Tragic Posture and Tragic Vision*, New York: Continuum.
Ruprecht, L. (1996), *Afterwords*, Albany: SUNY.
Russell, R.J., Murphy, N. and Peacocke, A. (eds) (1995), *Chaos and Complexity: Scientific Perspectives on Divine Action*, Berkeley: Vatican Observatory.
Schafer, D.P. (1998), *Culture, Beacon of the Future*, Westport, Conn.: Praeger.
Schillebeeckx, E. (1987), *Jesus in our Western Cultures*, London: SCM Press.

Schleiermacher, F. (1975), *The Life of Jesus*, ed. Jack Verheyden, Philadelphia: Fortress.

Schrag, C. (1997), *The Self after Postmodernity*, New Haven: Yale University Press.

Schreiter, Robert (1997), *The New Catholicity*, New York: Orbis.

Shriver, D. (1995), *An Ethic for Enemies*, New York: Oxford University Press.

Song, C.S. (1993), *Jesus and the Reign of God*, Minneapolis: Fortress Press.

Strinati, D. (1995), *Popular Culture*, London: Routledge.

Suchocki, M.H. (1982), *God – Christ – Church*, New York: Crossroad.

Surber, J.P. (1998), *Culture and Critique*, Boulder, CO.: Westview Press.

Tanner, Kathryn (1997), *Theories of Culture*, Minneapolis: Fortress.

Taylor, C. (1989), *Sources of the Self*, Cambridge: Cambridge University Press.

Taylor, Charles (1992), *Multiculturalism and the Politics of Recognition*, Princeton: Princeton University Press.

Taylor, Charles (1999), *A Catholic Modernity*, Oxford: Oxford University Press.

Taylor, M.K. (1990), *Remembering Esperanza*, Maryknoll, New York: Orbis Books.

Thiselton, A.C. (1992), *New Horizons in Hermeneutics*, New York: Harper Collins.

Thornhill J. (2000), *Modernity*, Grand Rapids: Eerdmans.

Tillich, P. (1959), *Theology of Culture*, New York: Oxford University Press.

Tillich, P. (1998), *Against the Third Reich*, Louisville: Westminster John Knox Press.

Tracy, D. (1987), *Plurality and Ambiguity*, San Francisco: Harper and Row.

Tylor, E.B. (1871), *Primitive Culture*, London: J. Murray.

Van Huyssteen, W. (1998), *Duet or Duel? Theology and Science in a Postmodern World*, Philadelphia: Trinity Press International.

Van Huyssteen, W. (1999), *The Nature of Rationality*, Grand Rapids: Eerdmans.

Vesey, G. (ed.) (1989), *The Philosophy in Christianity*, Cambridge: Cambridge University Press.

Vroom, H.M. (1996), *No Other Gods?*, Grand Rapids: Eerdmans.

Vroom. H M. (1989), *Religions and the Truth*, Grand Rapids: Eerdmans.

Ward, G. (2000), *Cities of God*, London: Routledge.

Ward, Keith. (1994), *Religion and Revelation*, Oxford: Oxford University Press.

Ward Keith. (1996), *Religion and Creation*, Oxford: Oxford University Press.

Ward, K. (1996), *God, Chance and Necessity*, Oxford: Oneworld.

Ward, K. (1998), *Religion and Human Nature*, Oxford: Oxford University Press.

Ward, K. (2000), *God, Faith and the New Millennium*, Oxford: Oneworld.

Webster, A. (1995), *Found Wanting*, London: Cassell.

Weil, S. (1957), 'The *Iliad*: Poem of Might', in *The Simone Weil Reader*, ed. G. Panichas, New York: McKay, 1977.

Weithman, P.J. (ed.) (1997), *Religion and Contemporary Liberalism*, Indiana: University of Notre Dame Press.

West, Cornel (1994), *Race Matters*, Boston: Beacon Press.

Westphal, M. (1999), *Postmodern Thought and Christian Philosophy*, Indianapolis: Indiana University Press.

Wildman, W.J. (1998), *Fidelity with Plausibility – Modest Christologies in the Twentieth Century*, New York: SUNY.

Williams, D.D. (1985), *Essays in Process Thought*, Chicago: Exploration Press.

Wittgenstein, L. (1980), *Culture and Value*, Chicago: Chicago University Press.

Wolterstorff, N. (1980), *Art in Action*, Grand Rapids: Eerdmans.

Wuthnow, R. (1996), *Christianity and Civil Society*, Philadelphia: Trinity Press International.

Index

Page numbers in **bold** indicate main discussion; *n/ns* refers to note/s.